The
Barefoot
Guide

to learning practices in organisations and social change

Praise for The Barefoot Guides

"The Barefoot Guides use simple methodologies that allow people to bring the best of their experiences to share through the book. They show that all we need is to be awake to learn, to create, to innovate and by the end of day we can create a transformational approach. All of us can do it, even those who do not know they can, truly they can do it too... all of us can change lives!"

MÁRIO ALBINO MACHIMBENE, KEPA, MAPUTO CITY, MOZAMBIQUE

"This exceptional series is hugely accessible yet deeply rooted in solid theory and extensive practice across a wide range of contexts and fields. Expect from it something truly unique in its combination of insight, reflection, experience and highly usable mixed text/visual presentation. It is not "dumbed down." I have seen it bite as deeply at high academic and professional level as well as at grassroots community leadership level ~ an astonishing achievement worth honouring."

JAMES R. COCHRANE, EMERITUS PROFESSOR, RELIGIOUS STUDIES, UNIVERSITY OF CAPE TOWN, AND ADJUNCT PROFESSOR, DEPT OF SOCIAL SCIENCES AND HEALTH POLICY, WAKE FOREST SCHOOL OF MEDICINE, USA.

"The Barefoot Guides are chock-full of practical wisdom. It has given more legitimacy to a way of working that has always felt 'true' and 'right' to me intuitively and that I have seen the effectiveness of in action."

TANA PADDOCK, ORGANIZATION UNBOUND, CAPE TOWN, SOUTH AFRICA

"The Barefoot Guide Connection has a unique and truly transformational approach to collaboration, learning and facilitating social, transformational change across borders."

TOBIAS TROLL, DIRECTOR, EDGE EUROPE AT EDGE FUNDERS ALLIANCE, BRUSSELS, BELGIUM

"The Barefoot Guides are an important reference for our international students in development studies. Crossing the border between academia and practitioners, they repeatedly prove to be a rich source of inspiration for those working with local communities and grassroots organizations"

DR KEES BIEKART, INTERNATIONAL INSTITUTE OF SOCIAL STUDIES (ISS) OF ERASMUS UNIVERSITY, THE HAGUE, NETHERLANDS

"The Barefoot Guides are a wonderful contribution to open access knowledge, grounded on a great depth of experience and horizontal learning from across the world."

SAMANTHA BUTTON, MALIASILI INITIATIVES, TANZANIA

the
barefoot
guide
to
learning
practices in
organisations
and social change

Written by the
Second Barefoot Guide Writers' Collective
Illustrated by Meg Jordi

PRACTICAL ACTION
Publishing

CONTENTS

Organisational Learning

and CONTENTS continued

Practical Action Publishing Ltd
25 Albert Street, Rugby, CV21 2SD, Warwickshire, UK
www.practicalactionpublishing.com

The Second Barefoot Guide Writers' Collective (2013) The Barefoot Guide 2: Learning Practices in Organisations and Social Change, Rugby, UK: Practical Action Publishing.

Since 1974, Practical Action Publishing has published and disseminated books and information in support of international development work throughout the world.
Practical Action Publishing is a trading name of Practical Action Publishing Ltd
(Company Reg. No. 1159018), the wholly owned publishing company of Practical Action.
Practical Action Publishing trades only in support of its parent charity objectives and any profits are covenanted back to Practical Action (Charity Reg. No. 247257,

Group VAT Registration No. 880 9924 76).

What is learning?

It's not a package tied with string,
or a machine with precise instructions.
It doesn't obey rules or masters.

No-one can patent it though many have tried.
It's never been captured and bottled,
or dissected, defined or delivered.

It has many colours and scents,
many flavours and textures,
it can speak in every language.

And every time people tell a story
and others give their whole selves
to listening, it can happen.

And every time someone asks real questions
and honours unexpected answers
then acts on them, it happens.

It's out there in the field, waiting for you,
like a juicy red fruit or a pale blue flower, or the raindrop
you can catch in your hand because you watched as it fell.

By Tracey Martin

Welcome!

...to the Barefoot Guide to Learning Practices in Organisations and Social Change

Wamkelekile!

This is a practical resource for leaders, facilitators and practitioners wanting to improve and enrich their learning processes. It is intended for individuals, organisations and for social change practice in the field.

This is not just another book on organisational learning and social change It is different in that it was not written by one person. Neither is it a collection of essays written by different people. This book is the joint effort of a group of development practitioners from across the globe. It was designed and written during three intensive, participatory writing workshops known as 'writeshops'. Through this process we have created something to help us and others to start, and continue, a more fruitful journey towards learning and social change.

We (the writers) are all passionate about learning and have brought our different experience and expertise to the book. It includes topics as diverse as community mobilising and development, adult learning, funding, evaluation, facilitation, and creative writing. In writing this book, we have tried to use accessible language and to avoid 'development speak'. We hope community leaders, field workers, NGO staff and donor agencies struggling to make their organisations more learning-oriented will find this book helpful, inspiring and thought-provoking.

Writing this guide has been a learning journey for us. Most of us haven't really been writers in our professional lives – although we happened to have some poets amongst us. Most of us had never met before going to Kleinmond (South Africa) for our first writeshop. And few had ever written a book together with others. To get acquainted and build trusting relationships, we shared our personal learning stories and practised the very values this book tries to inspire – knowing ourselves, creating safe spaces, losing our defenses, taking personal responsibility, creating reflection in action and celebrating diversity. We learned to develop our writing voice and to give each other honest feedback on our chapters. We even painted each other's portraits and learned to drum – all to get our creative energy flowing. Over time, we grew stronger as a team and felt less resistance about letting go of certain parts of our chapters ('killing our darlings') and integrating various chapters into new, exciting pieces of work. This was a real collaboration.

Although this book stands on its own, it is closely connected to the *Barefoot Guide to Working with Organisations and Social Change* (BFG1). The idea to write a second *Barefoot Guide on Learning Practices in Organisations and Social Change* (BFG2) was born when the writers of the first *Barefoot Guide* recognised that Chapter 7 on Learning and Innovating in Organisations ('Staying Alive to Change') could easily be a book in itself.

Many organisations aspire to be 'learning organisations' but there is very little practical guidance available, except from the business world. That guidance is difficult to interpret and apply to the more complex terrain of social change, and often guided by different priorities. This book seeks to fill that gap for civil society organisations, and, as the feedback about the BFG1 revealed, we will not be surprised if people in government and business also find it helpful.

A big part of this book is about learning and its importance in enabling organisations to contribute more effectively to positive and sustainable social change. Our aim is not to help you just create a beautiful Learning Organisation but to assist you in strengthening your organisation and its work, so that it has a positive and lasting impact on its surroundings. At the same time, social change is a diverse, multifaceted phenomenon. We can't think of any social change which does not have learning at its heart.

Learning is not a technical thing. We want to encourage you to embrace the strangeness. We hope to inspire you to not just wonder if you are doing your job in the right way, but to also ask the more

philosophical and political questions. We don't want to mainstream any 'best practice' – in fact we strongly believe that the idea of a global best practice is quite colonising! We each must develop good practices for our unique contexts and be open to learning from others in this process. We are aware that a lot of learning is already taking place in communities, organisations and social movements. Our aim is to appreciate what is already there and to enable organisations to learn even better. We want to contribute a new flavour to what is already good.

This book is filled with real-life stories, images and ideas, and while it will not always answer your questions it will, we hope, help you to ask better ones. It will not tell you how your organisation ought to be but it will support the path towards becoming more effective and reflective. Towards more positive and sustainable social change.

You probably won't read this book from cover to cover. You will need to make your own unique journey through it. But don't worry; there are plenty of signposts to help you. Remember that the end will just be the beginning – for you, for your organisation and for your relationship with the people you are working with to bring about social change.

We have used many stories – our own learning stories and stories that others have told us. We are aware of the fact that stories are very powerful. However, their power can have both positive and negative consequences. There is a danger in telling a single story, as it easily leads to generalisations and stereotyping. We know that in telling stories, we are always selective. We make our own stories depending on our world view, our interpretations and our assumptions. Especially when working with other people's stories, we have a great responsibility to tell them and use them with care and respect. We hope we have managed to tackle this ethical question in a responsible way, by using only stories that we know people have told us in good faith.

Finally, this book is humble in its aspirations. We know we have only touched upon a small part of knowledge and experience existing among the many development practitioners around the world. To build on the BFG2 and continuously expand it, we strongly encourage you to contribute your own learning story and experiences to the book or website, and to connect with other people and organisations that have similar questions to yours. It is our desire that the content of the book is continually evolving and enriched. Our learning journey has only just started and we encourage you to take it one step further!

We'd like to hear your feedback

1. Has the *Guide* inspired any changes in how you do something or approach your work? It would be helpful if you could tell us a brief story of how you have used it and what responses it has had.

2. Which chapters have been particularly helpful? Why?

3. Is there anything else that you would like to see in the *Guide*?

4. Is there any part of the *Guide* that you have found difficult to understand?

5. Is there anything that you disagree with? Please tell us why and feel free to contribute alternatives.

Send your feedback to feedback@barefootguide.org.

Contribute your tools and resources

We also welcome additional materials for future editions and for the website. These could be activities, readings, case stories or even poems or images that you have found useful, and that might be useful to others. We can't promise that we will always include them, but each contribution will be seriously considered and acknowledged, if used. Email your contributions to contact@barefootguide.org.

The People of the Second Barefoot Collective

The Writers:
Aissata Dia - Action Aid
Akke Schuurmans - PSO
Alfred Kuma - VSO
Arja Aarnoudse - PSO
Doug Reeler - CDRA
Jan van Ongevalle - HIVA/KULeuven
Malcolm McKinlay - IFRC
Maria Cascant (Kas) - CIRAC
Marianne Brittijn - Cordaid
Martine Koopman - IICD
Nomvula Dlamini - CDRA
Pamela Atieno-Olwal - EASUN
Philippa Kabali Kagwa
          - Namutebi & Associates
Quang Ho Sy - MCNV
Sandra Hill - CDRA
Tony Saddington
Tracey Martin - VSO
Tripti Rai - Action Aid

The Editorial Team:
Arja Aarnoudse, Doug Reeler,
Tracey Martin

The Illustrator:
Meg Jordi

The Layout Artist:
Paula Wood (Paula Wood Design)

The Copy Editor:
Judy Norton

The Proof-reader:
Siobhain Pothier - CDRA

Administration:
Marlene Tromp - CDRA

First steps:
preparing for our learning journey

Trying out new learning approaches

A few years ago we asked ourselves questions like these: 'What is our real work now? Where do we need to give attention to learning? How are we already learning? Where does our organisational culture support or block learning?' These questions were intended to help us to slow down and deal with our needs more thoughtfully. After a foundation workshop to build ideas and ownership we decided to put aside three days a month to start trying out some new learning approaches.

It took us a few months to find a way that works for us, but now it is helping us to bring a different quality to our practice. We are less stressed and more co-operative and productive. Even our reports to donors are more interesting because they contain richer information about what we are doing, learning and achieving.

Where do we begin?

You might be asking: 'How can we start to become a healthier learning organisation?' Most of us would like an easy recipe for this ... but it's not that simple. Each organisation is different and will have to work out its own way. The one key ingredient, however, is that there must be strong desire and support from leadership to put some time and resources aside to invest in learning processes. Otherwise it's just a good idea.

In this chapter we describe some of the helpful principles, creative ideas and experiences that we have gathered which you might find useful to get yourself going and to guide you along the way. It will also help you to plan your own journey through this guide and to decide which parts are most relevant for you.

We are all learning, almost all the time.

Appreciating and strengthening how we are already learning

You are already a learning organisation! Does that surprise you? Every organisation learns: some well, some not so well, some consciously, some unconsciously.

We are all learning, almost all the time. Usually this is unconscious. Our minds are continuously taking in what we see, hear, feel, taste and smell and they are sorting this information in many ways, storing it in different places, trying to make sense of it. This happens while we are awake and asleep. Organisations do this too.

Because we are already learning, our first challenge is to recognise the learning and be more aware of how we are able to do this so that we can strengthen what is working and stop what is not working. For example, one of your staff members may already be using a journal to note what happens while working in the field. She then uses it to write her reports. If more of you did this it might help to enrich your meetings and reports because you bring better observations to share with each other.

Following are some places to look for how we already learn.

Learning from and with communities

Do we allow what we hear from communities to guide our next actions? This is possibly the most important learning we do. Value it, become more aware of it and ask how you could do it even better. Ask: 'How can we listen more attentively, more deeply?'

Do the people you lead or work with *know* that you are interested in their observations and ideas and need to learn from them? Perhaps if the community knows this then they would be more open and informative. They may also feel more valued and be encouraged to take their own listening and learning more seriously.

Learning informally with colleagues

Perhaps as co-workers we share impressions and ideas in the car, on the way home from the field, while the experience is still vivid and our feelings are alive to what has just happened. How can we improve these conversations, ask better questions and value and share with others what we learn here?

During tea breaks colleagues may chat informally about work. How valuable is this? Do we have informal meeting areas that encourage spontaneous conversations? Are people allowed to mingle and chat about their work or do they feel they have to be seen working alone at their desks?

Remember that some people will more easily express their thoughts and feelings over tea rather than in meetings or workshops. So if we want to have a 'learningful' conversation with them then we might make them a cup of tea and chat about work. Drawing out and appreciating their thoughts in this way may help them to participate more openly in more formal situations.

Learning in our work meetings

Meetings can be enormous opportunities for learning; they can also be boring and a waste of time. In our meetings what do people enjoy and value most? What do they like that helps them to be more thoughtful? What should we do more of?

> *Do we allow what we hear from communities to guide our next actions?*

> *Remember that some people will more easily express their thoughts and feelings over tea rather than in meetings or workshops.*

Learning through personal supervision, mentoring and coaching

In our organisations we use different combinations of personal supervision, coaching and mentoring to support individual staff members. In some organisations these are formalised, in others very informal and sporadic. Is your organisation using these vital sources of support and productivity in the most fruitful way? Making them more formal and regular may really help to improve both individual and organisational performance.

Four paths to choose from

Surfacing and strengthening learning practices that are already working may be enough. But if you want to do more then you need to think about where to go next. Consider which of the following four situations most applies to you, as an organisation wanting to learn.

A. We are okay for now… but maybe we can try a few things.

B. We are okay… but we want to really up our game.

C. We are not okay. We really need to change things around here.

D. We are not sure…

A. We are okay for now… but maybe we can try a few things

Your organisation is in reasonably good shape; you are working well. Perhaps you have come through some big changes in the past year and you just need to focus on your work. Quite possibly you are learning lots while you work, in the field and inside the organisation. You and your colleagues do not feel any pressure to put special time into learning. If you are a new or *pioneering* organisation this makes sense (see below). Perhaps others you work with want you to do something new (for example donors want a monitoring system), but you feel happy with what you are doing. If this is the case, by all means look through this book – but bear in mind that we are not saying all organisations need to change how they learn, or even learn more consciously. Perhaps next year will be different, when the situation you are working in changes. But for the moment – ignore this book. Get back to work!

However, if you have the feeling that you could improve some aspects, possibly introduce a small reflective practice here or there, then this book may be helpful. Look over the rest of this chapter, see what makes sense, ignore what does not speak to you.

If you are a relatively new pioneering organisation then consider these two challenges following.

See Barefoot Guide 1, page 75, for a good description.

Challenges of learning in a pioneering organisation

1. Learning on your feet

Pioneering organisations are young organisations. They are often small and flexible and spend lots of time experimenting out in the field. They are often a little unstructured and plan as they are working, make it up as they go along.

These organisations can appear from the outside to be disorganised, but actually may be highly effective and efficient – the very opposite of heavy, over-organised bureaucracies. They are often nimble, adaptive and innovative. Outsiders find them confusing, especially donors and governments, who assume that they are not reliable or sustainable. However, because they don't work by conventional rules, young organisations can be very effective.

Are they learning organisations? Yes, they are learning organisations, of a special kind – they learn mostly by doing! They do this in an intuitive, unconscious way, not knowing that they are learning. As they have an informal culture and systems, information can move around in all sorts of ways, unrestricted by rules and hierarchies. This enables a great deal of learning to take place.

Sometimes donors insist on planning, monitoring and evaluation systems that bureaucratise and undermine learning in these organisations.

Your challenge: Are you facing pressure to be more structured and systematic than you feel is necessary? How can you help others to understand what you need and what you don't need?

Being a transparent organisation is the most effective way to encourage learning in your organisation.

2. Keep the windows and doors open!

Even though communication flows freely, pioneering organisations can still have communication difficulties. Because they communicate informally, people can be left out of the loop unintentionally. This blocks learning. Perhaps those with easy email access get to hear about things first and this undermines the inclusion and participation of others. Perhaps some members don't live or work close to the HQ or office and don't learn about important meetings until it is too late. Perhaps some chats only happen over tea with certain people. This can exclude some from taking part in important conversations, both formal and informal, where others are learning about things that matter to the organisation.

Being a transparent organisation is the most effective way to encourage learning in your organisation. People cannot learn if they are not informed.

Your challenge: How can you be more transparent and actively communicate with and include more people?

As an organisation you are in fairly good shape. You have moved beyond your pioneering years and have become more organised. You have a sense that lots of learning is happening in the field but it's quite haphazard or possibly a bit too mechanistic or lifeless. You are ready to learn in more conscious, creative and disciplined ways but you do not know where to begin. Or perhaps you have made a start but things are not really working out because you did not have enough ideas to develop fruitful learning practices. Maybe you want to implement a good planning, monitoring and evaluation system.

If any of these apply to your organisation then this book has lots for you to work with.

Even though you are in good shape, be careful not to take things for granted. It's not just about learning a few quick methods. Resistance to learning is often stronger than anyone realises. If you ignore it then it will suck the life out of your attempts to learn. If you surface and acknowledge resistances to learning, and work through them, then you will generate good energy for learning.

Challenges of learning in a more complex organisation and context

1. Developing clarity about roles is capacity-building

I remember working in an organisation that grew quickly from one year to the next. We suddenly realised the need for us to develop more specialised roles, each with a new range of skills. Until then we all did a bit of everything – no-one had a definite or exclusive role. So we developed new roles and capacities. The different roles we settled on were decided quickly. Then we looked for ways to get the right skills. Some people went on courses; others had to read up for themselves. We organised some exchange visits as well. For the most part, though, people had to learn on-the-job and from each other. All of these were helpful but actually we made a mistake.

The problem was that we did not have a clear idea of our new roles. We had rushed the process. Of course we were not working in a stable situation so roles were never going to be fixed. But we should still have spent more time thinking about who was doing what and what the real work was for each role.

I had to raise funds and went on a fund raising course – but I learnt little of value; it was all quite obvious. So we sat down to figure out for ourselves what the role of a fund raiser was. Through discussion we realised that fund raising was only one of the end products of my job; my real role was to help to mobilise resources and resourcefulness, both inside and outside the organisation. It was to keep alive conversations about the real purpose of the organisation and deepen our understanding of our approach, both to improve our practice and to inspire donors; to build relationships and network;

to connect our organisation to strategic conversations in the sector so that we could collaborate; to empower others to think about resourcing and so on. These are not capacities but roles. Often the key capacity is clarity about the real work of that role, and with that clarity comes the confidence and the ability to do the work. So if people say that they are feeling insecure about their skills, first check to see if they know what is expected of them.

Clear roles will help people to assess whether they already have the necessary capacities (skills, knowledge, experience) to meet these expectations. Quite often the capacities they need are already there, unknown to them, and just need to be taken out and polished a little. If not then the organisation can arrange coaching, exposure visits, workshops, courses, self study and so on.

2. Who else can you learn from?

Although you will always have to rely on your own experience to improve your practice, it is quite likely that you will become stuck at times – things are often too complex for any one organisation to understand sufficiently. Reading books with other ideas and experiences is always a good idea. But many people struggle to read a lot or to engage with readings collectively.

It is worth finding out who else is working in your field and arranging exchange visits to learn from their experiences and share yours. Horizontal Learning is a powerful alternative to training.

Of course exchange learning means letting go of any hidden competitive instincts. Opening up for learning from others implies that you are comfortable admitting your ignorance and difficulties and willing to discuss them with others!

'Listening is a magnetic and strange thing, a creative force. The friends who listen to us are the ones we move toward. When we are listened to, it creates us, makes us unfold and expand.'

Karl Menninger

Quite often the capacities they need are already there, unknown to them, and just need to be taken out and polished a little.

3. Learn to collaborate

Collaboration is a fashionable buzzword – and for good reason. We simply have to work with a wide range of people and organisations to be able to contribute towards real and sustainable results. But collaborating is difficult. It's hard enough for people inside an organisation to collaborate, let alone get two or more organisations to work together.

This is where learning together has a valuable role to play. There is now enough experience to show that *if organisations (or communities) learn together*, sharing their practices and experiences, their reflections and learnings, then this starts to *lay a foundation for collaboration*. It helps people to learn about each other and understand each other before they decide to work together.

Invest in a culture of listening and questioning

Perhaps the most useful thing to improve learning in your organisation is to cultivate good listening and questioning culture and skills. A good listening culture is one where people are really interested in each other, in what they think, what they feel and what they want. Good leaders usually take the time to sit with their members or staff and encourage them to speak from the 'head, heart and feet' (see *Barefoot Guide* 1 pages 29–32), and also encourage them to do the same with each other. Not only will they learn from each other, getting more important information and ideas, but they will also help to cultivate a more thoughtful, caring and enthusiastic culture which is likely to make people happier and more productive.

Of course better listening is also helped by people asking each other better questions – you are more likely to get a good answer if you ask a good question – and so it is worth investing in developing better questioning skills.

Chapter 2 in the Barefoot Guide 1 has some ideas for encouraging good listening. The website has great exercises to try out.

C. We are not okay. We really need to change things around here

Your organisation needs a lot of work. Things are more complex than they used to be and you know you need to be not only learning, but also rethinking the way you work.

But people are too busy to stop and learn together. You all need to take time to improve your organisation's collective approach and practice. However there just doesn't seem to be enough time, or perhaps some are not interested. You may have tried reflective activities, in the field or inside the organisation, but they did not help, or even made things worse.

Maybe there is resistance to learning from some people, or there is not sufficient trust or self-confidence for people to open themselves up to each other, to openly share their successes and failures and learn from them. Perhaps your organisation is so results-driven that people do not want to share their struggles or 'failures' for fear they will lose their jobs, pay rises or promotions.

Every organisation finds itself in this situation at one time or another – but don't panic, it's a quite natural state. If you are able to resolve it then it can lay the basis for a very fruitful next stage of development.

It might also be that your organisation is moving from one phase in its development to another, needing to transform itself in fundamental ways, and so learning is only a part of the challenge. If this is true then it might be a good idea to read the first *Barefoot Guide* on the challenges of organisational transformation – see Chapters 4–6.

Even if only some of this is true then do proceed with this book, but pay particular attention to the challenges of addressing those aspects of your organisational culture that support or hinder individual and collective learning.

The challenges of learning in a transition or a crisis situation

1. DON'T PANIC!

The first thing to realise is that being in a crisis is not always a bad thing. Often a crisis has many opportunities for change, even though it can feel so painful and difficult. Remember that where there is pain there is a good reason to change. The trouble is that leaders are often blamed, or blame themselves or their staff members when things are not working. This is unfortunate because crisis is natural.

The challenge here is: Get some understanding of what crisis, and being stuck, mean.

Have a look at pages 74-79 of Barefoot Guide 1, for a view of the typical crises that organisations go through, and how to deal with them.

2. It's not about learning, but unlearning

The most interesting thing about being in transition (a polite word) or stuck or in crisis is that learning can only help a bit. The problem is not what you don't know and think you need to learn – it's what you already know or what you are so used to doing that you may need to *unlearn*. Sometimes we are stuck in our habits, doing things in ways that used to work, things that we have got the skills for and that we are experienced in, even if they are no longer needed. Yet the situation out there has changed and so must we. If we want to use new ideas and skills we have to get rid of some of the old ones that no longer work. This is more about unlearning than about learning.

There are different kinds of things we may have to let go of. Sometimes they lie in our practice, or perhaps in our purpose or approaches or strategies. Sometimes we have to let go of things inside our organisations, our culture, values, the structure, relationships, roles or processes that we are so used to.

For example, we may be used to calling communities to attend review meetings that we organise, design and facilitate. This gives us more control over the outcomes and might help us to meet our obligations to donors. Then we may realise that it would be more empowering if we participated in their processes rather than they in ours. So, we try to encourage them to introduce review questions into their own meetings, in their way – but only if they want to and if they find it helpful. Which means that we lose control over the feedback we need for donors, and a new level of engagement and relationship with the community is now required.

It is always a good thing to look first at your practice or your work, and when this has been reworked or transformed then you can look at reshaping the organisation to better support new work practices.

See Chapter 10 in this book which focuses on unlearning and also look up the U-process on pages 112-117 of Barefoot Guide 1 for some ideas about how to help organisations/people to unlearn.

… sometimes too much change is stressful – it's called 'change fatigue'

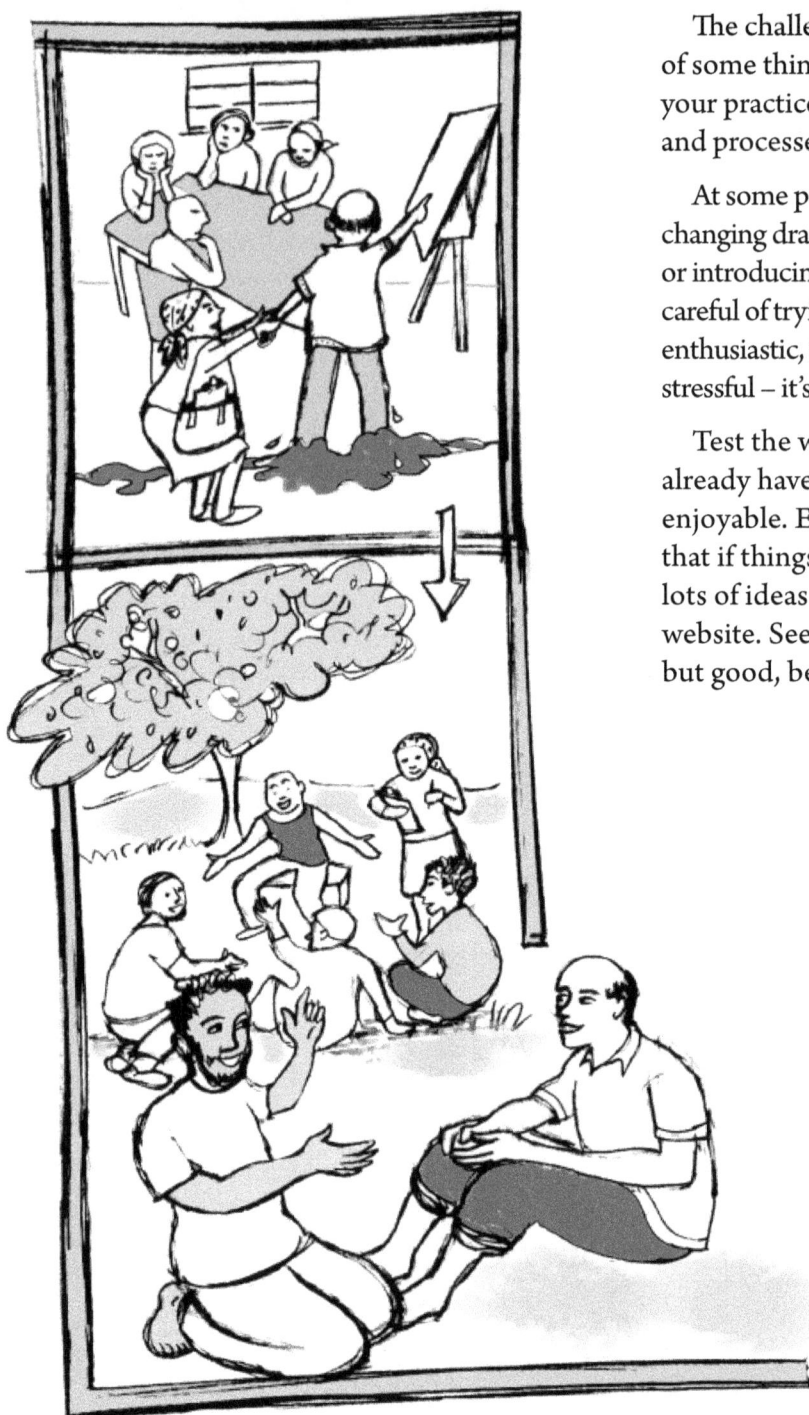

The challenge here is: Prepare yourselves to let go of some things that are important to you, starting with your practice and then with the organisational forms and processes that support practice. (Not everything!)

At some point in your change process, if things are changing dramatically, you may want to focus on adapting or introducing some conscious learning practices. But be careful of trying to do too much. If everyone is ready and enthusiastic, that's fine, but sometimes too much change is stressful – it's called 'change fatigue'.

Test the waters first, strengthen anything that you already have and then maybe add something easy and enjoyable. Encourage a spirit of experimentation so that if things don't work first time, it's okay. There are lots of ideas in this book and on the Barefoot Guide website. See which one or two might work as a small, but good, beginning.

D. We are not sure…

If you do not fit into the above descriptions then open up a conversation with your colleagues, asking them where they think your learning challenges lie. If you are worried that people are not speaking up then you could discuss things in smaller groups or one-to-one, testing some questions and ideas. You may want to bring in an outsider to interview everyone and see what all the thoughts, feelings and wills of people are towards being a more conscious learning organisation.

Enabling change to happen

For many people change is a *cause and effect thing*: you name the problem (effect), look for causes and then design and implement a fix (a new cause and effect). Or you decide what you want, perhaps a vision of the future (a desired effect), and then plan the steps to get there (causes). Often change is seen as more complex and circular, with many interacting causes and effects.

But there are other ways to think about change. It's not that cause and effect thinking is all wrong, but perhaps there are better ways. One way is to be interested not only in how or why things change but how or why they *do not* change. People, individually and collectively, are so active and dynamic, giving rise to so much activity and movement, that we should not be surprised by change; it is almost unceasing. Actually it's when things do not change, when they are stuck, that we should be most surprised, and curious about what it is that is preventing change. We should be curious about the *blockages or hindrances* to the kind of future situation we want.

Here is an example to make this a bit clearer. Think of a 'stuck' situation in your organisation that needs to change, such as not enough conscious learning. It might well be that the potential and energy for change is already there, that this situation is filled with possibilities. These different possible futures are, at the moment, prevented from happening by certain blockages. These constraints are holding the situation, keeping it from changing. There could be unhealthy power relations that shut down communication, or a value that puts results above honesty, or a fear of being criticised, or no time allocated for learning. It might be that people are keen to learn with each other but many things are in the way.

You can see this in cause and effect terms but this does not help you to see the potential for change and therefore to understand what the key blockages or hindrances are.

The first challenge is together to look for a possible desired future situation – something inspiring, but also something that feels possible. Once you have this the task is to understand what is blocking the desired future and to look for ways of dealing with it.

In summary, you don't always have to make it all happen, but rather to allow it to happen, to unlock the possibility that you collectively desire.

What is our practice? Where should we focus our learning?

This Barefoot Guide was developed to help organisations become healthier and more conscious learning organisations. The purpose of becoming a learning organisation is to become more effective in our work, to improve our practice in the field. So the first questions would be:

'What is our practice?' and 'Where in our practice should we focus our learning?'

Once we have answered these questions we can ask:

'What kind of learning will best help us to improve our practice?'

> *What exactly is it that we need to support through good learning?*

Surfacing our practice – where is the real work?

Some of us might say, 'Oh we know what our practice is already; it's in our strategic plans, so let's move onto the next question…' But wait a bit. It makes good sense to begin by revisiting our practice, to remind ourselves, collectively, what our real work is. What exactly is it that we need to support through good learning? We don't want to waste time working on aspects of our practice that don't need it.

> Start with what you actually do, not what you intend to do. This is a fundamental principle of an Action Learning approach.

Two 'maps' to identify the learning focus in your practice

First map: Exploring what you actually do

There is often a difference between your plans or proposals and your actual work. Your plans and funding proposals may contain your thinking, even your theories of change, but what do you actually do and what is the thinking you do in the field? What is your theory of change in practice? This is what needs to be uncovered.

For some this might be obvious, but for most practitioners what they do is often intuitive or unconscious and what they end up doing by the end of each day is different from what they planned.

Try working in a group to surface a map, or picture, of your practice:

1. *Describe to each other* what you actually do. Give time for people to prepare for this (individually or as work teams). Tell each other a detailed story of your most typical work, preferably something already completed.

2. While the story is being told your colleagues should *listen intently* with particular questions in mind, for example:
Where is a difference being made?
What contribution is being made here?
What needs are really being addressed?
What is the real work that matters here?
How is this being addressed?
Whose energy is driving the process?

3. After collecting their thoughts individually, your colleagues can now *reflect what they have heard* that felt important, what grabbed their attention.

4. This can then *open up a conversation* that looks for the answers to the questions:
So what are we really doing – what's our real work here?
Where do we have concerns?
What does this mean for my future practice?

   This can happen for each member of the team. And so a picture builds of what the practice of the organisation is.

   There are many different ways to do this. We could ask different people to prepare presentations and open up questions and discussions. We could use a World Café process (see website) to further explore the different connections in our work.

5. *Now see where to focus your learning* – the pictures of your practice that emerge will help you to decide where. Perhaps you want to continue to share your stories to deepen your understanding of your work. Perhaps you can see that you need to be clearer about what needs you are addressing and to put more thought into your purpose. Perhaps this reveals a need to develop certain skills that are lacking.

> Before opening up for group conversations it is always useful to give people a little time to collect their thoughts, to think about what they want to say.

Whose energy is driving this process?

Where is a difference being made?

How is this being addressed?

The Five Elements of a Developmental Approach

Another way to find focus for practice learning is to explore the Five Elements of a Developmental Approach and to see where your practice needs more learning attention. These threads are typical of most developmental field practices:

1. Building relationships – developing trust and clarity
2. Gaining understanding – enabling people to surface and understand their reality
3. Facilitating change – enabling shifts and breakthroughs
4. Supporting change – practical implementation
5. Reviewing change – assessing progress and looking ahead.

We begin by building relationships. But these threads usually happen concurrently, although at certain steps in an intervention there may be more emphasis on one or another. As soon as we start building relationships with the people we may work with, we start to gain some understanding of what is happening. This relationship-building continues all through the process.

Share and discuss these threads with colleagues and then work with the questions for each, exploring and assessing your own practice.

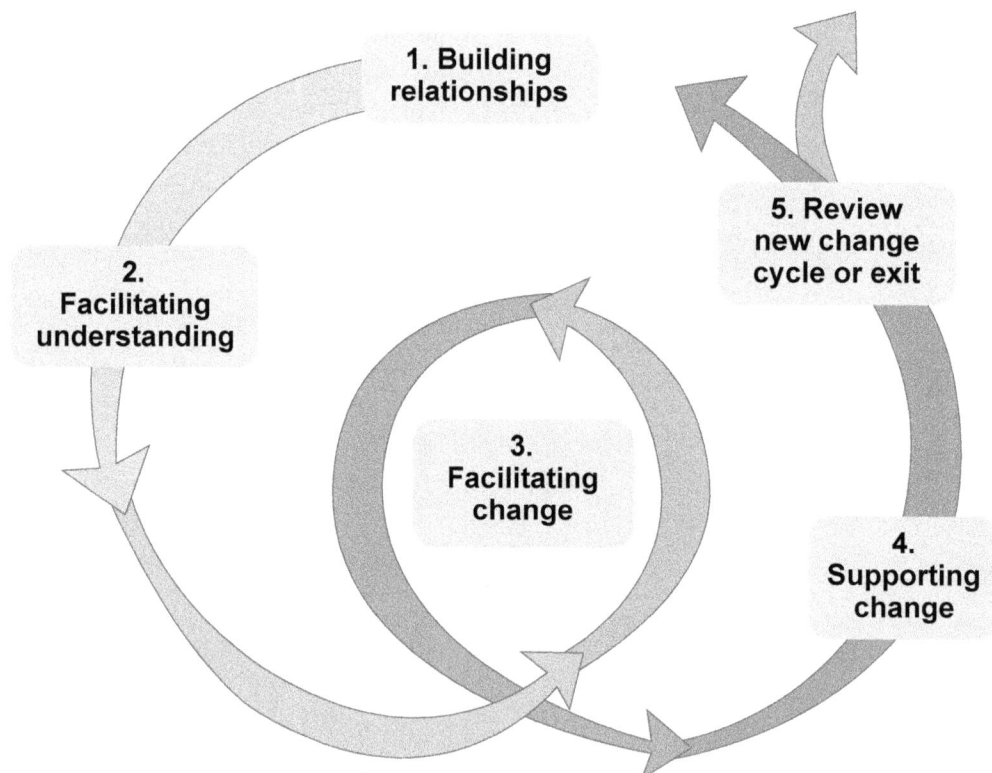

1. Building relationships

2. Facilitating understanding

3. Facilitating change

4. Supporting change

5. Review new change cycle or exit

1. Building relationships

Change begins and ends with relationship and the need to establish, firstly, the warm human conditions of trust to enable honesty and good co-operation. Without this the people we work with will be closed to us and we will find ourselves unable to work effectively. Secondly, there is a need for openness and transparency, so that what people think, feel and want are sufficiently clear to be able to proceed.

Often the real work that needs to happen is at a relationship level. Power lives in relationships – so if there is the abuse of power, or if power needs to be more equalised then the key work that needs to happen is at a relationship level. The questions to ask are:

- How do we build relationships with the people we work with, so that they trust and understand us?

- How are we affecting their relationships with themselves and with others?

2. Gaining understanding

Understanding what it is that we are really working with is a primary challenge. Behind what we think is happening often lie deeper issues. These must be surfaced and understood, not only by the practitioner, but more importantly, by people we are working with so that they may see for themselves more clearly what matters. Then they can more easily see and lead their own change process.

Helping people to see themselves and their situation more clearly enables them to achieve acceptance of what kind of change they may need to face and what may need to be done.

Interestingly, the processes of building relationships and of gaining understanding not only prepare the way for facilitating change but often produce immediate changes – especially where the problems are about relationships, lack of clarity and misunderstandings. The questions to ask are:

- How are we contributing to people understanding their situation for themselves?

- How are we helping them to continue to learn about themselves?

- What kind of change conditions exist?

- How does this help us understand our real work?

See Barefoot Guide 1, Chapter 3, for an exploration of power and relationships.

Change begins and ends with relationship...

3. Facilitating change

Being stuck, rigidity, clinging to the old, refusing to relinquish past perceptions and hurts, difficult relationships, inappropriate structures, cultures, strategies and ways of seeing the world – all must be loosened, opened, so that new life may emerge. Some of these may be resolved through learning in better ways, which we call Action Learning.

But sometimes the stuck feeling, or crisis, first requires unlearning. The old ways of relating and seeing must be let go of to make space for the new, thus creating the conditions for visioning a new future. The questions to ask are:

- What role do we play in helping people to change themselves, their relationships or the conditions in which they live or work?
- How are we helping them to unlearn what needs to be unlearned and to learn what needs to be learned?

4. Supporting and grounding change

After having committed to change and starting to implement it, people may easily slip back into old patterns and habits. Change needs to be grounded: the new situation must be given roots to stabilise and new structures to hold onto. New skills and capacities may need to be developed to enable the new plans to be activated and implemented. Leaders may need mentoring and progress may need to be reviewed and consolidated. The questions to ask are:

- How are we assisting people to turn their intentions and plans into actions and achievements?
- Is there sustainability?

Change needs to be grounded: the new situation must be given roots to stabilise and new structures to hold onto

5. Reviewing

In leading or facilitating change we need to pause regularly to review the process, reflecting on how things are going, monitoring progress to make sure things are on a positive track. This should be happening continuously, but then at key points there may be deeper reviews to decide whether to move into another cycle of change or to exit. Empowering people to be reflective builds independence and sustainability for the future, enabling them to understand change processes for themselves. The questions to ask are:

- Are we building in sufficient time and space for people to reflect on and learn from experience?
- Are the review processes we support of good quality?
- Are we empowering others to facilitate their own reflection and learning processes?

What does this mean for learning?

Once you have worked through the Five Elements of a Developmental Approach, you can add a sixth step: 'What does this mean for learning?' Exploring these five elements in your practice is itself a learning process, but will also point you to the aspects of your practice that need attention. This could be to strengthen, improve or even to transform different aspects. Useful questions to ask now could be:

What should we do more of?

What should we do less of?

What should we start doing?

What should we stop doing?

Different places to focus learning

Here are several of the most important areas on which you could focus organisational learning.

- **Developing purpose and our theories of change**

  What really matters to us? Where we can make our most useful contribution to the world?

- **Understanding what social change is**

  Deepening the theories of change that connect the work we do with the contribution we want to make.

- **Developing practical approaches, strategies and methods**

  – for specific interventions, programmes or projects

  What is the real need, and our real work, in this situation? What have we learned from experience here so far, and what does it mean for our next action? How can we improve our approach to this situation? What can we learn from others?

- **Giving and receiving feedback**

  How can we help people to see and understand their contribution and to get helpful and specific feedback through which they can learn, both individually and collectively? How can feedback be received as a gift (even if challenging) and not a criticism?

- **Building specific skills**

  What skills need to be strengthened? What skills need to be acquired?

- **Building good support systems and procedures**

  How can we design our support systems and procedures to serve the needs and to suit the realities of our practice?

- **Innovating and designing**

  How can we encourage innovation, creativity and risk-taking? How can we use our collaborative potential to spark new ideas, designs and initiatives?

- **Overcoming conflicts and resentments**

  How can we surface and deal with conflict and resentments?

- **Building authentic community**

  How can we regularly renew relationships and enthusiasm for working together? How can we pay attention to the emotional health of the organisation and its people?

- **Developing healthy living and working paths**

  How can we help people, as individuals, to vision and plan their working lives and to grow themselves more fully as human beings? How can we help them to find healthy balances between work and personal lives?

I am, we are:
linking individual and organisational learning

Meltdown – times three!

'We have fired the CEO. He embezzled funds, the financial management records are in chaos, the office was used for inappropriate purposes and most of the staff were not showing up for work. We had no choice. We had to fire him. Now he's taking us to court for unfair dismissal.'

The chairperson of this humanitarian organisation, a former politician, an honest and imposing man, was exasperated. 'We trusted him. He was "one of us". We should have been more vigilant.' He shook his head, avoiding our eyes. We weren't too sure where to look. One couldn't help but notice the mess around the office – piles of paper everywhere. His organisation seemed to be in meltdown in front of our eyes. My boss and I were both fairly new to our roles and this was our first meeting with the chairperson. It seemed to us that a rescue package would be required.

Several international partners and donors were determined that the organisation in question would not fail. And our job as the Organisational Development (OD) specialists was to co-ordinate the partners to put this rescue package together.

One of the partners agreed to send an experienced manager to the country for three months, to help the organisation get back on its feet. New staff were hired, an external bookkeeper was employed, and staff regulations were created as well as policies and procedures on a wide range of key issues. A new local CEO was recruited, with a mentoring programme to ensure the person was supported. And so, humanitarian programmes in the community began again. There had been no board meetings for months; these were restarted. The constitution was revised and it was agreed that an annual general meeting would be held with elections for all the governing board posts.

We wondered if part of the problem was the current chairperson, who had been there for twenty years and was reluctant to move on. At the same time, he seemed to be the only person keeping what was left of the organisation together.

The annual general meeting attracted some new talent to the board, including a new chairperson. Governance training was carried out. It seemed that everything was back up and running again.

We congratulated ourselves on a job well done. Our task here was over... except that three years later, the organisation was in meltdown once again. The CEO had been accused of financial mismanagement and had disappeared; the board was riven with conflict and had ceased to achieve a quorum for several months; most of the staff had left. To be honest, the picture didn't look much different from three years earlier. But by this time, both my boss and I had moved on.

However, there were some new OD specialists on hand to help them. I heard that a similar rescue package was put together (which saw the former chairperson being re-elected). And the organisation was back on its feet.

Until three years later...

> *Organisational learning is difficult where there is no organisational memory.*

There seemed to be no organisational learning in this story – neither in the local organisation, nor in the international partners who were supporting it. The same problems were recurring and the same 'solutions' were being applied with the same results.

Yet, individual learning was taking place. In the local organisation, programme staff were on steep learning curves and were leaving to more responsible jobs elsewhere. The senior leaders were learning that their international partners would not let them go under. But there didn't seem to be any learning that enriched the life of the organisation itself, or enabled it to negotiate its way through rocky periods.

Individual learning was also taking place within the international partners. But the typical contract length of their staff was two years. So by the time of the second meltdown, every single person in the support organisations was new to the situation. No one was in a position to recognise the recurring pattern.

This sad lack of organisational memory resulted in the international partners responding in an almost identical way to their predecessors. It was as if a sandcastle had been wiped out by the high tide, and we had simply rebuilt it on the same spot, ignorant of the tidal pattern. Organisational learning is difficult where there is no organisational memory.

What's in this chapter?

This chapter explores the connection between individual learning and organisational learning. After exploring three 'traditional' approaches to improving organisational learning and their pitfalls, it considers how we can take individual learning more seriously. It then shares stories of individual learning and how these have succeeded or failed in bringing about organisational learning. I hope these stories will enrich your thinking about improving your organisation's learning. Finally, the chapter introduces the importance of 'organisational culture' as a key enabler or inhibiter of organisational learning.

Three traditional approaches to organisational learning

> *Training can support an individual's learning – or can be irrelevant to it.*

1. Training – 'quick fix' learning

When an organisation recognises its need to learn, one of the most common tactics is to send people on training courses. In many countries, a wide range of training opportunities are on offer and international partners are sometimes willing to fund participants to attend training in other countries. But the depressing truth is that often the impact of the training is questionable.

I knew one organisation that had sent 30 staff on international training courses funded by their international partners, over the course of a year. And yet no one could identify any changes in the way this organisation carried out its work.

Those who see training as the great hope assume that if participants deepen their knowledge in their technical area, they will be in a position to change the way they work. One unfortunate dimension of 'workshop culture' is the implication that learning is something that happens in a workshop or a special event. Once the workshop is over, the learning is over and it is time to go back to your normal job where an inbox full of correspondence needs attention and where there is no opportunity to inspire wider learning in the organisation.

'Training' and 'learning' are very different things. Learning involves a process of change that can transform individuals. Training can support an individual's learning – or can be irrelevant to it.

2. Consultant evaluation – an external fix

Another popular way to address the needs of organisational learning is to recruit an external consultant to carry out a review. This can result in an intense experience of research and learning – for the consultant! But this consultant then leaves the organisation with a report which can all too easily be filed alongside the other consultant reports that no one refers to.

I was involved in planning a review of a colleague's work, inspired because the work was innovative. The primary purpose was to see what could be learned from his experience and whether his approach could be applied more broadly in the organisation. This review included all the dead ends and failed approaches as well as the successes. My colleague was enthusiastic and expected to be heavily involved.

However, the terms of reference was altered to allow an external consultant to evaluate the impact of his work (for the purposes of accountability). My colleague's attitude changed instantly and visibly; he now put his best face forward, rather than reveal his struggles and doubts. It's a natural reaction when you think your job is under threat.

Such is the tension between accountability and learning. Most of the evaluations I've seen have been funded and inspired by donors for the purpose of accountability. The primary question for the community organisation then becomes whether they can put a sufficiently good face forward to win a continuation of their funding. While the donor might encourage their partner to see it as a learning experience, it rarely is. Learning requires honesty, vulnerability and a safe environment. An evaluation can challenge the survival of an organisation – which by definition is a threatening situation, not a safe one.

3. IT solutions – a technological fix

A third popular approach is to seek a technological solution to addressing organisational learning issues.

The Z-drive that no one used

I know of one organisation where the expectation was that each staff member file their work onto a hard drive on a common computer server that they called the 'Z-drive'. This would make 'knowledge' available and easily accessible to everyone else in this networked organisation.

Unfortunately the Z-drive became a confusion of different filing systems 'designed' by people from the past and the present. If anyone attempted to access other people's files, the time required to find their way meant they were unlikely to try that approach a second time. While cleaning up the Z-drive was often talked about, it never climbed high enough up the priority list. Whenever it became full most people simply deleted their predecessors' files, without even examining them to see if they were useful and should be kept.

One day, a staff member decided to look on the Z-drive for something that they had put there years earlier. To their surprise, their computer couldn't seem to connect to it at all. When they told the IT person, he explained that 'the pathways' to the drive had been changed three months ago.

'Does that mean no one has been able to access the Z-drive for three months?'

'Yes. And you are the first person who has come to ask us about it,' he grinned broadly.

Many organisations have experimented with more sophisticated IT solutions than a common 'Z-drive'. But it is surprisingly rare to find people who are satisfied with their knowledge management systems. These systems should link to organisational learning, but the link is often not clear or doesn't work. Knowledge management as a strategy to promote organisational learning fails when it doesn't recognise the human side of the organisation. The leadership may hope that the difficulties are merely technical, not wanting to be drawn into the messy mix of egos, ambition, rivalry, jealousy, gossip, frustration, anxiety... all the relationships and politics in the organisation that determine the potential for organisational learning to take place.

The prospect of a quick fix is always appealing and setting up an external consultancy, sending people on a training course, or implementing a new IT solution all seem to offer good outcomes at first glance, but deliver disappointing results in the longer term.

Recognising the human side of organisational learning

Recognising the human side of an organisation can cause something more effective and lasting to happen. One colleague set up a programme to provide water supplies to communities severely affected by a major natural disaster. He knew it was a programme that would run for up to five years and that significant staff turnover was likely. So an early priority was to set up a system whereby the story of this project and what had been learned along the way could be documented.

One of the key challenges was to create something that people would enjoy contributing to and exploring. Asking people to write more documents and reports was not going to elicit any kind of enthusiasm.

His approach was to employ a full-time staff member who operated like a journalist within the programme. Whenever someone returned from an important meeting or event, this 'internal journalist' would interview them and write the story. Whenever someone submitted an important report, the journalist would ask them about the background, why it was written and what the key issues were that the report grappled with. The journalist would compile all the interviews, 'introductions' to documents and other information into a filing system using some mind mapping software, with a structure that all the staff had discussed and agreed on.

The result was a popular information resource that told the story of the programme from beginning to end. It created a rich layer of personal reflections that were not captured in the official reports. And staff enjoyed contributing to it. The internal journalist was a friendly and positive character in the office. People enjoyed being interviewed by her and would seek her out when they had something interesting to report on. They also felt that the system was encouraging them to reflect and it was generating interesting conversations, rather than simply demanding more reports.

It was the non-technological dimension of this technological solution that made it successful.

Taking individual learning seriously

Without individual learning, there is no possibility for organisational learning. So in the next section, we consider some ideas around individual learning.

Individual learning – out of the classroom and into the... swamp

How can individual learning flourish in situations of great complexity, where technical solutions rarely work, and where the arena of social change feels more like a swamp than a classroom? Many practitioners come to grief in the swamp, trying to get control over that which refuses to be tamed, with the risk of becoming weary, and finally resigning. Yet for others, the swamp can become a beautiful wetland, full of interesting life and unique possibilities.

Learning from experience – Action Learning

When dealing with 'messy' realities, learning from experience is often the only option.

For some years I saw the Action Learning model (planning, action, reflection, learning, planning and so on) as too simplistic, too obvious to be worth my attention. However, I came to understand its value when I realised that in my own work I was almost always flitting back and forth between action and planning. And often they would be happening at the same time. At the busiest times, I'd receive an email informing me that the deadline for next year's plans had arrived – and I was nowhere near ready! I'm not proud of some of the plans I've made simply to satisfy the requirements of 'the machine'.

The Action Learning cycle includes a period of deeper reflection after a period of action, rather than reflecting-on-the-run and quickly moving on to plan the next piece of work. The time after the action has taken place is the best opportunity to become more conscious of what happened and of the dynamics that were at play, before you start forgetting.

'In the varied topography of professional practice, there is a high, hard ground overlooking a swamp. On the high ground, manageable problems lend themselves to solutions through the application of research-based theory and technique. In the swampy lowland, messy, confusing problems defy technical solutions. The irony of this situation is that the problems of the high ground tend to be relatively unimportant to individuals or society at large, however great their technical interest may be, while in the swamp lie the problems of greatest human concern. The practitioner must choose. Shall he remain on the high ground where he can solve relatively unimportant problems according to prevailing standards of rigor, or shall he descend to the swamp of important problems and non-rigorous inquiry?'

Donald A Schön

> More about the Action Learning cycle and helping questions can be found in Chapter 12. 'How do we learn?'

In recent years, I have organised an annual event which involves participants from a dozen different countries. I got into the habit of documenting my reflections on the event the week after it had finished, and I always surprised myself with how much I wrote.

'That activity didn't really work. Why was that, I wonder?'

'Having this type of discussion after lunch is a bad idea. Next time, we should keep this for the morning and be more physically active in the afternoons.'

'We should have been clearer with the hotel on catering for people with different dietary requirements.'

'The group discussion activity brought out a lot of energy, but we finished it too early.'

My non-official document proved very useful when planning the event the following year. It was rich with reflections and suggestions, about big and small issues, which I never would have remembered otherwise.

Some simple helping questions to encourage reflection are:

- What happened?
- Did everything happen as expected? What was unexpected?
- What did not happen?
- What still puzzles you? Is there anything that concerns you?

The depth of any learning from experience is directly related to the depth of reflection. 'Learning' is the process of distilling your reflections. After giving due time to reflection and learning, the planning phase provides an opportunity to translate your insights into action.

> ‘ *The depth of any learning from experience is directly related to the depth of reflection.* ’

Mentoring and coaching

A mentoring or coaching relationship can yield rich learning for an individual. Whereas a training course will start with a subject and a range of participants with a variety of expertise and experience, a mentor or coach is focused on the individual person and the specific issues and questions they bring.

Peter was an older man who had been in his organisation for a long time. He worked in the finance department but his career had not kept him office-bound. He was not your typical finance person. He had spent a number of years working closely with people in all parts of the organisation. And he had lots of ideas for how to improve things. He was one of ten people in his organisation who was given a coach.

Through coaching, he realised that he needed to learn how to bring others on board regarding his plans; to also see things from their perspective; and to help them see the bigger picture.

Peter became increasingly inspired by the communication practices he was learning through coaching: improving communication with others, asking questions, listening closely and explaining his perspective instead of assuming that people understood him.

He wanted to try out this communication practice and started with a non-threatening situation. He had a young assistant who was not very efficient. She tended to miss things that he took for granted, which resulted in lots of mistakes. He decided to build his relationship with her. Every morning he would come in, say hello and invite her to have coffee with him while they spoke about what was going on in the work space. This was completely different from the way senior people usually spoke to their subordinates, but this informality created a relaxed and comfortable atmosphere to work in. His next step was to use a coaching-style approach – to first listen and understand what she thought, and what her questions were. She slowly began to ask questions, and sometimes to explain why she had done things differently. He was delighted to notice how much her effectiveness began to improve. (Part 2 is on page 12.)

The value of a good coaching or mentoring relationship extends beyond the content of the conversations. It has the potential to model a way of relating and a style of leadership.

Creativity, the brain and learning

A considerable amount has been written about individual learning styles. Yet, a huge amount of training, and many conferences, still leave you with the impression that if you pack a programme with as much information as you can, people will learn.

In recent years, I've experienced training and conferences that emphasise a more creative approach to learning. I've found myself being invited to articulate my own question, to use clay, draw with crayons, and learn dance steps, all to encourage a different way of seeing and thinking about my work. Not long ago, I would have viewed such activities as either a break from the real learning, or if I was in an uncharitable mood, as a waste of time.

However as I reflect I realise that those learning experiences that have thoughtfully incorporated creative experiences have influenced me and contributed to changes in the way I work far more deeply than all the information-packed days of PowerPoint presentations I've sat through.

What if you worked with the poise of a dancer?

- You never compromise your centre of balance. In all moves, you pass through your centre. Each partner retains their balance while creating tension through which they can communicate. If you sacrifice your centre to 'give yourself to your partner' or to pull away – releasing the tension – it becomes impossible for communication to take place.

- The leader has a moment, a natural pause between moves. This is a decision-making moment, a moment to determine and demonstrate intention before going on.

- The leader needs to physically communicate their intention clearly and lead through invitation.

- The follower needs to foster the skill of following a lead while maintaining their own centre. They need to be sensitive and responsive to the invitation. They need to trust the leader for direction and not make assumptions.

- Partners need to trust each other, lean into each other and commit to each other.

- You always maintain your own dignity and safeguard the dignity of your partner.

- An overly strong desire to 'do it right' can be inhibiting. It is not about the steps. It is about the connection with your partner. The steps merely provide a framework. If you aren't in your centre, the steps cannot help you.

- It is necessary to cultivate a sense of trust in yourself and in what you already know.

I wonder, is this to do with the way our brains operate? Psychiatrist Iain McGilchrist argues in his 2009 book, *The Master and His Emissary*, that while the two hemispheres of the human brain are both employed in any mental activity (be it language, mathematics or painting), the way they process information is quite different. The right hemisphere is best able to recognise something as a whole, related to its context. It can take a broad view, seeing patterns, thinking creatively and working easily with metaphors. The left hemisphere focuses on the parts of the new information. It is more interested in function and analysis and is comfortable with syntax and grammar.

McGilchrist argues that for learning to take place, both hemispheres of the brain need to be engaged. But if the left hemisphere (the one that focuses on the parts) is engaged first, it easily dominates the thinking process, believing it also has the whole picture. Yet, all invention, creativity and innovation occur in the right hemisphere.

Could this be the reason that learning experiences involving creative expression (in addition to employing my better-developed analytical skills) have proved so powerful? Perhaps they activate an under-utilised and powerful side of my brain.

I attended a conference for organisational development practitioners at which the central activity was an art elective. I chose dance. Each day of the conference I attended Argentine Tango classes. While no one mentioned professional practice during the class, I began to reflect on my work in light of what I was learning about dance.

The connections between individual learning and organisational learning

I remember growing frustration over a period of years, feeling that my approach to my work was not achieving the results I had hoped for. The work was demanding and difficult. And I was deeply unsatisfied. Nevertheless, my boss was happy with my efforts to date and trusted my instincts, which created a sufficiently safe environment for me.

One day, I decided to put my normal work on hold. I cleared everything off my desk, closed the door to my office, and tried to clarify what my difficulties were. It took a couple of hours of solitude for my questions to crystallise. But once they had, everything changed for me. Some questions arose that got to the root of my frustration. I felt that if I could make progress in those areas, I could transform my working life. I did have some fear though. Shouldn't I know these things already? Should I reveal to others that I don't have the answers I need to be effective in my job?

> *Learning is a vulnerable process. It requires courage to face reality.*

Nevertheless, I found myself on a fresh journey. My questions helped to focus my thoughts. I began to test them with others. Far from being accused of 'not knowing enough', some people were energised by my questions. They recognised the value of my journey, both for myself and for the organisation, and suggested possible avenues for me to explore. Some were inspired by my honesty, and asked to be kept up to date on my progress. New professional relationships emerged. I read one colleague's PhD thesis and began to follow up some of his sources. An email exchange with one of these sources profoundly deepened my questions and led to further reading, thinking and training opportunities.

> *If an organisation doesn't have a culture of learning, it is extremely difficult for individual learning to inspire organisational learning.*

This was very different to being sent on a training course someone else had chosen for me. The training was directly related to my questions and the journey I was on. These lead to further new connections.

It was a rich time of individual learning. But did it lead to organisational learning?

It led to both organisational learning and organisational conflict. My enthusiasm attracted those with similar questions, and those dissatisfied with how things were being done. I was able to create some environments for others to engage with new ideas and practices. Many were excited to experiment with new ways of thinking and working.

However, as my enthusiasm for a new way of working built momentum, my critique of former ways of working also became stronger. Not everyone shared my disenchantment. Some people now saw me as being negative and overly critical of their approaches and ways of thinking about the work. This resulted in some uncomfortable professional relationships and misunderstandings.

In retrospect, I could have dealt with these more constructively, but I wonder if we had a real culture of learning. If an organisation doesn't have a culture of learning, it is extremely difficult for individual learning to inspire organisational learning.

Peter and coaching Part 2

After gaining confidence from his coaching experience, Peter decided to tackle a larger organisational problem.

The organisation was trying hard to create systems that were more efficient and user-friendly. He had an idea that he knew would work, but he had to get all the relevant units to agree to test this out. Peter realised that all the departments he needed to speak to were represented in his coaching circle (the group of ten in the organisation who were all receiving coaching).

His normal way of addressing this would have been to just change it, and then fight his way through, because consulting with each department individually would be too time consuming. This time he decided to bring the other people on board. Through a dialogue within the coaching circle, he was able to share his idea and get input from everyone. Collectively they developed a solution, and committed to sharing this with the necessary decision-makers.

When he finally made a proposal to the senior management team, it was approved without a fight. This was the first time anyone had used an inter-departmental team to address an issue, and soon others explored this approach.

Recognising the underlying organisational culture

One afternoon I went on a walk through a river valley with a water ecologist. She explained how she was trained to observe nature. Given a landscape to examine, she would pay careful attention to the patterns that were visible. She would then identify the relationships between different parts of the landscape, in all their complexity – in a river valley everything is connected. She would then try and work out the underlying processes taking place. 'Pattern' and 'process' are key concepts.

An ecologist should never intervene in a landscape without having developed an understanding of the underlying processes. Simply working on the visible patterns is normally a waste of time. Instead, one should work with the underlying processes to achieve an objective, rather than work against them.

At one point while walking through the river valley, we got lost. 'Ecologists always get lost,' she said reassuringly.

Organisations have an underlying culture that powerfully shapes the way things are done. Some dimensions strike you immediately: one organisation will only take you seriously if you are dressed in a suit and tie; another sees anything beyond a shirt, shorts and sandals as an obstacle to conversation – a demonstration of how out of touch you are.

In the same way that it is pointless working on the visible dimensions of a river valley if you don't understand the underlying processes at work, it is pointless trying to improve organisational learning if you haven't grasped the organisation's underlying culture – especially those dimensions that either enable or inhibit learning.

Recognising and describing an organisation's culture is not easy and takes well-developed skills of observation and insight. Like ecologists walking through river valleys, it is easy to get lost.

> *We should have probed its history, allowing recent patterns ... to come to light.*

In Chapter 3 we will consider how to recognise, and work with, an organisation's culture, and explore how to generate a 'culture of learning'.

Revisiting the 'meltdown' story

Let us return to the story that began this chapter. As OD specialists, we could have done a much better job of supporting learning and bringing about a deeper change in the life of the organisation. For a start, we could have seen part of our purpose as being to promote organisational learning, rather than simply trying to solve a sticky problem. We should have probed its history, allowing recent patterns of 'collapse and rescue' to come to light. This may have uncovered the underlying assumptions, beliefs and values at play in the organisation. We could have explored the relational patterns between all the key players, and attempted to see the deeper culture of the organisation.

By surfacing these deep realities in the organisation's life, the leadership would have come to recognise that a simple diagnosis and the usual rescue package were not the answers. As individuals, they could have seen their organisation and their role in it differently. As an organisation, they would have had an opportunity to address the deeper dynamics that seemed to regularly bring them into crisis. They would have experienced serious organisational learning.

It would have been a painful process, but when people recognise an organisational pattern which extends beyond individuals, it can transform relationships.

And what of the international partners, staffed with people on two-year contracts? Their lack of organisational memory made it more difficult to be a good partner. Organisational memory would have helped them recognise collective failure, rather than simply pointing the finger at the implementing organisation.

Given the regular turnover of staff, it is even more important for the support organisations to maintain a living analysis of their relationship with local partners. They need to understand the history and the power dynamics between the key stakeholders, what had been done in the past, and what had been learned. They should find ways of nourishing this understanding so that it can live beyond the individuals who come and go. And they need to be particularly accurate at harvesting the reflections and learnings of their staff as they get to the end of their two-year term. Otherwise, learning remains forever with departing individuals and never becomes 'organisational learning'.

These international partners have no less a need to develop their own culture of learning. If they began to model a more effective culture of learning, their staff would be in a much better position to encourage their partners in the same direction.

Other sections of this guide will explore ways of supporting learning facilitators, what unlearning is and how to facilitate it, how to open learning processes, and how to incorporate learning into existing systems. Some of these approaches can help an organisation develop a culture of learning – but none of them will be effective in an organisation that clings to an anti-learning culture.

CHAPTER 3

Lively spaces:
creating a learning culture

Case studies for the sake of … what?

I was once asked to work with some organisations to develop case studies, so that their 'learning' could be shared with others. However, no one felt at all comfortable documenting any decisions or actions that could reflect badly on themselves, their organisations or their bosses. And so the result was a collection of 'success stories' devoid of any failure or sense of struggle. Unfortunately, they probably wouldn't be particularly useful to readers either. What were missing from the collection were the stories of failure and struggle – the experiences that prepared the ground for success to bloom. *Those* stories many readers would have related to.

One of the things that makes every organisation unique is its own culture. Some can be relaxed and friendly while others can be formal and businesslike. Some may be transparent and inclusive about how they make decisions whilst others may only allow certain people access to vital information. Or some may have quite competitive relationships and others co-operative relationships. There are numerous things like this. Like people, each organisation has its own character and personality.

This chapter focuses on 'learning culture', which are those aspects of organisational culture that affect learning, whether they be supporting or hindering it.

A *conscious* and *healthy* learning culture is a set of practised values, conditions and behaviours that are *agreed* upon by a group of willing learners. This culture also supports the learners to regularly, honestly and effectively reflect on *how* they learn together to improve their practice.

Why is it important to pay attention to learning culture?

Monday – learning day

We all agreed that we would put aside three hours each Monday to share what we were doing and look for learnings, connections and support from each other. But when the next Monday came, only half the people were there. When they were later asked what happened one said, 'I assumed it was optional, that I could come if I wanted to or not,' and another said, 'I didn't want to come because last year when we did something like this I was criticised for mistakes I had made. I felt really undermined.'

The first response here reveals an aspect of culture that is free but individualistic, where people are encouraged – but not expected – to co-operate and can 'do their own thing'. They enjoy their freedom, which feeds their individual commitment, but they lack organisational commitment. How do we ensure both individual and organisational commitment in an age where the needs of individuals are gaining increasing priority?

The second response reveals a culture of critique, very different from a safe place for honest sharing. Learning only becomes possible if people feel safe to share their experiences, questions and ideas freely. People must be rewarded for honesty, not punished. They must be encouraged to share their struggles and mistakes. Only then can learning take place. An environment in which 'success stories' are the only acceptable ones undermines a culture of learning.

In these two responses we touch upon several *dimensions* of a learning culture, as outlined by John Farago and David Skyrme in their 1995 internet article, *The Learning Organisation*. In balancing the individual and organisational commitment and creating a fruitful environment for learning we must think about the following aspects.

Future, external orientation

The organisation must commit time to keeping an eye on the future, on what is moving towards the organisation from the outside. It must open up to outside feedback and support and challenges.

Free, horizontal exchange and flow of information

Organisational processes and systems must be in place to ensure that experience and expertise is available where it is needed. Individuals must be helped to network extensively, crossing organisational boundaries, to develop their knowledge and expertise.

Commitment to learning and personal development

Learning requires support from top management and people at all levels being encouraged to learn regularly. Learning is rewarded and there is time to think and learn – to understand, explore, reflect, and develop.

Valuing people and their inborn creativity

Ideas, creativity and 'imaginative capabilities' are stimulated, made use of and developed. Diversity is recognised as a strength. Views can be challenged.

A climate of openness and trust

Individuals are encouraged to develop ideas, to speak out, to challenge actions.

Learning from experience

Learning is acknowledged as happening from successes and mistakes. Failure is tolerated, provided lessons are learnt.

What to keep in mind when thinking about a learning culture

When thinking about developing learning in an organisation, the following points should inform your ideas:

- An organisation's culture is mostly unconscious and invisible to its own people, which can make the culture difficult to change. Before it can be changed it needs to be made more visible. (The section below – 'Find out your own learning culture', might be helpful.).

- Culture is not a uniform thing. There are often competing sub-cultures, different groupings of people who experience the organisation very differently. Don't assume that everyone has the same experience of the organisation.

- Most people want to co-operate and learn from each other, and they will do so if the conditions are right.

- Staff members are complex human beings who question, learn and form relationships. The co-operative quality of these relationships is key to a culture of learning. This view can be contrasted to treating staff as 'human resources' who perform like machines and need an occasional 'tune up', for example a training course, or a good talking to.

> *The co-operative quality of these relationships is key to a culture of learning.*

Hofstede's model of organisational culture

Organisational sociologist Professor Geert Hofstede has identified five dimensions of national culture. He organised his findings into a framework that reveals the expectations people have of leadership and management within an organisation. The diagram below shows the range of positions in relation to each other.

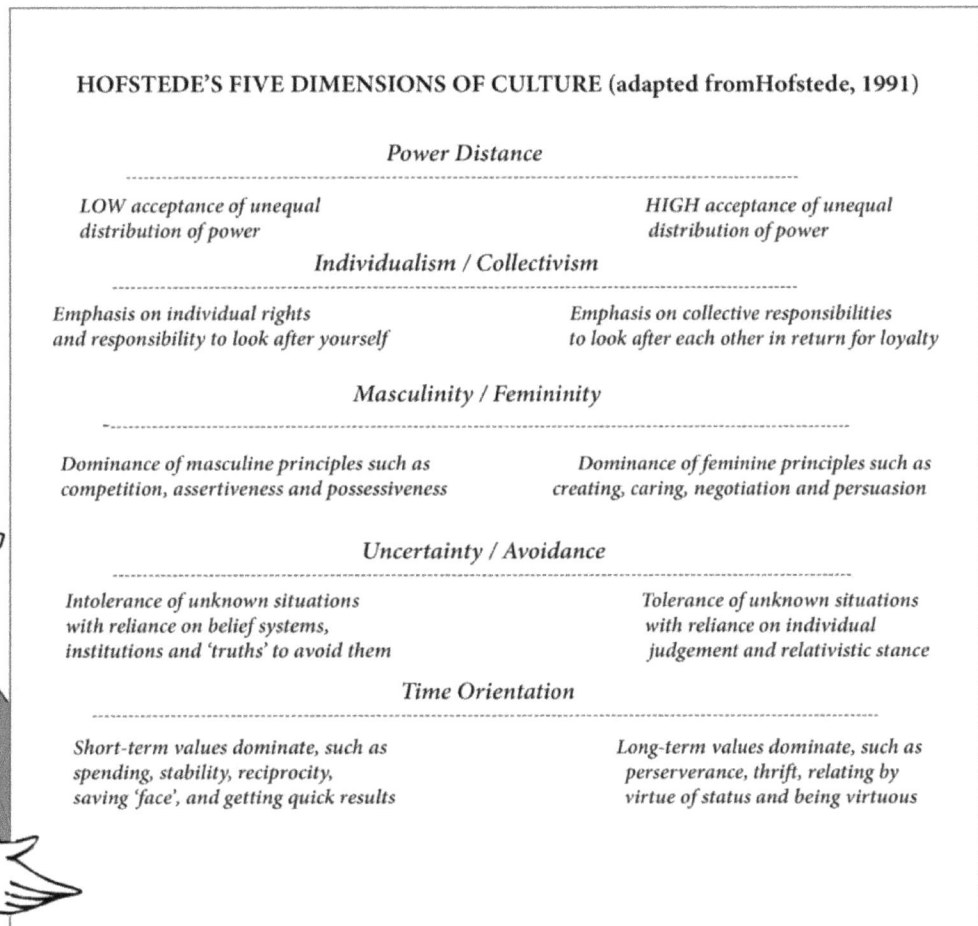

HOFSTEDE'S FIVE DIMENSIONS OF CULTURE (adapted fromHofstede, 1991)

Power Distance

LOW acceptance of unequal distribution of power

HIGH acceptance of unequal distribution of power

Individualism / Collectivism

Emphasis on individual rights and responsibility to look after yourself

Emphasis on collective responsibilities to look after each other in return for loyalty

Masculinity / Femininity

Dominance of masculine principles such as competition, assertiveness and possessiveness

Dominance of feminine principles such as creating, caring, negotiation and persuasion

Uncertainty / Avoidance

Intolerance of unknown situations with reliance on belief systems, institutions and 'truths' to avoid them

Tolerance of unknown situations with reliance on individual judgement and relativistic stance

Time Orientation

Short-term values dominate, such as spending, stability, reciprocity, saving 'face', and getting quick results

Long-term values dominate, such as perserverance, thrift, relating by virtue of status and being virtuous

How can you use this model to stimulate a learning culture?

- Ask each staff member to place a mark along each line at the point which they think accurately describes the organisation's culture. For example, is it more individual or more collective?

- Compare these answers and ask people to motivate their own, using *real examples* to illustrate their answers.

- Ask each other how the organisation's culture affects its ability to learn.

This exercise should lead to some interesting observations and reflections, and enable the organisation to think about what needs to change in order for it to become a more learning organisation.

Find out your own learning culture

Learning lives all over an organisation, so we can look in different places. What would happen if you asked yourselves these questions?

How participative are meetings? Do only the experienced speak, or do most people have a chance to have their say?

If people see a colleague is messing up their work, what do they do? Ignore it, gossip amongst each other, confront them, or speak to them supportively?

If people have been struggling with their own work, what happens? Do they feel safe to admit it freely and ask for support or ideas, or do they keep it to themselves for fear of losing people's respect or that promotion?

If people have done a good job, what happens? Is this ignored or celebrated? Are their efforts appreciated, or do their colleagues resent their success?

After interesting experiences in the field, what happens? Is time put aside to learn from it, or are deadlines too tight to stop and reflect?

Whose experience and ideas matter most? Outside consultants, the team leader, those who talk the most, or all staff?

How much attention is paid to individual development? Very little? Now and again if there is funding? Is there effective induction of new staff? How about regular individual development planning?

How are decisions actually made? By the managers, collectively by consensus or behind the scenes? Perhaps by those most affected by the decision?

If people feel unfairly treated how do they explain it? Because they are women, because they are black, because they are white, because they are less experienced?

These questions explore aspects of organisational culture that directly affect the ability of people and the organisation to learn effectively.

A culture of learning demands that people take a long term perspective. If the pressure is always on to deal with the next crisis, it becomes difficult for people to take a step back and reflect on the bigger picture.

> *A culture of learning demands that people take a long term perspective.*

Lessons not yet learned

A colleague once told me, 'If you looked back at all the major projects we have carried out in the last fifteen years, you will find the same issues rising up again and again under the "lessons learned" section at the back of the external evaluation report. This section should be renamed "lessons not yet learned".'

Types of learning that a learning culture should support

Being a learning organisation is not about 'more training'. While training does help develop certain types of skill, being a learning organisation involves developing higher levels of knowledge and skill. These are the types to support:

Type 1 – Learning essential facts, knowledge and procedures Does your culture support people getting to know the basics?

Type 2 – Learning to transfer experience and skills to other situations Does your culture encourage people to think about how what they learn can apply to other challenges?

Type 3 – Learning to adapt Does your culture support experimentation, and deriving lessons from success and failure?

Type 4 – Learning to learn and innovate Does your culture reward taking risks, being innovative and creative? Do you design the future rather than merely adapt to it? In this learning assumptions are challenged and knowledge is reframed.

These four types of learning can be applied to several areas: to the learning of individuals, of teams and of organisations. Organisations that achieve learning to the level of Type 4 will reinvent not just their organisation but their industry.

Letting go… letting come…

Getting your learning culture right may mean taking on new attitudes, behaviours and skills but it may also mean letting go of – or unlearning! – things as well.

Letting go…

For many organisations, developing a learning culture requires 'letting go' of things that undermine learning. Consider:

- Competition between staff (often very hidden) that undermines co-operative and collective sharing and learning.
- Success is seen as more important than admitting failure.
- The idea that time for learning is a luxury we cannot afford.
- An unsafe culture where criticism is mistaken for honesty.
- Over-activism and idealism that sacrifices the personal health and needs of individuals, often leading to burnout.
- Hierarchies that value the experience and ideas of some over others.
- A situation in which the leaders don't feel the need to participate in learning, because they know it all. (See 'Star learner syndrome' in *Barefoot Guide 1*, page 144.)

See 'Star learner syndrome' in Barefoot Guide 1, page 144.

Letting come…

A space is now created into which can 'come' and grow the following qualities and resources. They enable individual and collective will and ability to learn.

- Commitment to time – regular, dedicated time.

- Empathy – a most important value. It enables us to identify at the deepest level and through this really learn from each other.

- Curiosity – being fascinated with all experience and insights.

- Appreciating honesty – once fear and destructive competition disappears then honesty can be unlocked and open the way for transparency. Everyone can reveal their stories.

- Equality – everybody's experience is valuable.

- Enjoyment – a space is created to enjoy meaningful learning.

Improving the learning culture

There are many ways to improve the learning culture – but no tricks or quick fixes! It takes effort, commitment and time, and needs at least the following factors to be in place.

Willing leaders

Willing leaders let go of certain attitudes and inspire new ones. If the directors, managers or co-ordinators are not really interested, then this is a losing battle. Does the leadership accept that the organisation isn't learning, or has a culture that inhibits learning? Do they recognise the consequences? Are they willing to explore the underlying assumptions? Are they willing to model an approach to learning that will demonstrate that they too are learners? It may be that you need to engage the leadership with these questions. Without their enthusiasm and energy, you will risk exhausting yourself, swimming against a tide.

Frank and open conversations

These lay good learning foundations beneath and between all members. They ask the kinds of self-reflective questions we suggest above. If there is strong resistance to collective learning then you can take yourselves through a 'U-process'. This is an unlearning and creative process which helps you to let go of what does not help learning. It also helps you to renew existing values and create new ones, plus practices and behaviours that will better support good organisational learning. It can lay a good foundation for launching your organisation into a more 'learningful' future. (See pages 112–17 of *Barefoot Guide 1*).

'We learn through all our experiences and they enrich our store of knowledge. But in order that we may learn on the Earth, we must be allured by and involved in enjoyment.'

Rudolf Steiner

See pages 112-17 of Barefoot Guide 1.

Taking time to reflect and learn more deeply as a team

The Action Learning cycle was introduced earlier as a model for individual learning. Its power magnifies if done in a team or a group. But it is often used in a shallow way. Does your team find itself constantly moving from planning to action and back into planning, without really stopping to think and reflect? Do you have the influence to include times of reflection and learning into the normal rhythms of work? How can you ask more penetrating and revealing questions to get to the real challenges and prevent your organisation repeating the same mistakes?

Friday – learning day on the verandah

A colleague of mine used to work in a culture where politeness and 'saving face' were critical dimensions to work. This made it difficult to address problems and failures because they were never recognised as such – they were always written up as 'successes' with a list of a few 'lessons learned'. He began to take his team out of the office onto a verandah every Friday afternoon. This took everyone away from the formality that normally accompanied their meetings. And they learned to speak frankly with each other about the week:

'I don't like that way you spoke to our visitor on Tuesday. You were too aggressive. He didn't say anything, but I'm sure he was offended. I could see it in his face.'

'Well he had been telling lies about me to our colleagues. I know I was aggressive with him. But I was angry.'

This routine evolved to ensure that all the 'dirty washing' was regularly brought out and the team became aware of important ways in which they related. It also built up the trust among this team considerably. They learned to be very open with each other. This became their venue for sharing reflections and exploring what they had learned. My colleague was surprised at the strength the team drew from these sessions.

'There won't be a moment when the stars align and you'll know it's time to start. In today's rapidly changing world, real-world practice never presents itself as a collection of precise problems but as messy, indeterminate situations. It's everyone's job to develop better ways to deal with the unstructured, the undefined, and the unknown. Ralph Waldo Emerson once noted that there are always two parties: the movement and the establishment. Which one are you a part of? Unless you're an active learner, you're part of the establishment and are likely stifling learning in ways you don't understand.'

Marcia L. Conner and James G. Clawson

To conclude, you *can* make a new start as a leader in a learning organisation. What you need is the courage to look at your own learning habits and to try new things. When you start others will follow. And the moment you start is always the right moment.

Moving tapestries:
learning in
organisational systems

Things are going well. You have worked hard, studied your organisation, understand how individuals learn, know your context well. With the leadership on your side, you have developed a plan of action to ensure your organisation can learn effectively. There are learning events planned throughout the year and the Action Learning cycle is incorporated into meetings. The first big event is tomorrow. Development practitioners from different levels and offices are coming together to understand better what they have been doing, and how effective it is. You have had a good response. Every place is taken. You have spent a long time preparing materials. The day before, you prepared the room. It is airy and light, looking on to a garden where people will be able to work in groups. There are chocolates and biscuits on the tables. You have paints and crayons and clay. The walls are adorned with pictures and quotes that should get people thinking.

Today you had a couple of cancellations. Sorry, they say, but they have deadlines to meet, or another department has organised an urgent meeting. Nothing to worry about, you reassure yourself, the room will still be full.

On the first day of the workshop you arrive early. The first two people arrive, quite excited by this new opportunity. The third comes straight up to you and explains that he will need to leave early. The accounts department needs some figures urgently; no-one else can do it except him. More people come looking keen, but flustered. A few people don't show up. When you are laying the ground rules, everyone agrees that it would be better to finish an hour earlier than you had planned. And do we really need a full day on Friday? Wouldn't it be better to finish at lunch time? The deadline for appraisal reports is Monday. And then there's month end…

It's not that we don't want to learn, they say, it's just that we have all these deadlines to meet.

What's happening here?

As an organisation grows, it needs to develop processes that support the work we do. These administrative support systems enable us to recruit the people we need, report to our donors, decide how to allocate our resources. In big organisations there are teams of people working on these systems full-time.

Support processes and systems

Communications

Fund raising

Administrative support systems are typically a product of left-brain thinking (see Chapter 15.). They enable us to put information into categories, prioritise it and bring order to our world. Even small organisations need systems to help them make sense of an increasingly complex world. They also enable us to be accountable to other organisations that support and legitimise us: the tax office, the donor, the regulatory body.

Without systems, we could not function; they help us to manage our world in replicable ways. There is a danger, though, that we begin to see the systems as more important than the reality they help us manage. We start acting as though the world really can be divided into discrete pieces of information that can be counted and analysed. Activities that are not easily fitted into time-bound processes with clear deadlines – relationship-building, creative thinking, learning, even social change itself – struggle to find space in this world. The time available for them shrinks. Or, their value is recognised and

Information technology

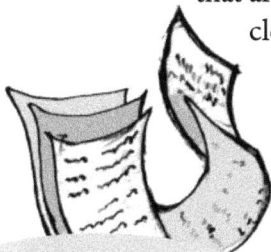

Human resources

Finance

Marketing & publicity

an attempt is made to fit them into a system: 'By Sept next year we will have developed ten good relationships with community-based organisations'. But the time allocated makes it impossible for us to do this in a meaningful way. We visit a community-based organisation once, and the second time we arrive with partnership agreement in hand – 'sign this' – so we can tick them off the list. The organisation wants to measure in steps and end points, whereas a lot of change is incremental, happening bit-by-bit, barely visible unless we stay with it and watch it over time.

Instead of serving us, the system becomes the master.

But systems are living things too...

The support systems we are looking at are part of a larger system, the organisation, which in turn is part of an even bigger system, the environment in which it operates. So systems are living things too. They grow and develop over time and, well-tended, they can flourish. But without care they can become monsters, killing other living things around them. If we want to make them healthier and more effective, we can't just replace a broken part or tighten a screw. We need to look at the organisation as a whole and understand that changes made in one place will affect the whole organisation, because it is held together by relationships and connections.

Are there systems that you have set up that have slowly encroached on the rest of your work? Simple solutions may have grown into complex monsters over time. If you find yourself saying, 'We can't do strategic planning now because we have to fill in our timesheets this week,' you might like to examine your systems more closely and see how much time you spend on them.

Getting rid of such systems is not the answer. Good administrative support systems help us to organise our work so we can use time most effectively doing the things we want to do. Good systems mean we don't spend the last month of the year scrambling to report to our donors. What we need to ensure is that all these systems enable the people who use them to learn from them and that they are regularly adapted, based on our learning. That they provide space and information for learning. That they also do not take up so much time that the vital functions of the organisation, the processes that bring about social change, are unable to take place. But systems are complex. Where do we start?

Physicist and author Fritjof Capra states that there is no distinction between living and learning, 'A living system is a learning system.' If we don't begin to seriously focus on learning in our organisations, there is no way we can bring them to life.

Margaret J Wheatley and Myron Kellner-Rogers

Some principles for working to change organisational systems

1. Participation is not a choice

People support what they create. Every person in the organisation needs to be involved in thinking about how the organisation can learn, and how working with the systems they are responsible for can enable this learning to happen.

2. People react to directives, they never obey them

We must offer our thoughts and ideas to people to invite them to be involved and co-create. We cannot tell people to change; we need to work with them to enable change to happen.

3. We do not see 'reality'; we each create our own interpretation of what's real

You may see a system that is slowing fieldwork down and tying the staff up when they should be out working with communities. Others may see a system that is providing information to people who need it to raise money so that fieldwork can continue, or so that informed decisions can be made about how resources should be best allocated to benefit communities. Unless we listen to how others see the system then we can't work together to make it a learning system.

4. Systems improve themselves by connecting with all the parts and listening

Systems are capable of changing themselves if they get better and richer information from within themselves. But often this information resides with people who have not always been understood to be part of the system – for example, the communities the organisation is working for. In schools this might mean listening to children; in factories listening to workers and customers; and in organisations listening to all staff and the people we are working with to bring about social change.

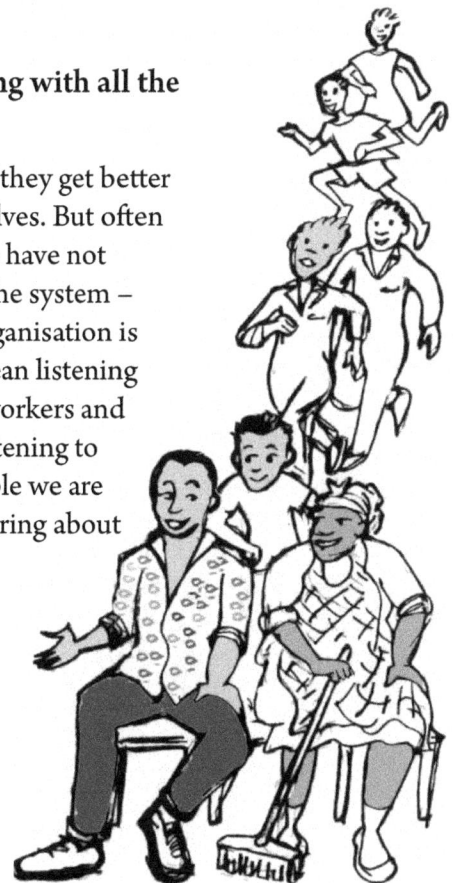

Systems are about people

If an organisation's main purpose is to enable social change, shouldn't every person contribute to this purpose? Just as we have spent a lot of time trying to understand ourselves and our context, we must make sure we understand ourselves as a whole organisation. This includes understanding all our current systems and processes, not only those that relate directly to social change. (If you have done this when analysing your organisation and the context in which you work, then you can skip this bit!)

Smaller organisations may think: this does not concern us, we don't have a human resources or an IT department. This may be true, but it's good to check whether you have really involved everyone in the process so far. Have you considered the accountant? Or the cleaner? Have you talked to your members or the people you work with in communities? What systems do you have? Why? Are they helping you to learn?

As long as the beakers are clean...

A soil scientist was volunteering in a government soil science research station in Thailand. He was working with the researchers to improve research techniques, and carry out research that would provide information to local farmers on crop management. The station had been carrying out research for years. The volunteer got to know the laboratory technicians. They were not well paid and their status was low because they did not have a university education. However, they were responsible for the day-to-day running of the laboratories and a lot of the repetitive tasks associated with the research. One day he was shocked to find them rinsing out test tubes and beakers they were using for an experiment, under the tap.

'Don't you use distilled water?' he asked.

'We used to,' they replied. 'But it ran out and we thought it would be easier just to use tap water – cheaper too.'

The researchers had told them to use distilled water but not why this was critically important – to avoid introducing unknown bacteria into the research samples and skewing the results. It turned out the lab technicians had been using tap water for five years and no one had noticed.

All the research done during this time was invalid because no-one had thought to tell the lab technicians why using distilled water was important, or to recognise the value of their work.

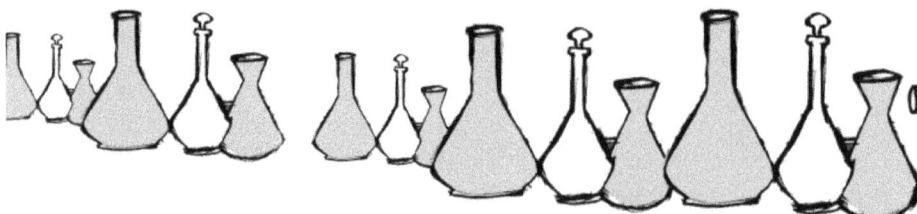

> *Systems, like organisations, depend on people.*

Those of us who work in the field have a tendency to complain about systems, to feel that others are not doing enough to help us. We say, 'IT are so slow and when you do get them on the phone, you can't understand what they are talking about,' or 'Who invents these spreadsheets?' It is easy to complain about systems. Or use them as an excuse for not learning. But unless we change them we will not address the issue. And to do that we need to engage with the people who run them. Systems, like organisations, depend on people. We need to understand them and what they use the systems for and why they developed in this way.

Working with different parts of the organisation may be new. Staff working in the field may have little knowledge of the organisation as a whole, especially if the service departments are located in another country. Bureaucracies can easily lead to people working in isolation, just concentrating on doing their own job well, without thinking of the wider implications of what they do. Administrative and programme staff in the same office can be surprisingly unaware of what each other's jobs involve. Starting to work with a department of the organisation or a person that you don't know very well is not so different from being a facilitator of change in an organisation other than your own. The processes described in the *Barefoot Guide 1* regarding organisations and social change can be helpful here, especially Chapter 3 about creating and working with relationships in organisations. First of all, build up relationships; get to know what people do and what is important to them. What are they passionate about? What excites them?

Understanding each other's role

In a smaller organisation, a facilitator asked each department to pretend they were a radio station – they were to broadcast key statements about what they felt was important about their work. With the staff sitting at their usual desks, the facilitator tuned in and out of different 'stations' so all could hear about each other's work, and everyone was given space to describe their reality. This opened the way for debate and increased people's understanding of each other's role in the organisation.

Recently I was lucky enough to be involved in a strategic planning process that brought together people from all parts of my organisation. It was an opportunity to talk to them and find out what they value in their work, their successes and the challenges they face. Most of the people I spoke to have what Buddhists call 'right intention' and are proud of what the organisation does. They want the work they do to meet the standards that are considered acceptable in their field, for example equality in human resources practices, accountability and transparency in financial management.

They also want their work to contribute to the work of the organisation as a whole. For some people this seems to be about the organisation being seen as one that is good at what it does and achieves what it has set out to do. For others this is directly about making the world a better place and changing people's lives for the better. Building relationships, listening and learning is the first step towards mutual understanding and change.

Don't forget the leaders!

Once we have understood the people who manage and develop the systems better, the leaders of the organisation need to be brought on board. There needs to be a commitment to change systems so that they are *learning systems* that allow learning for social change to take place; recognition that learning involves the whole organisation and is not something that can just be tacked on. To achieve this you may want to give a presentation to senior management or the board, or invite them to your events. It's helpful if you can show how a specific system is hindering learning.

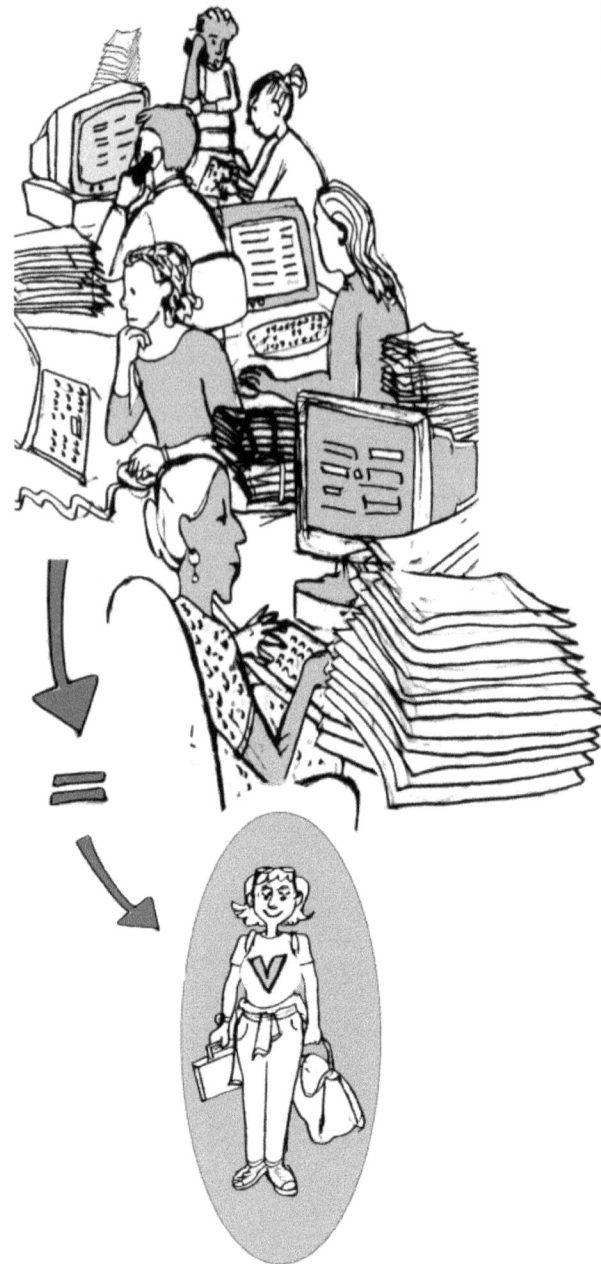

A burdensome support system

At a strategic planning meeting one group presented a dialogue between two staff members. It showed clearly how the system for recruiting volunteers involved many members of staff, many emails and meant that partners had to wait a long time before they got the person they needed. People could see immediately that the current system had become ineffective and burdensome. The dialogue succeeded in getting people thinking about ways in which they could do things differently.

Systems for learning, systems for social change

We need to remind ourselves what our systems are for. Our systems and processes should be based on the values we espouse and the vision to which we aspire.

This seems so obvious but it is surprising how many organisations do not even think about this when they develop administrative systems. We lecture our partners or the communities we work with on the importance of learning, but we use systems that hinder our own learning, or ignore learning.

We are organisations working on social change. Our systems need to enable us to make social change happen. In order to do that, we need to learn. It might be useful to ask:

- How do our systems enable us to bring about social change?

- How do our systems enable us to learn?

- How do our systems stop us from learning?

- How do our systems stop us from bringing about social change?

> *Sometimes systems are so deeply ingrained in our work that we don't even notice how they influence us.*

www.appreciativeinquiry.case.edu – is a worldwide portal devoted to the fullest sharing of academic resources and practical tools on Appreciative Inquiry.

This keeps our focus on our purpose better than questions such as, 'What kind of accounting system do we need so that we can report to donors properly?' or 'What's the cheapest way in which we can communicate with each other?' These questions have their place but it is important to return to the wider questions above, so we don't end up with a cheap communication system that makes it difficult for people to learn from each other or that takes up time that could be better used working on social change.

Each system needs to be looked at rigorously. An Appreciative Inquiry approach may be useful here (see box). It enables us to see where there is potential for learning and build on this. And there needs also to be a letting-go; an unlearning. Sometimes systems are so deeply ingrained in our work that we don't even notice how they influence us. For example, the tax year in the country where the head office is based has an influence on financial reporting. This then tends to influence the timing of narrative reporting – which then influences the activities in the field – and monitoring and evaluation activities are timed to take place so that they can feed into reports – plus small grants to partners must be spent before the financial year ends. In some countries this will mean that money is available at the time of year when it is difficult for partners to do activities, perhaps because it is the rainy season so travel is difficult, or because it coincides with major festivals or intense agricultural work. It may mean that we are asking partners to be involved in learning activities when they would prefer to be carrying out activities with communities. Often it is only when we look at the effect systems have on the context where we are trying to enable social change that we can see the inadvertent damage they might be doing.

The cumulative effect of systems also needs to be examined. If the financial and narrative reports and appraisals are all due in at nearly the same time, staff in a small programme office may have several months in the year where they are not able to carry out any activities with partners or communities at all. If a fieldworker is spending more time at a computer than with the community then we have to ask ourselves if this is really the ratio of action to administration that will be most effective. We expect teachers to spend most of their time with their students and doctors to spend most of their time with their patients, so development fieldworkers might reasonably be expected to spend most of their time with the people they are working for.

In praise of simple systems

We can become very attached to the systems we use, especially
if we have invested a lot of energy in them.

We like systems

A staff member from head office tells about how systems can give you a false sense of work done: 'Systems are
not threatening; they're comfortable. They give a meaning to the hours we are required to spend in the office. We
like to look busy, to be busy and the best way for that is to spend as much time as possible working in the system,
belonging to it, nurturing it, growing it.'

He goes on to reflect how he has his best ideas when running on the treadmill in the gym in the mornings – time
he is not paid for in a place where no one sees him working. It is not the systems that are making him effective – it
is activities that give him space to reflect and think.

What might this story mean for an effective working culture? To
make time for reflection and learning, basic systems – reporting,
data input, accounting – need to be pared back to the minimum
needed to keep the organisation functioning. They need to be as
simple as possible. They need to be regularly reviewed to make
sure they are not inadvertently preventing learning.

A note of warning

Simplifying and streamlining systems can mean we don't need
so many people to run the systems. If you are a fieldworker
you may end up with more time to learn and to be in the
field. But the IT worker and the accounts officer may end up
without a job. How are you going to manage this situation?
A learning organisation needs to give people the skills and
experience they need to make a career change or find similar
work. A learning organisation cares about people and has
invested in their learning – not just for the organisation's benefit
but for the individual's benefit too.

Other systems that may need attention

If you ask someone, 'Who is responsible for learning in your organisation?' it is very likely
that they will say the 'staff development team' or the 'monitoring and evaluation advisors' or
even the 'knowledge management people' or the 'data management section'. But no one can
learn for us. We cannot give the responsibility for our own learning to someone else nor can
we expect someone else to take the responsibility for sharing our learning with others.

The role of these teams is to enable learning and to ensure that individual learning
translates into organisational learning. In addition, learning facilitators or leaders can keep
learning alive within the organisation. It is important to work with the people who have
been given this responsibility to make sure their systems are encouraging and valuing
learning – helping to create the conditions for it to happen.

For ideas on working with this, read the chapter 'How do we learn?' in Pearson's paper. It also has more thoughts about enabling conditions for learning, for example, 'Who decides about the learning needs?'

Staff development

Staff development teams traditionally operate as part of the human resources function of the organisation. Their role is to ensure that all staff members have the knowledge and capacity to do their jobs effectively. They are responsible for organising and co-ordinating professional development at two levels: individual and organisational. At the individual level, it can happen by providing funds for a member of staff to attend a relevant course, or matching them up with a mentor for example. At the organisational level it may be, for example, by developing and running training courses to familiarise all relevant staff with new systems or ways of working.

There are a number of things to look out for if you want to understand whether current staff development is really enhancing learning.

1. What kinds of staff development are currently preferred and who decides about the learning needs?

If the majority of resources are spent on traditional training courses then there is a danger that individual learning is not being translated into organisational learning. Jenny Pearson points out, in her 2010 book *Seeking Better Practices for Capacity Development: Training & Beyond*, that traditional training has been shown to have a limited effect on translating individual capacity into organisational development. Staff members are often unable to take and use the skills they have learned into the workplace, because there is not the time or understanding to support this.

2. Is the link between learning and social change made?

Staff of an organisation that is involved in social change need to understand how social change happens and have an understanding of the communities or organisations the organisation is working with. It may not be possible for the accountant to visit every partner or community but it is essential for them to spend time with one and speak with the people there. This is not a touchy-feely exercise in participation – it is fundamental if we are going to develop systems that are informed by our values and the aspirations of those who we seek to work with to bring about social change. If it is impractical to fly everyone round the world to visit the actual places where we are working, then watching films, listening to interviews and speaking to fieldworkers are all useful exercises. Organisations that work with volunteers can create volunteering opportunities for their staff.

3. Is enough time spent on learning from those we are working with?

Many NGOs, both local and international, act as though learning and the exchange of knowledge are one-way processes – they talk about what they are bringing to communities and rarely about what their staff and their organisation is learning from them. Time spent in communities, listening to what they have to say and looking at their systems and processes to see what we can learn from them is hugely important. Listening is a way of being accountable to the people we work for – it shows that we value their learning and skills and knowledge as much as we expect them to value ours. It acknowledges that we are able to bring resources and expertise to social change because we are privileged and because the balance of power is uneven, not because we are intrinsically better than they are. It recognises that it is the mobilisation of local expertise and knowledge that is the key driver in bringing about social change.

Monitoring and Evaluation

It is often assumed that the Monitoring and Evaluation (M&E) department or activity is where the majority of learning in an organisation takes place. However, the very words (monitoring = checking that something is happening; evaluation = giving a value to the results of an activity or project) suggest that this is often not so. It is perfectly possible to have a learning-free M&E system! Most of our systems actually are not promoting learning because they have some characteristics that do not help us learn.

Firstly the focus is on getting reports in on time rather than the process of collecting, analysing and understanding information in order to improve our work.

Secondly, M&E processes and events are carried out in an identical manner in every community, province, district or country. The focus is on comparing the data we collect with other data, or aggregating it until it becomes a meaningless statistic, rather than on enabling the communities and the organisations to learn from them.

Thirdly the M&E system has been developed to meet the requirements of the donor only: it is for accountability purposes. There need to be learning processes too.

And finally the M&E system is separate from the planning system, so no changes are made as a result of the information collected and analysed.

Other chapters will deal with M&E in more detail.

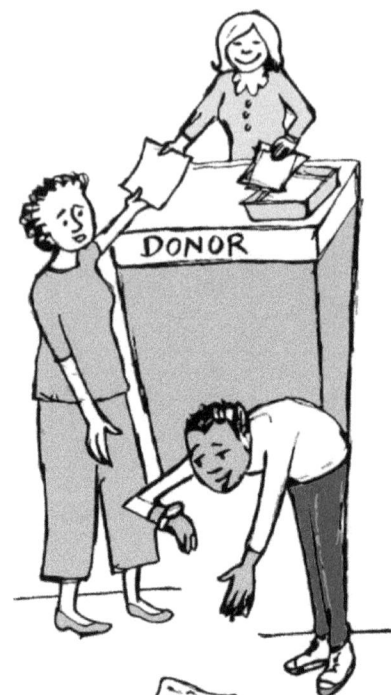

Knowledge management

Some organisations have knowledge management functions, either within M&E or separate from it. Knowledge management is often the reserve of people with good IT skills and involves setting up databases or virtual storage sites of information. Knowledge is, of course, important for learning and organisations need to document learning and make sure it is available to others, both inside and outside the organisation. But technology is only a tool, not a solution.

Information and knowledge are not learning. Learning is a process that is ongoing and requires access to information and knowledge, gained from our own experience or that of other people.

QUALITIES OF A GOOD KNOWLEDGE MANAGEMENT SYSTEM

- Accessible to everyone who needs it.

- Organises information and knowledge in ways that are understandable to all. For example, giving documents numbers only would be restrictive; using technical language may be exclusive.

- Has a human face – people have limited time to search for information and much of it may be hidden within documents. In most organisations there are people who are 'repositories of knowledge'. They do not know everything but they have been around long enough to remember pieces of work and projects that we can still learn from. Such people could be available to advise people on where to look for information. In bigger organisations, it might even be worth having someone employed full-time to look through the database for specific information as it is requested – just as researchers for a television programme set in a historical period will be employed to find out what kind of clothes the characters would wear and check for historical accuracy.

- Supplements learning between and within people, but is not learning itself. If the knowledge management budget is equated with the learning budget you will end up with an expensive tool that is not fully used.

Joining up the learning dots

Staff development, M&E and knowledge management tend to sit in different departments and be organised by different people. They may even operate entirely separately from one another. This makes it very hard for individual and organisational learning to be connected and for the two to inform one another. The individual attending a training course may not be able to connect what they have learned with the needs of the organisation and communities. The learning from the communities and practice from other parts of the organisation may not be shared with individuals.

The knowledge management, staff development and M&E people should work together. They could be the learning team – champions of learning across the organisation, and able to facilitate and enable everyone to learn.

Getting creative about systems!

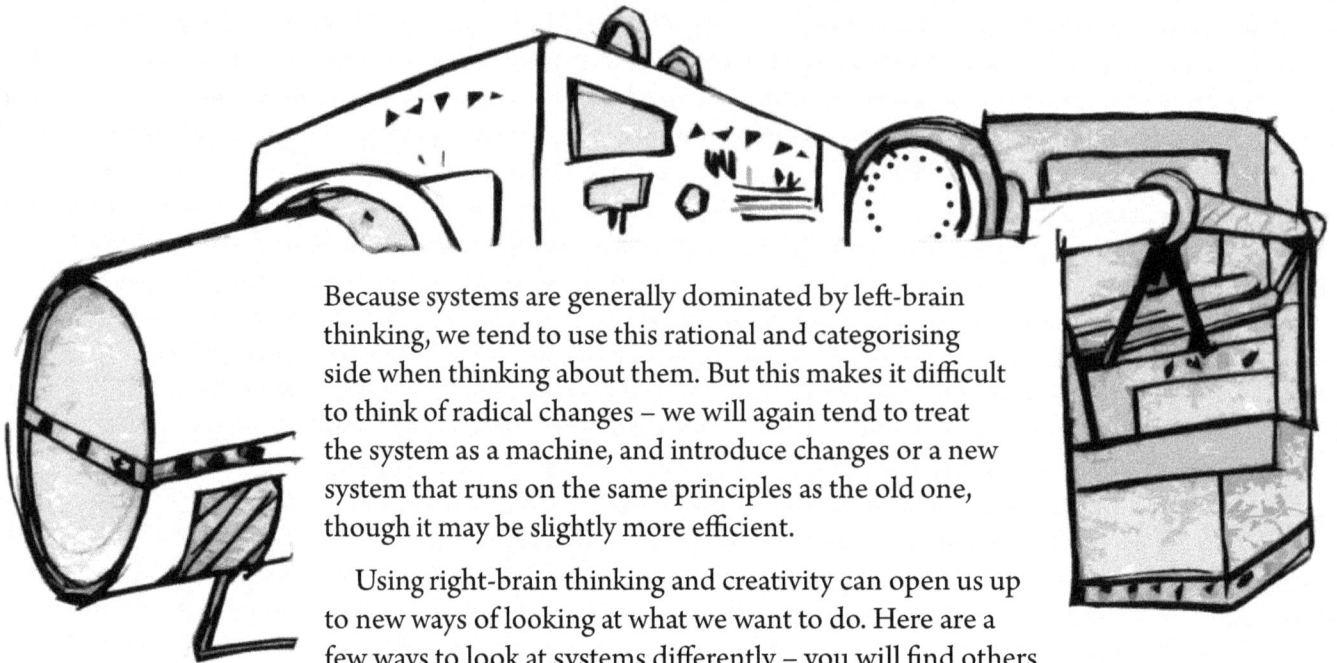

Because systems are generally dominated by left-brain thinking, we tend to use this rational and categorising side when thinking about them. But this makes it difficult to think of radical changes – we will again tend to treat the system as a machine, and introduce changes or a new system that runs on the same principles as the old one, though it may be slightly more efficient.

Using right-brain thinking and creativity can open us up to new ways of looking at what we want to do. Here are a few ways to look at systems differently – you will find others in other parts of the book.

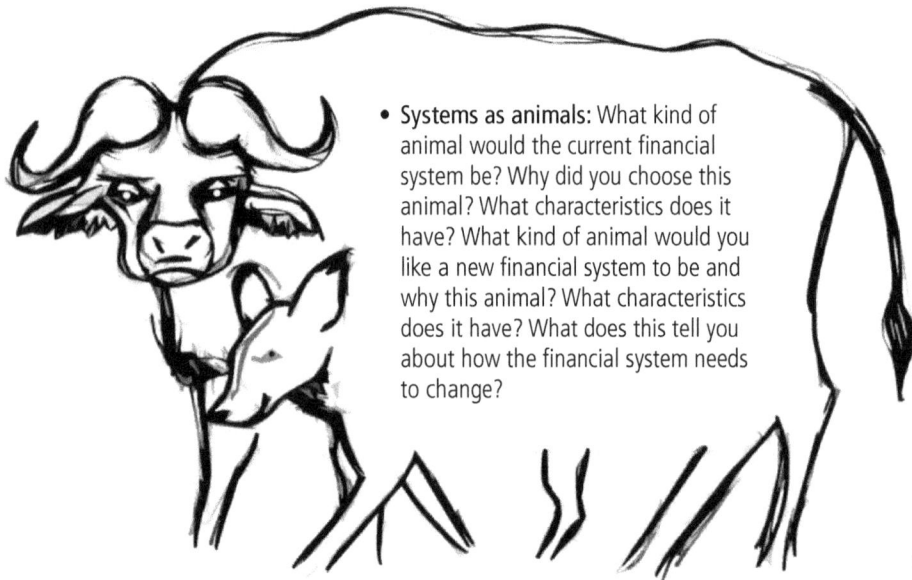

- **Systems as animals:** What kind of animal would the current financial system be? Why did you choose this animal? What characteristics does it have? What kind of animal would you like a new financial system to be and why this animal? What characteristics does it have? What does this tell you about how the financial system needs to change?

- **System painting:** gather people from different parts of the organisation in the room and ask them to use crayons to draw a picture of the fund raising department. It should be abstract and done quickly. They then describe their picture to a partner and the pair makes notes on the characteristics of the department that are coming out. These should then be shared with the whole group. What picture is emerging? How different is it from how the fund raising team sees itself?

- **A visitor from Mars:** a Martian is visiting the planet and decides to apply for a job in your organisation. Write a description of the process from the Martian's point of view. What does this tell you about how people might see the organisation and what messages you are inadvertently sending to prospective employees?

Systems fit for purpose

The fundamental question is: 'What kind of system will best enable us to bring about social change?' Those who are responsible for making sure the system works effectively may also need to adapt for their particular situation. The 'perfect' accounts system, one that meets all internationally-recognised standards of accountability and transparency, may not look the same in a Western urban context as it will look in a development context. But both systems can still be meeting international standards.

Accounting for context, accounting in context

The Karen Womens Organisation (KWO), a refugee-women's organisation that works in refugee camps along the Thai-Burma border, does not have its own vehicle. Much of its work is done in the refugee camps that are a long way from the town offices, and in hard-to-access terrain. To visit most of the camps KWO project co-ordinators rent a car and must stay overnight, because a round trip is not possible in one day, for most of the year, due to the bad road conditions. In the rainy season the journey takes even longer. Only a small number of the staff members have documents to allow them to travel freely in, or between, provinces. In response to international accounting standards, and in order to have good controls in place, the KWO finance team prefer that the projects which receive external funding submit all receipts to them monthly at the central office. However, given the logistical challenges, it must also be possible for the system to work with receipts that arrive in the accountant's hands after two months. The financial staff and the managers agreed that even with receipts every two months, they could still monitor their budgets, report to donors, and be cost-effective. It would also provide better working conditions for staff by reducing time away in risky travel conditions, and away from family. The finance staff recognised that their financial system might not always be as rigorous as they would like and the managers accepted that they would have to wait for some financial information longer than was ideal. However, in both cases, the outcome was good enough and was achievable in their situation. KWO's donors are satisfied with the financial reports they receive and the system meets international standards.

There are some things, like tax years, that we just can't change. The potential negative impact they can have on social change must therefore be minimised, for example dealing with three-year budgets and decoupling narrative from financial reporting. However, in some cases donors impose systems that are simply not workable in the context and it may be worth lobbying them to allow more flexible systems, perhaps with other organisations that are facing the same issues.

All change, all learn

The Karen Human Rights Group (KHRG) is an organisation that documents human rights abuses in eastern Burma, and how local communities protect themselves against the abuses. The group became concerned about the effect of the resettlement of key members of refugee staff to other countries, such as the US and Australia(Some of its staff are registered refugees and are eligible for asylum abroad).

They were also concerned about the need for local staff now running the organisation to learn from foreign staff members who came to the organisation to provide expertise that was not locally available. How could KHRG make sure that learning was not lost to the organisation but rather stayed with staff, within the organisation, and that the capacity it had developed continued to grow? Staff members together developed the Handover Project. Clear guidelines were set for when it was appropriate to employ foreign staff and it was made clear that their role involved sharing skills with local staff in a systematic way. Local staff members eligible for resettlement are also required to share their skills with others. A system of training and mentoring has been developed to make sure that there is a pool of people able to take on key tasks. Lessons learned from these activities are thoroughly documented in an operations manual that serves as a living document, to ensure that all staff and the organisation are continuously developing good practices and building upon lessons learned.

Key principles for systems

It is not an easy process, and changing systems may take several years. However, involving people across the organisation from the start and agreeing on the key principles that should underlie all the systems will help.

What should those principles be? They may differ from organisation to organisation but here are a few that should be considered.

Systems should:

- Reflect the organisation's core values.
- Have built into them processes that enable learning, both to improve the system itself and to improve the organisation's abilities to bring about social change.
- Take as little time and resources as possible away from direct action to bring about social change.
- Be respectful of the people who use them. If this sounds crazy, then think about conversations you have had with automated voices on the telephone – if they have been designed with the customer in mind then you hardly notice you are not talking to a real person. If not, then you end up shouting. Avoiding the use of jargon, an awareness of the context in which the system will be used – simple things like this can make all the difference.

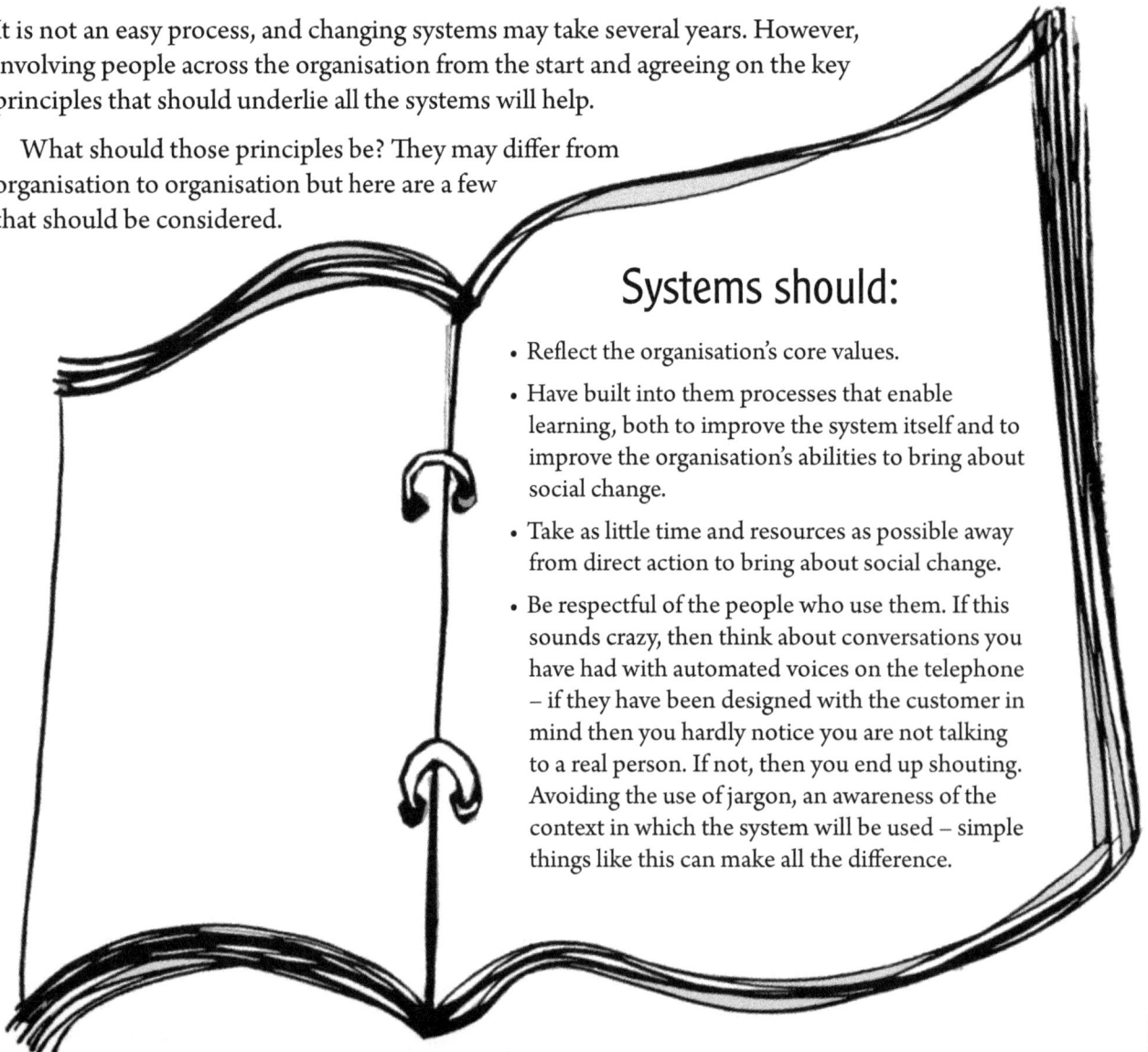

The people we expect to use the system should understand why it is important. If you are filling in a database, you are much more likely to fill it in correctly if you know what the information is used for. Deadlines are also more understandable if you know why they have been set, for example: 'The funding committee meets next week' or 'It takes up to four weeks for the logistics people to be able to buy a particular item'. The people responsible for the system will design better systems if they are familiar with the work of the organisation.

Finally

Changing systems is not easy. There are no shortcuts if you want to have systems that people really buy into and use for learning. A country can change the side of the road it drives on overnight, but not without huge education programmes, changes in signposts and traffic systems and accepting the inevitability of a certain number of accidents. You cannot change your systems overnight and you cannot change them all at once. It might be useful to identify the system where changes will have the most significant impact and start there. Changing one system will inevitably have a knock-on effect on others – both good and bad. Done with care, this will bring the incentive for further change.

In his 1994 book *Maverick*, Ricardo Semler describes how his company, Semco, changed from one that was governed by rules and compliance to one that was governed by principles and values. Semco is a successful company that also values its employees and enables them to learn for themselves how best to do their jobs. If this is possible in the private sector, surely it is possible in the social change sector!

Finally, finally...

Learning systems cannot survive without a learning culture (see Chapter 3). And vice versa. Working on these two must go hand in hand, with each supporting the other to enable the organisation to learn and act on its learning.

CHAPTER 5

Weaving learning into change:

planning, monitoring and evaluation alternatives

'We are overloaded with all kinds of documents for different purposes... planning, monitoring and reporting. It feels like the vision of the programme has shifted to the background in all these planning activities.' It was a bit of shock to hear these statements. I thought that the planning workshop had gone quite well.

But this is what we then did: we put all the planning documents aside and went into a process of exploring the actual content of our programme. We organised three consultative workshops with important stakeholders, including partners, to explore what we really meant by 'vulnerability' and how exactly we could address vulnerability issues through teacher education. This allowed us to gain a deeper understanding of the vision of the programme. It also helped us to link this understanding with our planning, and to help programme support staff and our partners to feel they also owned the plans. Misunderstandings that had built up between programme support team members during the planning could also be discussed. This allowed us to build an environment of trust in the programme support team.

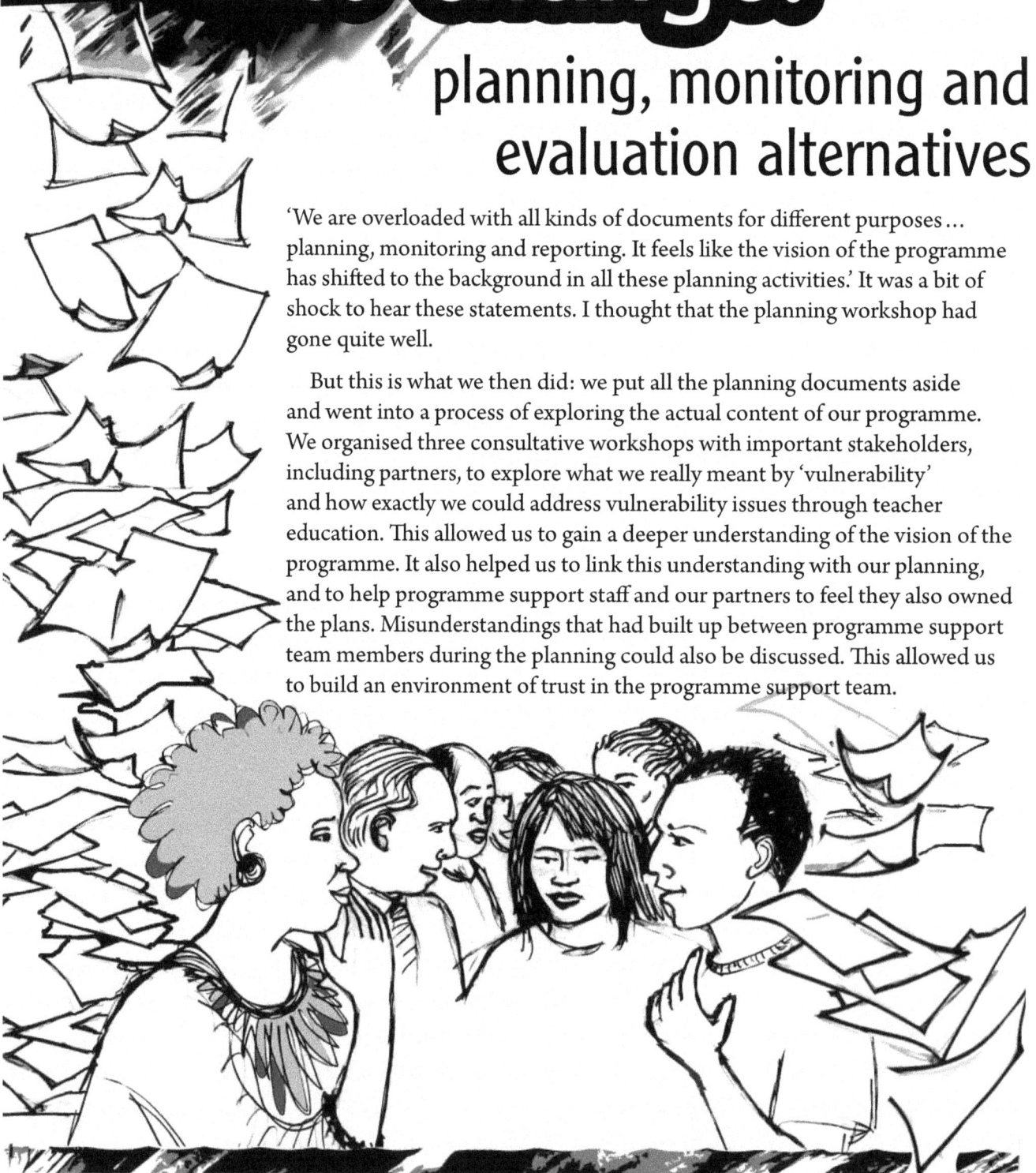

Is social change 'complicated'? Or is it 'complex'?

Many people think that thorough planning, based on a detailed analysis of the problem, is the key for developing good programmes that support social change. How I wish this was true! If it were then many of our development challenges would have been solved by now. The problem with this idea is that people think that development is a *complicated technical process*, like fixing a faulty aeroplane. In reality social change is a *complex social process*, not the same at all. When fixing an aeroplane an expert starts by doing a thorough problem analysis and then develops a plan before doing the repairs. Other experts can evaluate the work until all agree that the aeroplane is properly fixed according to some internationally-agreed, good practice standard. Very complicated, but not complex.

Most social change processes are completely different – they are complex, not just complicated. There can be no master plan to reach the desired goals. There are too many things that are unknown and unpredictable along the way. Indeed, many things are unknowable! Many organisations or communities, under pressure from donors, spend years developing complicated plans. Then unpredictable things happen. Re-planning is needed – often again and again – wasting energy and frustrating everyone. Sometimes, people are blamed for failing to properly implement 'The Plan', often developed by experts who are out of touch with complex realities on the ground. Sometimes communities are blamed for not responding well to a 'good' plan.

However, we *can* do good preparation. Often preparation is more important than planning, because it helps us to deal with a variety of situations, to face things as they change, to explore possibilities. If we are well-prepared we can plan our next few steps. Then, as we implement our plans we feel the water, trying things out. We are constantly observing the effects of what we have just done, finding out what works and what doesn't, thinking about what is happening and what we could do next. And we do this together, involving many players. This is not just a good approach to complex social change – it is how social change happens anyway. It's about working with reality.

This is a learning approach to planning and social change. You could call it an Action Learning approach.

> *Often preparation is more important than planning...*

Four stories of learning

These stories will help you to unpack the meaning and the importance of learning for social change. They set the stage for another set of stories about making our Planning, Monitoring and Evaluation (PME) systems more learning-centred. As you'll notice, this chapter is not another PME manual – it is stories of practice that show the crucial value of learning in PME, in support of complex processes of social change.

Story 1: Multiple perspectives – valid and inevitable

A local community is trying to save a wetland in Harare, the capital city of Zimbabwe. Residents around the wetland engage with some environmental NGOs and neighbouring schools to create an education programme. They want to alert policy makers and residents to the ecological value of the wetland and the natural protection it offers against flooding.

Home developers are eyeing new areas for building houses. Residents from a neighbouring high density suburb are eyeing the wetland to grow food. Becoming aware of opposing points of view and motives occurs through active engagement between the various stakeholders – often through conflict in the field. For example, local residents rush to the wetland to fight bush fires set by would-be urban farmers.

No formal workshops here, just raw action. In a context of social change, multiple perspectives are inevitable and valid, even if contradictory: a problem for some can be a favourable situation for others.

> *Instead of having a big master plan they move forward step by step ... reinforcing what seems to work.*

> *... learning does not have to come from books or experts or happen in classrooms.*

> *... deep listening, strong observation and sense-making...*

Story 2: In the absence of a technical plan – a dream

The Wetlands Protection Committee in Harare engages in a variety of activities, from removing alien species to educational walks and collaborating in research projects with students from local universities. Instead of having a big master plan they move forward step by step, growing stronger in numbers and learning as they act, reinforcing what seems to work. They learn that their work around income generation through innovative composting techniques can help them in their public awareness campaigns. The team is guided by the dream of a healthy wetland. It gives them energy and a reference for reflecting on their progress. There is no master plan or strict project time frame, but without this initiative, an irreplaceable natural resource could be lost.

Many of the problems that we face in our societies or communities, worldwide, cannot be solved by calling in the experts. Neither would I bet my money on a conventional project approach, with predefined outcome and impact indicators, to safeguard the wetland in this story. Chances of success are probably slim for starters, depending on many unpredictable factors and actors.

Story 3: Adapting and surviving in a changing world

In their 2006 book *Getting to maybe*, Westeley, Zimmerman and Patton tell the story of the Afaris, a nomadic tribe in Ethiopia, who see it as a sacred responsibility to share '*dagu*'. Dagu means 'information' if translated to English. But it's much more than just facts. When Afari families meet while travelling from place to place with their cattle, they sit down to talk and listen, usually for hours, sharing *dagu*. The Afaris have an expression: '*Dagu* is life'. In the process of sharing *dagu*, they share what they have seen and heard about the environment, about health issues related to people and cattle, about political tensions and about new relationships. So during this process, they provide facts and also their interpretation of these facts. They collectively make sense of the patterns that are emerging. '*Dagu* is life' illustrates that *dagu* is more than sharing facts but also involves deep listening, strong observation, and sense-making or pattern recognition. *Dagu* is at the heart of the Afaris' ability to adapt to and survive in a changing world.

It was early 2009 in Zimbabwe, during a cholera outbreak. On a sunny morning in one of the green, leafy suburbs of Harare, lecturers from teacher education colleges and some NGO staff got together to take the first steps in developing a cholera-awareness training programme for teachers. People were worried because many had relatives living in cholera-affected areas.

The facilitator started by inviting the participants to share stories about their experiences with the cholera epidemic. I was struck by two things that the facilitator did.

Firstly, he acknowledged each of the storytellers, praising them for the beauty and the importance of their stories. He motivated people to be very free to share their specific experiences, and some stories were very personal and emotional. But it was okay, because people felt safe and respected.

Secondly, while people were telling their stories, the facilitator captured points under headings on flipcharts. And so a clear and structured story about cholera emerged. We could see different themes, such as causes, symptoms, prevention, traditional practices that help prevention, and what can be done in case of infection. In front of my eyes was a story of empowerment; a story of people coming up with the solution, informed by practical experience and cultural practice. We felt great! We were ready, and confident about dealing with cholera.

One thread through the four stories is that learning does not have to come from books or experts or happen in classrooms. It can happen out of day-to-day experience, guided by shared vision – such as the conservation of a wetland or the survival of the tribe through exchanging dagu or determination to defeat cholera. Each story is an example of horizontal learning in which ordinary people learn from, and with, ordinary people. Experiences of different people are shared, leading to new insights and new actions. The stories show that development or social change is driven by the energy of people genuinely concerned about something dear to them. It is a complex process with no predetermined master plans and is characterised by horizontal learning processes. These are some of the raw building blocks of learning for social change.

As facilitators – whether leaders, practitioners or donors – how can we initiate or support more learning-centred approaches that can better work with the unfolding reality of social change?

'Each context demands its own tailor-made approach; begin working with what people already know; understand how they perceive their predicament; do not impose solutions; work with the method and media they prefer; be prepared to make mistakes; engage people as much as is practical.'

Wendy Quarry and Ricardo Ramirez

QUESTIONS
TO THINK ABOUT

- Can you observe common elements across the four stories?

- How do the stories relate to your own learning practice in your work?

Horizontal learning is learning from the experiences of others, not only your own experiences. Examples are peer learning, community exchanges or farmer learning groups – powerful forms of practical and rapid learning. This kind of learning can also reduce community isolation and build solidarity. Storytelling is a powerful method for horizontal learning.

Why do we need Planning, Monitoring, Evaluation and Reporting?

Planning, monitoring, evaluation and reporting helps us to manage, improve, rethink and account for our practice, over time. Let's take a closer look at each of these:

Managing practice

Through cycles of planning, monitoring and re-planning we are able to keep track of what we do and make necessary adjustments. It is rather like steering a ship with a hand on the wheel, one eye on the compass and one eye on the horizon, constantly adjusting and checking to keep on course.

Improving practice

Through good monitoring and evaluating processes we can reflect on our experience, learn from our mistakes, capitalise on our successes, deepen our understanding of our work and continuously develop, strengthen and enhance our practice.

Rethinking practice

Through good evaluation, whether short- or long-term, we are able to rethink our practice, as the context and needs change, and as we change. The context is getting more and more changeable, requiring us to rethink almost continuously.

Accounting (and reporting) for practice

We do not work in isolation. If we are leading or assisting people then we should be accountable to them for the quality of our leadership or help, to ensure that we are doing no harm. The best way to do this is to ask for and give honest feedback. If we are getting funds from others we need to account for these, not only to donors but also to communities in whose name we raise the funding.

How results-based management undermines results

Donors are understandably anxious for proof of results. But focusing on results written up in a report is a bit like trying to understand the life of butterflies by studying dead specimens pinned to a board. In fact, donors are more likely to get results if they ask for a different kind of proof. They should be more interested in how 'butterflies' actually live: in honest accounts, real stories of what really happened. They should be interested in reflections and learnings and how these are being translated into improving or rethinking practice. Not only would learning be encouraged; it is far more likely that good results would be achieved and would be easier to show.

The unintended consequences of results-based management are that people ignore interesting failures and exaggerate their successes as they try desperately to safeguard their funding. Ironically, this undermines the very results that donors desire. It is their biggest mistake.

The challenge for donors is to help their partners to invest in PME systems and cultures that are centred on learning, not results or impact.

'The highest level of accountability is not that you did what you said you would, but that you are getting better at serving the underlying intent of what you said you were going to do.'

Terry Smutylo

From M&E to PME – bringing the 'P' back into M&E?

I was asked to develop a Monitoring and Evaluation (M&E) system for a country programme. I was impressed by its work – assisting community schools and supporting continuous professional development of teachers. But, I wasn't sure that my input would be helpful because I didn't see myself as an M&E expert. I prepared these questions to discuss during the first two days of our three-day workshop:

1. Who are the partners that the project is working with directly?

2. What would the programme like to see changing in the practice and relationships between these partners?

3. What activities would the programme use to support its direct partners?

My colleagues were a little taken aback at the simplicity of the agenda outline. But as we discussed the first question it quickly became obvious that the answer was not all that straightforward. Some were surprised to realise that the programme was not able to work directly with its ultimate beneficiaries, such as teachers and pupils. It could only support its direct partners – such as continuous professional development committees in the teacher education colleges or the school parent committees. Team members also talked about their deeper vision, about the 'why' questions, and by the end of the first day, we had a flipchart specifying direct partners. 'So when are we going to start working on our monitoring and evaluation system?' one participant now asked.

'We have already started,' I replied, 'by working on the "P" of PME, the "P" of planning with a difference.'

'Planning with a difference?' the participant asked.

'Yes,' I said. 'Planning our intervention logic, or our theory of change, in which we have clarified the responsibilities and expectations of the programme support team and the local partners we can work with directly. We must bring the people back into the centre of our planning. This forms the basis for the M&E plan that we will develop tomorrow.'

> *We must bring the people back into the centre of our planning.*

> 'Imagine a map ... drawn from your memory instead of from the atlas. It is made of strong places stitched together by the vivid threads of transforming journeys. It contains all the things you learned from the land and shows where you learned them. ... Think of this map as a living thing, not a chart but a tissue of stories that grows half-consciously with each experience. It tells where and who you are with respect to the earth, and in times of stress or disorientation it gives you the bearings you need in order to move on. We all carry such maps within us as sentient and reflective beings, and we depend upon them unthinkingly, as we do upon language or thought. ... And it is part of wisdom, to consider this ecological aspect of our identity.'
>
> John Tallmadge, *Meeting the Tree of Life*. 1997: IX

Developing a shared theory of change

What is the thinking that lies behind your planning? How do you understand social change to happen? What unfolding processes cause people to think, feel or behave differently, in different situations? Where is the real work? What is your practice?

Every plan has an underlying theory or idea of change, but very few people take the time to surface and understand this. Many work intuitively, from the gut. Sometimes this works. But sometimes we apply (favourite) approaches that work in one context but not another – and we cannot understand why they do not always work.

If we work on developing our theories of change or our intervention logic then we become less dependent on detailed plans and more able to work with what emerges, as thinking leaders and practitioners.

How can we do this? One way is for each team member to share their understanding of their expectations, roles and responsibilities. This will reveal where their energies are likely to go and show what kinds of change are possible – and possibilities and ideas for change will grow. It is important that this is a shared process, so that you don't have some clever people cooking up cunning plans through which they can 'facipulate' change!

Where is the map?

One day my friend asked if I would like to learn how to make a 'change map'. I looked up, puzzled. My friend smiled. 'A map for planning, monitoring and evaluation,' he said and his smile grew wider. Several years later, I am still on a learning journey and have come to appreciate the wisdom of Marcel Proust: 'The only real voyage of discovery exists, not in seeing new landscapes, but in having new eyes.'

Mapping one's change process – a people-centred remedy for 'indicatoritis'

This story is for those who are looking for alternatives to the usual logframe-type indicators:

Using our maps of change for monitoring

The time had now come to reflect on the progress of our programme and to learn from each other about how we were doing. Our colleague who facilitated the reflection meeting asked us to get into groups and to discuss the changes in behaviour that we set ourselves last year. We were given half an hour. We took more than two hours.

'We have a functioning staff development committee!' one lecturer exclaimed. 'I keep the minutes of our monthly meetings and do you remember the full day training session that we organised for the staff on how to assess students on teaching practice?'

'But we didn't do anything related to vulnerability, as we thought we would,' said another.

> *... we become less dependent on detailed plans and more able to work with what emerges, as thinking leaders and practitioners.*

Mapping change

'We had a dream! A dream of colleges as places of safety and respect for staff and students. I remember us doing the 'River of Life' activity, exploring key life moments that lifted us up or brought us down. We came to the insight that the solution for making our colleges better places could be found in ourselves – by changing our own behaviour towards our colleagues or students, not waiting for some kind of system change.

Some would call it strategic planning – we called it making a map. We mapped the changes to our practice and our relations with others that we thought were needed. The first changes could be small steps, such as college lecturers attending the syllabus review meetings. These first steps are the foundation to build deeper changes, like adjusting classroom practice to cater for the different learning needs of students. So, now, looking for the change in behaviour of college lecturers is the basis for our monitoring system.'

Our facilitator explained that having a functional staff development committee provides the foundation for moving a step further. We could now look for ways to strengthen the capacity of the lecturers to address vulnerability.

'Why don't we use teachers from the school for the blind to workshop with our lecturers?'

'We could ask the programme support team to come and help us develop a workshop on how to accommodate learning differences in our classrooms.'

The new ideas were written down in the change map so that they could be followed up in the next reflection meeting.

Women's dialogue groups in a conflict management programme in Zimbabwe identified the following milestones to map their own change process:

ENGAGE LOCAL AUTHORITIES IN CONFLICT ISSUES AFFECTING THE COMMUNITY

USE DIFFERENT CONFLICT TRANSFORMATION TOOLS FOR RESOLVING CONFLICTS WITHIN THE GROUP

MEET GROUP COSTS THROUGH INCOME-GENERATING PROJECTS

SEEK SUPPORT FROM LOCAL AUTHORITIES FOR OUR CLUB ACTIVITIES

CREATE CONSTITUTIONS FOR OUR GROUPS

FACILITATE COMMUNITY DIALOGUES

A map of one 'change process'

It is not so difficult to become the learning or PME expert yourself...

The story about change in a training college illustrates two important principles of learning within social change:

- It is a process over time in which social actors do things differently from before.

- People take charge of their own change process.

Did you notice that there is no M&E expert at work in the story? How often do we develop complex PME systems that only the M&E experts can understand? But real learning takes place among the people who are involved in the action, working towards the change they believe in. It is not so difficult to become the learning or PME expert yourself, like the people in the story.

People-centred approaches to PME

Outcome mapping

Outcome mapping encourages you to develop progress markers that pinpoint the change in behaviour of the partners whom a support programme or project is working with directly. As we have seen in the previous section on 'mapping change', progress markers do not represent targets, but rather points of reference that help to monitor and reflect on progress. They are developed by the partners as a framework for dialogue and learning. They are a little like resting places on a long journey, places to reflect and review progress. The following progress markers were identified by college administrators in an environmental education project in Zimbabwe:

- Provide office space and equipment for the environmental education co-ordinators.

- Allow lecturers to participate in environmental education activities.

- Facilitate a reduced teaching load for the college co-ordinators.

- Attend environmental education activities.

- Support college-based environmental education policy development and implementation.

- Provide transport, finances and other resources for environmental education activities.

- Include environmental education on the agenda of staff meetings.

- Incorporate environmental education in the college strategic plan.

- Appoint full time environmental education co-ordinators.

Progress markers are different from indicators in the following ways:

- They do not describe a change in state (e.g. income levels increased), but rather changes in behaviour or relationships of those individuals or groups that a programme supports directly.

- They describe a gradual change process.

- As a set, progress markers help to illustrate the complexity of the change process.

- They can be adjusted during the implementation of the project (mid-course corrections).

- They are *not* a checklist of accomplishments or targets to be reached.

- They provide a basis for dialogue about progress.

'The focus of Outcome Mapping is on people and organisations. The originality of the methodology is its shift away from assessing the products of a programme (e.g., policy relevance, poverty alleviation, reduced conflict) to focus on changes in behaviours, relationships, actions, and/or activities of the people and organisations with whom a development programme works directly.'

Barefoot Guide I, page 155, 2009.

'Most Significant Change' stories – learning from beneficiaries

'So how do we know if the changes in our direct partners contribute to some positive change for students and lecturers?' This question came up again and again during our work in the teacher training college in Zimbabwe. For some time defensive reactions were heard:

'We don't have any contact with our partner's beneficiaries so it's impossible to monitor at that level.'

'They are outside our sphere of influence.'

'We don't have the means to monitor at that level.'

After a team member participated in a Most Significant Change workshop, a student on attachment was asked to collect stories. These were to be stories from students or lecturers about how they felt the programme had affected their lives. We are still struggling to get useful stories, but slowly we are getting better at it. The most significant stories are selected during a reflection meeting. Feedback about why a story was selected is given to the storyteller and to the donor head office. Learning happens mainly during the discussion of the story selection process. We learned, for example, about help needed by college-based support groups to ensure balanced diets and psychosocial support for students or lecturers who disclosed their HIV status.

Some people feel that working with 'Most Significant Change' stories only brings the positive out. Some also wonder how to analyse large numbers of collected stories. The answers lie in how people learn as they discuss the stories. The story above illustrates how this learning resulted in the insight that college-based support structures were needed. This is not a celebration of the success of the programme – it was shown to have paid little attention to such support structures, but was now going to take it up in its future plans. The story also illustrates that it need not be about analysing huge amounts of data. Learning and change can be triggered by just one powerful story!

> *Learning and change can be triggered by just one powerful story!* "

During an end-of-year reflection meeting, the issue of monitoring and evaluation came up. The programme co-ordinator gently explained: 'We have specific indicators that allow us to track our progress,' she explained. 'Our friends from our donor fill in the monitoring report every three months and send it to their headquarters. The college principals also get a copy. We have copies of all the monitoring reports in our programme file at the colleges and you are very free to come and see them.'

'So does that mean that only the donors learn from the monitoring system?' someone asked. The co-ordinator asked me to answer this question.

There I was, at a loss about what to say, startled by the sudden insight that was so clearly levelled out for the whole group! The insight that our monitoring system was, indeed, not a learning system but an administrative reporting mechanism.

'Let's move on!' someone shouted. 'Let them do their reports because this will keep them happy. Let's move on with our workshop and our planning for next year.'

Testing the will to learn

A challenge for the programme in Zimbabwean colleges was to motivate local partners to participate. Big NGOs had been in the habit of 'motivating' people with considerable allowances in the past.

Faced with this, the Action Aid team decided to reflect on their assumptions about why people should be motivated to participate. They decided that no allowances would be paid; the programme would only work with genuinely-interested people. This was a risky decision in a context of economic meltdown in the country, but was in line with the programme's vision. In fact, the reflection blew some new life into this vision. It was difficult at the beginning, but the monitoring process showed that, step-by-step, this approach resulted in a growing group of active college students and lecturers. They had genuine interest in the activities, such as the life skills training workshops. Feedback of these insights to administrators and local authorities resulted in more support and them contributing more of their own scarce resources.

> ' *So does that mean that only the donors learn from the monitoring system?' someone asked.*

Finding a rhythm and space to share our learnings

We need to find good rhythm for our learning, to ensure that we have regular, safe and reliable space which people can look forward to for support, refreshment and inspiration, as in these observations:

'Every Monday morning all members of the programme support team meet in the Harare head office to reflect on the previous week and to look at the plans for the coming week. Besides highlighting the major activities undertaken, every team member is expected to share any lessons learned that they think are significant for the programme. This routine has helped team members to become more reflective.'

'Somehow the weekly reflection meeting has helped to pull us out of our comfort zones and to stimulate us to be on the lookout for unexpected insights and lessons and to document them so that we can share them during our weekly reflection meetings with our colleagues.'

'Important lessons are documented during the meeting and feed ongoing management meetings and the six-monthly monitoring cycles.'

'We put aside three days every month to develop our practice. Half of this the time is spent with personal reflective reports and feedback for each practitioner, a space where they can honestly bring their experience, for all to learn from, be inspired and to get ideas and advice. Case studies and strategy discussions are also common, depending on what is needed that month. We also have some time to reconnect, to build personal trust which helps with our learning culture.'

Planning, Monitoring and Evaluation – the real challenge

For many of us PME processes are add-on activities that only support our work. But this is like saying that our bones or our blood circulation are there only to support our bodies! If we want our practice to stay alive and relevant we need PME approaches that are deeply woven into practice, where working and learning are part of the same process. In this way PME does not have to be the deadly dull processes that we have to do to please others, but can continually help to refresh and stimulate our work, enabling it to stay alive to the ever-changing circumstances of life.

QUESTIONS
TO THINK ABOUT

- How do you feel about the learning approaches described in the stories?

- Can you think of opportunities to nurture learning and learning rhythms in your organisation?

CHAPTER 6

Humble offerings:
donors' practice and learning

Donor

A person who gives money or goods to an organisation

– Cambridge Advanced Learners' Dictionary

One that contributes something, such as money, to a cause or fund

– The Free Dictionary

This chapter discusses ways in which donors hinder or help learning, and suggests how a donor organisation can itself learn, and enable learning. It seeks to go beyond the 'us and them' mentality that one often finds with the relationship between donor and recipient, and to explore ways that they can learn from, and with, each other.

'Donor' tends to be a word that we use to describe *others* rather than to describe ourselves. But there are very few organisations that only donate money. Most of them – whether they are the development arm of a national government, a multilateral organisation such as the World Bank, or a private foundation – do other things as well. They may implement their own projects, alone or with others; publish research; lobby for policy change or network with other similar organisations to bring about change. But, if they give money to my organisation, I will call them a 'donor' and group them with all the other organisations that give money to me, however different they may be. And to confuse matters, as soon as *my* organisation starts to distribute that money to others, however small the grant may be, in the eyes of those who receive the money, I too become a donor.

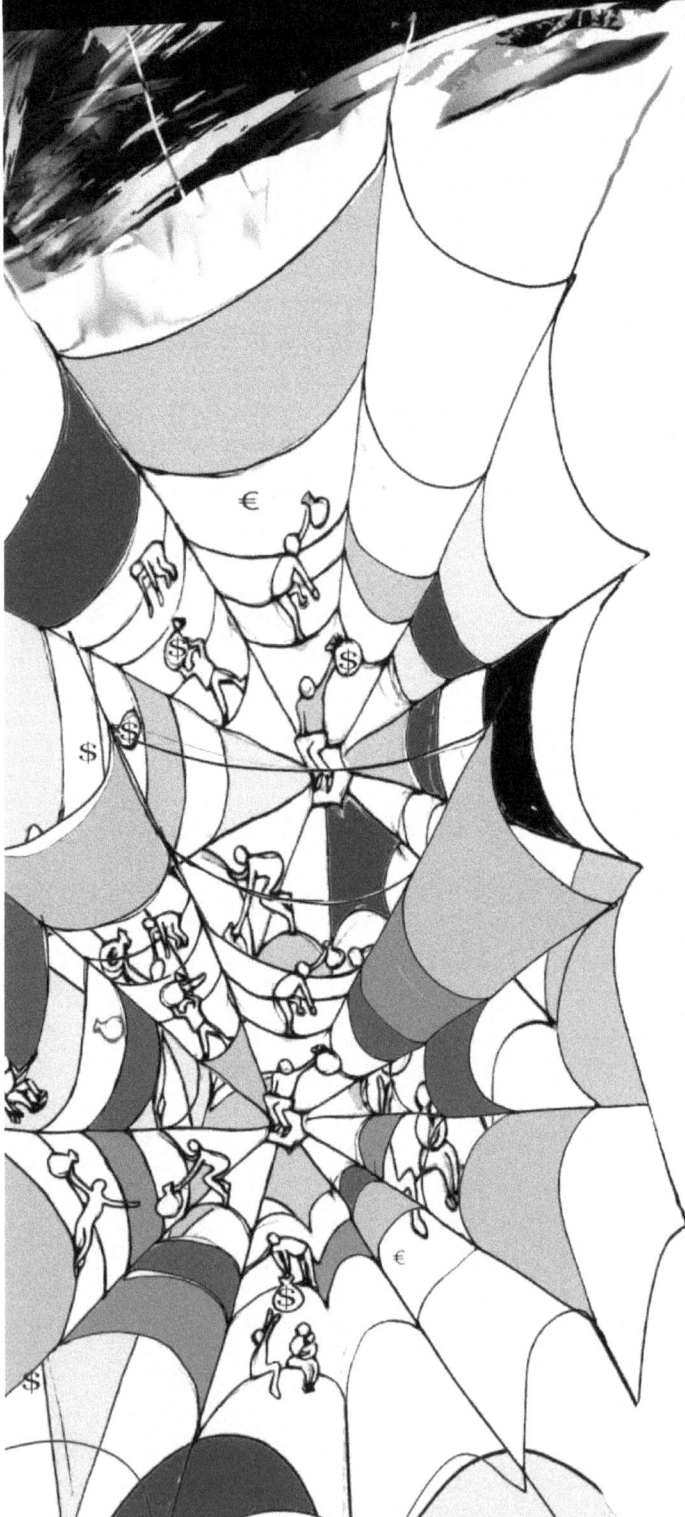

I suspect that the majority of the people who read this chapter are donors, either individually (perhaps you sponsor a child or give regularly to a favourite charity), or as part of an organisation that gives money or expertise or equipment to others. And most of us work for organisations that are part of a web of donors. We may be responsible for allocating money from a national development budget or a private foundation. We may give money that has been donated to us by individuals, or by governments to local organisations. Or we may receive money that has trickled down through a number of organisations before reaching us.

The donor web can be quite complex. For simplicity, in this chapter we refer to organisations who are primarily disbursers of money from national or international development budgets, or from the private sector, as 'primary donors'. Those who have to apply for this money and then themselves disburse it to local organisations or communities are 'secondary donors'. For example, an international development organisation that gets its money from the development agency of a national government and disburses this money to local organisations is a secondary donor, whereas the development agency itself is a primary donor.

The challenge – cut reporting, increase learning

'From the perspective of the [field] officers, two months (October and November) are devoted to reviewing and reporting on past performance; the next four months (December through April) are pretty much devoted to budget and implementation proposals… And of course the final two months of each fiscal year (August and September) are devoted to preparation and signing of contracts and grants… Almost eight months of every fiscal year are dominated by reporting and budget processes, leaving program and technical experts precious little time to design new programs and monitor the implementation of ongoing programs.'

Ken Schofield, head of the Philippines USAID mission, 4 March 2010

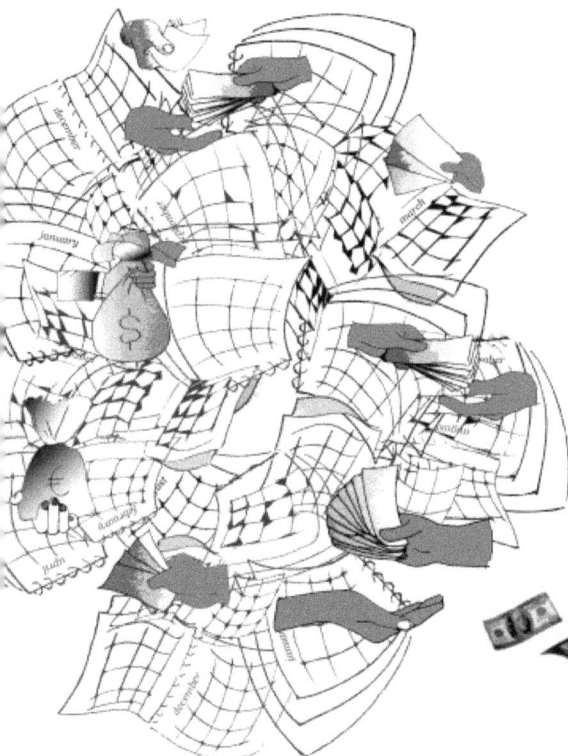

Andrew Natsios, director of USAID during the George W Bush administration, has coined the term 'counter-bureaucracy' – that is, bureaucratic systems and departments whose only purpose is to ensure compliance and to enable measurement of progress. The primary role of these systems is not to get things done, but to reduce risk. They are not intended to be learning systems, nor are they aimed at ensuring sustainable development. He argues that USAID is becoming less effective because of these systems.

Measurability (or accountability) does not equal developmental effectiveness. Natsios gives an example of a billion-dollar service delivery programme, the Bush Malaria Initiative. The initiative did achieve what it was designed to do: reduce infection rates. But these lower rates were not maintained because the programme had ignored the development of local institutions and organisations required to sustain them in the future. Without local institutions and organisations, initiatives of this nature usually collapse as soon as funding declines or ends, even though they did meet their measurable targets.

Development processes of policy dialogue and reform, as well as support to local institutions or organisations, are generally more developmentally successful than service delivery. However their success, which is often qualitative, is not easy to measure in the short term and can't be directly attributed in the long term.

USAID is not the only national development agency that is increasingly hampered by counter-bureaucracy. It is true of most major national and multilateral development agencies. They are reacting to governments, who are responding to an understandable demand by tax payers to show that they are spending money effectively. But most national development agencies give much of their budget to *other* local and international organisations in the form of grants. The net effect is a system of multiple and time-consuming reporting that trickles down right to community level. What effect does this have on learning?

'Those development programs that are most precisely and easily measured are the least transformational, and those programs that are most transformational are the least measurable.'

Andrew Natsios

Effects on learning in recipient organisations

An organisation working on providing support to people living with HIV and Aids has ten staff. They run a successful drop-in centre, testing service and outreach clinics. The organisation wants to expand and so, with some technical assistance from the donor, they put in a large number of grant applications. They get funding from four donors from four different countries. This will allow them to double the number of people they reach, pay their staff regular salaries and buy some much-needed equipment.

One of the donors raises most of its money from members. They want personal stories of change they can share and use for fund raising purposes. Another is a philanthropic foundation. They want photos of buildings with their name on them and photos of pieces of funded equipment being used. Neither of these donors is willing to pay overhead costs.

The third donor got the money it is disbursing from a government agency. This means that the compliance procedures of this government must be followed, including an annual audit, documentation for all transactions and activities, time sheets for all staff members and so on.

The fourth donor is only interested in the numbers of people who use services, but they want detailed information about the age, gender and ethnicity of the users. They also have the expectation that the numbers using the service will increase every three months, as a result of their support.

The grants allow the organisation to recruit two new members of staff. One of them works full-time on project finance and the other works full-time on monitoring and evaluation – collecting all the different types of information required by the donors.

Increasing the number of service users requires a lot of outreach work and development of facilities.

This is extra work, but must be done by the same number of staff. Staff now also spend a lot more time on accounting for expenditure and collecting information for donors.

In the past, the staff had time to talk to service users, learning about their concerns and needs. This information was shared in a monthly meeting where all staff got together to talk about issues that were emerging and how they could improve their services. Now this meeting is taken up with each member of staff reporting on what they have done and whether they are reaching donor targets and spending the budget as planned.

The director, who used to spend a lot of time visiting staff at the centre and attending outreach clinics, now spends most of the day at the computer, editing everyone's reports and communicating with the donors. He realises that some of the projects are not working well, learning is not happening, and changes are needed but he is not sure whether he can talk to the donors about this. They are new donors and he does not want to create a bad impression.

The service users have consistently told staff that one reason they use the drop-in centre is because of the face to face support they receive, the chance to meet with other people and discuss the issues in their community. The staff now generally have less time to allocate to face to face support, plus the emphasis on numbers of people 'served' means they are under pressure to minimise the time they spend with individuals.

The centre has inspired a number of self-help and income-generation groups that are much appreciated. These are never reported to the donors. Why? Because they are not listed as indicators of success.

Does the situation above sound familiar? It is important that we are accountable for the money we spend and it is important that we are spending money on bringing about social change. But the culture of compliance and short-term, results-orientated reporting means government development agencies are under pressure to perform. They pass these requirements on to big development organisations that often pass them on to smaller, local organisations. Administrative systems are therefore imposed on organisations. They take no account of the local context or of enabling learning in that context. The organisation still learns – but it learns how to meet donor requirements rather than how to be more effective in its work! And time for essential listening and reflection is lost.

Effects on learning by primary donors – questioning our assumptions about donors

Recipient organisations give donors the information they ask for, because they are afraid of not getting funding in the future. They answer the donor's questions rather than their own. This means they do not engage in deep learning rooted in their local context and, even if they are still able to do this, they do not share it with donors. With the aim of improving accuracy and effectiveness, donors have, according to DSA/IGS in 2010, 'created a situation whereby the reporting and accountability is actually less accurate in reflecting the reality on the ground, and less effective in achieving the desired ends.' Learning from what does not work, from our mistakes, is often the most fruitful type of learning. However both the reporting system and the perceived unequal relationship between donor and recipient make recipient organisations reluctant to share this kind of learning.

The donor organisation also wants to report success to its sources of funding, so it also has an incentive to not share the learning from projects that haven't worked. Thus important learning is not discussed with the wider community.

... government development agencies are under pressure to perform. They pass these requirements on to big development organisations that often pass them on to smaller, local organisations.

And yet it is learning itself that makes us accountable. By demonstrating that we truly understand the situation and seek to learn from it, we show that we are committed to using money responsibly.

It is very easy for recipient organisations to complain about donors. But learning is about understanding the context we work in, and donors are part of that context. We need to challenge our assumptions and understand better what it means to be a donor in order to learn from and with donors, and be learning donors ourselves. Let's look at some assumptions about primary donors and how we can move beyond them.

Assumption 1: Donors have more power to change things than recipients.

Donors, like any other type of organisation, are faced with barriers to learning, especially when they deal with big amounts of money and are large, centralised systems. These factors mean they are closely examined by the media or regulatory bodies, so they become slow and cautious.

Barriers multiply when it comes to government aid agencies, such as USAID and DFID). Bill Gates of Microsoft can decide where he spends his money, but agencies must report to the government and ultimately to the tax payers. They want results for voters. These need to be achieved in the time span of an elected government. But development takes time – the long term is its rule, not its mistake. And, as Natsios points out, 'the weaker or more fragile a state, the longer the time lag will be in showing program results'.

Donor governments tend to apply the same checks and balances to all departments. But development, again, proves different. Planned results can be reasonable in relatively stable contexts but unachievable in unstable political, economic and environmental contexts. Development is messy: supporting constant re-planning is a coherent objective, not an administrative mistake.

Add to this the geographical and political separation between large national and multinational donor organisations and poor people in recipient countries. Poor people have no political influence over donors, and donors may have poor information about, and no accountability to, poor people. This lack of accountability is mainly a problem of foreign aid, as compared to public services within a donor country, where tax payers, voters and service users are the same people.

And yet, even though there are all these limitations and dependencies, national development agencies do fund research and evaluations, and do spend time and money trying to understand what is working and what isn't. The 2005 Paris Declaration on Aid Effectiveness, whatever its weaknesses, was born out of a realisation that donors need to work together and learn from each other, rather than work in isolation when they are all trying to address the same issues.

Assumption 2: Donors are bureaucrats, not development workers.

Many people who work in donor agencies know that development is messy and complicated and that it takes time. Many enter the agencies with a strong belief in social justice and with degrees that taught them to innovate and take risks. Some also have extensive field experience. They have to try and reconcile these with a managerial and bureaucratic system with no space for manoeuvre. They often become frustrated and disillusioned.

But this does not prevent them from resisting. An Ethiopian proverb says that when the great lord passes the wise peasant bows deeply and silently farts. Andrew Natsios observes that, 'subordinates are not without their own resources ("they want stats, we'll give 'em stats"); others will subvert the management strategy by ignoring measured activities (thus jeopardizing their own chances for advancement) or by generating enough stats to keep management happy while they get on with their own definition of what constitutes good work'.

Recipients can help the staff of donor agencies to maintain their integrity and see themselves as development practitioners first and foremost. Because donors disburse money, their relationships are especially power-ridden. They need to be transparent but also manage complex political contexts. They are not the bankers of development, but practitioners who need to learn from experience, as all practitioners do.

By demonstrating that we truly understand the situation and seek to learn from it, we show that we are committed to using money responsibly.

Donors are not the bankers of development, but practitioners who need to learn from experience, as all practitioners do.

Assumption 3: If we don't do what donors tell us to do, we won't get the money.

Donors are not all the same – they differ in their intentions, objectives and actions. It is always worth talking to donors about how and why you have developed your accountability systems. You should tell them about how your learning practices enhance your work and make you more effective, as well as about ways of working that are context-specific but are also accountable.

Of course, some donors are themselves restricted (see above) and others just don't want to listen. But some will be sympathetic and open to adapting their processes so that you can keep the systems and practices that work for you. Nurture these donors and encourage them to talk to other donors about the change that can happen when you fund long term, promote difficult-to-measure processes, and encourage learning. Help them organise their own learning events and involve them in yours. Often the most flexible donors are modest – encourage them to publicise the changes they are supporting and share how this happens.

Enhancing donor learning

However small or large our organisation is and whatever portion of our time we spend as donors, we are all connected by the flow of aid money. We are all influenced by the way that money is spent and accounted for. We have seen what problems this may cause but it is also an opportunity for us to influence those who donate the most.

In particular, the distance between large donor organisations and people living in poverty needs to be reduced, through more conscious exposure and through learning processes, five of which are described in the next section.

Donors are not all the same – they differ in their intentions, objectives and actions.

1. Learning from poor people directly

Some big donor organisations have recognised the need to better understand poor people's lives in order to be more effective donors. Examples of ways to do this are immersions, narratives on donors, and poor people's evaluations.

Immersions

Organised immersions started in the 1980s in Germany. They are now used by many donor agencies and organisations. In an immersion, the visitor (senior staff from donor agencies, governments, NGOs, etc.) stays with a host family and gets involved in their daily activities for a number of days and nights. Tasks may include harvesting vegetables, cooking, learning to make butter, learning dance routines, having tea, having discussions with the host family and so on. Professional status, speeches, reports and other roles and work responsibilities are left behind. The aim in the immersion is to experience, feel and relate person to person.

Immersions are not at all like normal, brief field visits to monitor or evaluate a project. Those are 'red carpet' visits, in which the recipients are meant to please the donor and present a positive picture.

Immersions aim to make an impact at a personal level through direct, experiential learning; at an institutional level, through what visitors may later do in their organisations; and at a policy-making level, by putting a human face and on-the-ground reality to decisions, reports and policies back in the office.

A staff member of DFID China put it like this: 'We sit in Beijing, we talk, we discuss, and we analyse policy. We try to assume what the implications are for poverty without actually experiencing what poverty is... This immersion has served as an important reality check, but also to reinvigorate my commitment to the mission, goals and values of DFID China.'

Narratives on Donors

Although not physically linking donors and poor people, like an immersion, Narratives of Empowerment is another initiative that aims to help donor staff reflect about what they are doing and why. It was adopted in 2009 by the Development Assistance Committee Network on Poverty Reduction (DAC/Povnet) that was looking at how donors could better support and not undermine processes of empowerment. Stories (narratives) were identified in which decisions taken by the primary donor had had an influence on the funded secondary donors (recipient governments or larger NGOs) that, in turn, had been interacting with poor people.

For this, a method was commissioned from Rosalind Eyben in which the specific role of donors was emphasised in the narrative. Four versions or 'voices' were contrasted when relating the same story. Rather than recruiting a consultant, direct involvement in collecting and analysing stories by POVNET members (donors) was suggested.

The process recognises the possibility of many points of view in a story, but the initiative has not come without challenges – members of POVNET found it difficult to collect the stories themselves, because of time or resource constraints.

Poor people's own evaluations

Donors can also learn directly from poor people's own evaluations of how external-led programmes are affecting their lives. Another approach is to have a community carry out their own action plans and reflections (See Chapters 7 and 8 on community learning).

2. Learning from poor people through secondary donors

Grounded advocacy: When the seeds come too late you're part of the problem

Zimbabwe was once relatively food secure, but drought, economic decline, and the fourth-highest HIV infection rate in the world all combined to cause a decline in food security between 2000 and 2005. In recognition of these difficulties, the European Commission (EC) set up a multi-year NGO Food Security funding line in 2004. ActionAid (AA) Zimbabwe put forward a project to distribute drip-watering kits and seeds in five districts and planned to start it on 1 January 2005.

By February 2005, the start of the planting season, local partners were asking AA when the drip kits and seeds would be delivered. They warned that if they arrived too late, the harvest would be poor. In the event, the seeds were not delivered until July, nearly six months behind schedule. Research with target households revealed that when the seeds were eventually received, people washed and ate them, and were then forced to rely on emergency food relief.

In order to find out what should have been done differently, the AA team looked at where things had gone wrong. The results were surprising. It began by meeting with the Food Security manager at the local EC Delegation to talk though project progress and to ask why funding had been disbursed so late. There were a number of factors, most of which were beyond the control of the local office:

- a late European Council funding decision on this new budget line
- the Christmas holiday break in Brussels and at the local office
- an EC database off-line for two months due to necessary maintenance
- confusion at AA International over which deposit account to use, causing an extra three weeks of delay.

While acknowledging the EC's role, the EC manager asked why a large NGO such as AA had not covered the project's costs with its unrestricted money, until the EC funds arrived. Two things were clear. Firstly, AA needed to strengthen its internal processes and look at ways of pre-financing signed contracts when payment from the donor was delayed beyond the start of the project. Secondly, advocacy targeting the local office was important, but real change in the administration of funding would only come from the EC headquarters in Brussels.

The story above is an example of Grounded Advocacy (GA), which is used by AA to influence donor thinking policy, based on reality in the field. It starts with poor people identifying changes needed in the practices or policies of donor-funded projects that are negatively affecting them. A plan of action is then designed, to enable them to work with the donor to bring about this change.

AA reports that learning in this process has shown that donor in-country presence and ownership, rather than centralised policy-making, 'facilitates the promotion of tailored solutions to national or local-level dynamics ... opening up new opportunities for dialogue and making it easier to invite donors to participate in meetings'.

3. Agencies and secondary donors – strengthening a learning dialogue

As you have seen above, primary donors can be one of the main barriers for learning systems at the secondary donor level. But practices such as 'flexibility clauses', 'learning budgets' and 'open reports' can help pave the way towards a more open, trust-based relationship between primary and secondary donors. This in turn means that secondary donors don't pass on inappropriate accountability systems to the people and organisations receiving grants from them. This has the potential to rather become a creative web through which learning can be shared.

Flexibility clauses and learning budgets

A CDRA staff member reflects on flexibility, learning budgets and attitudes to donors

'Life used to be much simpler. I remember having a much clearer practice, working with one or two projects at a time. Planning was a relatively simple process and most of the learning we did was on-the-job and informal.

But these days it's a bit different. We spend much more time preparing, planning and reflecting, both on our own, and more and more with others. There are more of us and we are working with bigger programmes and collaborating with many organisations. We have to consider diverse and complex scenarios.

Gone are the days when you could construct a project plan and simply implement it. Things are too complex and unpredictable so we have to learn and re-plan our way along. A plan is okay but we are constantly having to change it. Planning is now a continual preparation and adapting process rather than a matter of plotting and implementing outputs and outcomes.

We do still come up with plans and budgets for our donors to secure resources, but we make sure that we discuss (and write in clauses about) how the plan will need to change. We negotiate a high degree of flexibility, so that we don't have to keep renegotiating our agreements with them.

Luckily we have some donors with enough experience. But we know that they are the exception rather than the rule. We have put some effort into helping them to learn about the realities we face, to enable them to develop a more developmental practice themselves. We regard them as fellow development practitioners who require our honesty so that they can be effective donors, just as we require their honesty. They have an unbelievably difficult practice of giving away money, developmentally, into poverty-stricken contexts, in ways that empower everyone rather than corrupt the few. We can help them do this.

We challenge donors and they appreciate this – in fact some of them have told us that they continue to fund us because we challenge them and also because our reports contain good reflections and learnings from our experience, not just lists of outputs or extravagant claims of outcomes.

What this all adds up to is that we are having to learn new things all the time, in new ways and with different people, in order to keep up with newly emerging and complex challenges. Indeed, we probably spend 20–25 per cent of our time in various planning, preparation, reflection and learning activities, both on our own and with collaborators.

So one of the things we have negotiated with some donors are good budget lines for learning. We are working on those who don't get the learning thing yet!

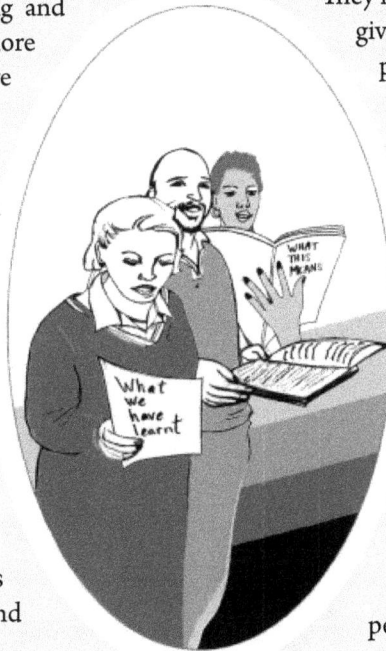

Open reports

Open reports are simply reports that explore what happened, and why, rather than answering set questions, or fitting what happened into prescribed boxes. Here are some ideas that might help you.

- Use the active rather than the passive voice: 'she did' rather than 'it was done'.

- Move from a focus on activities (by the NGO) to a focus on impact and change by people.

- Don't only look at what worked or happened, but at what made it possible.

- Give as much importance and normality to unexpected results as to expected ones.

- Include challenges, lessons learned and recommendations – what went well and what needs to improve.

4. Internal learning and learning from each other

Here are some examples of bilateral and multilateral learning initiatives between donor organisations.

Collective learning from experience and knowledge

Collective Learning Trajectories (CLTs) are organised around topical themes and issues by PSO – a learning and practice centre for Dutch development organisations. In a CLT people from several organisations come together for one, two or sometimes six days. The key to these Trajectories (pathways) is that, rather than bringing some relevant theory, the *experience* and *knowledge* of the participating organisations is shared. There is also always a link with one or more resource people from developing countries.

Last year, for example, there was a Trajectory about how to collaborate in networks with partners from north and south. All participants were involved with a north-south network, some as just members, some as donors, some as staff of the network secretariat. Everybody brought their own case study, and with the help of theory and

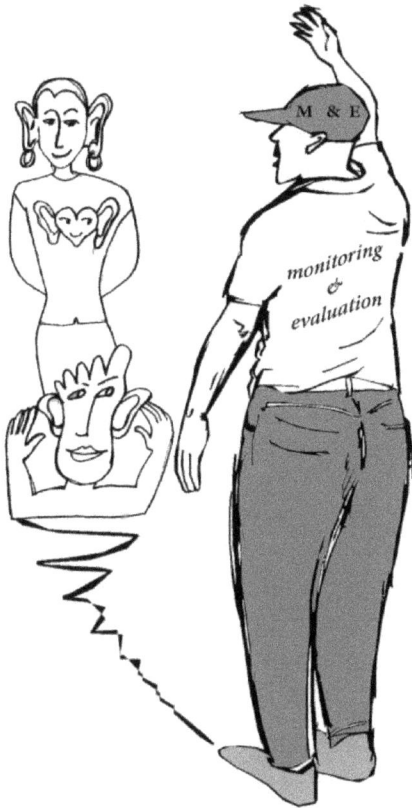

frameworks, they discussed their own practices as peers, and learned a lot from each other. For example:

- When you have the leadership role be transparent – do not confuse leadership and management.

- A network can be really needs-driven when you listen well at all levels (head, heart and feet) and you give attention to M&E. Be sure to include the target group.

- If the network becomes sustainable it is the end of the network. Take care: a network is not a programme!

- As a donor you must invest in communication. It is expensive, yet vital. Spend time with the secretary of the network, but also with the members. Chat, phone, Skype – be in contact!

One of the participants reflected: 'Through the things we learned in the Trajectory we decided to change our relationship with partners in the network. Now we are far more in the background and collaborate on the basis of equality, instead of taking a steering role.'

Lomeña describes a process of Internal Peer Review

Lomeña is a former consultant at the Inter-American Development Bank (IADB).

'During the Internal Peer Review process of evaluating documents (IADB evaluation office), we looked at the clarity of documents, methodology of evaluations, whether conclusions were well-sustained... it was a very technical and critical process, sometimes very controversial either because of disagreement about approaches or conceptual grounds amongst participants, but always very rich and interesting. These discussions could last from one to four hours, for the most controversial documents. At a personal and professional level, I learned a lot. The pressure of everybody having to make comments during the Internal Peer Review, from the very first day of your incorporation into the office evaluation team, raised the critical spirit and the motivation to present good documents for your colleagues' peer reviews. The later process of External Peer Reviews with the bank management, seem to me much more bureaucratic, and sometimes even political, but also full of learning about the relationship between the bank management and the independent "office of evaluation" of this international organisation'.

Guided Reading Weeks, as described by Rosalind Eyben, were initially developed for DFID Social Development advisers in 2005. Others, such as SIDA, have used them since. Their aims are to critically understand, engage with and apply recent conceptual approaches to themes such as power, social exclusion and gender. They have 5–10 participants and are organised as follows:

Sunday afternoon: Arrival. Participants are led through a session on collective, reflective learning and practice, and are encouraged to identify their own individual learning outcomes.

Monday – Friday: A specific theme is allocated to each day, with a participant assigned to take the lead on that theme by preparing a reading and presentation. The presentation should identify issues from the readings and the implications for both current organisational practice and for direct personal experience.

- Each morning is spent on individual study on the readings for that day. The facilitator very briefly introduces the readings to the group at breakfast. After breakfast the facilitator meets for about 90 minutes with the presenters of the day, who then work by themselves to finalise their presentations.

- The afternoon is for presentations followed by discussion. There is then a group walk of one to two hours during which participants often continue the discussions.

- Evenings are free unless the group decides otherwise. They might have informal talks around particular experiences, ask outside speakers to come and join them for drinks and dinner, and so on.

As with any other learning activity, these will work best if they are incorporated into the working system and supported by senior staff. In this case, it is important that the learning involves looking critically at how the process of donation is supporting or hindering development. They should not be an evaluation of any other organisation's work but a critical look at the donor agency's own practice and how it affects others. Special attention should be given to the effect on poor and marginalised people: those whose lives the donor is seeking to change.

5. Research on donor practice

Aidnography

Aidnography is a type of research, described by David Mosse in his 2005 book *Cultivating Development: An Ethnography of Aid Policy and Practice* as 'concerned not just with project objectives and outcomes but with questions about how such a development process unfolds'. This means understanding the relationship amongst the different actors in the aid web, such as donors, secondary donors and poor people.

There needs to be more research into how the practice of donors – the ways in which they disburse and account for money – affects development and social change.

This initiative was created by the Participation, Power and Social Change team at the Institute of Development Studies in Britain. A subsequent action research project aims to identify and demonstrate the effectiveness of alternative approaches to the results-orientated, target-driven reporting that is currently being demanded by many major donors.

Seventy development practitioners, researchers and funding agency professionals came together at a meeting in September 2010. They voiced their concern about the increasingly unrealistic results they were being asked to show, and the tendency for compliance to discourage work on transformational change. Some of the initiatives agreed were:

- Develop counter-narratives emphasising accountability to poor and excluded people and emphasising history over numbers.
- Develop different methods of reporting.
- Communicate that some aspects of development are not measurable.
- Collaborate with people inside the donor agencies who are dissatisfied with the 'audit culture'.
- Enhance organisational learning and reflective practice.

See www.bigpushforward.net

In conclusion...

Wherever we work, we have a responsibility to make sure that money that has been set aside for social change and development is used as effectively as possible. Complaining about donors, while passively complying with grant disbursement and reporting systems that undermine deep learning and meaningful social change, is not an honourable option. We may only be able to take small steps to begin with but we must be active in bringing about change.

Whenever we are a donor, whenever we give money, equipment or expertise to enable social change, we must ask ourselves: 'How can we do this in a way that ensures that communities and individuals can use it to learn for themselves and to act on their learning?' When we receive money for social change, we should ask: 'How can we use the money and account for it in a way that identifies and incorporates learning to bring about the most effective and sustainable change possible?'

CHAPTER 7

Our feet on the ground:
learning with communities

Talking with learners: A long process where education matters a lot!

In 2005 the women in the Reflect Circle in Diasson, Senegal, decided they wanted their own land for agricultural activities. They went to the local government with their demands and won legal entitlement to land. They got seeds, planted, harvested, managed the distribution themselves and many enjoyed a substantial increase in their earnings.

In 2006, the women asked for their own point of trade to sell groundnuts. This could have been seen as an insult to men because women had never before sold groundnuts. At first, the village chief refused to give them scales to organise the selling, and they had to hire equipment. One male operator lobbied the Governor of the region, and he stopped the women's business. But the women lobbied the Governor themselves and they gained his authorisation.

By 2007, seventeen women's Reflect Circles had acquired land and built a 'transformation unit' for processing food products into more commercially profitable products. Women now control their own farming and marketing activities and have their own bank accounts. Men give them greater respect in decision-making. This means women can help girls go to, and continue at, school. Nobody could have imagined these achievements in 2002.

In Reflect Circles facilitators from a community raise women's consciousness by linking adult learning to empowerment. They create a democratic space that strengthens people's ability to speak for themselves. Women learn to read, write and calculate, how to speak up and learn to be leaders, how to manage organisations and how to participate in an election.

It just has to be there!

Go to the people
Live with them
Learn from them
Love them
Start with what they know
Build with what they have
But with the best leader.
When the work is done
The task is accomplished
The people say:
'We have done this ourselves.'

Lao Tzu,
Chinese philosopher
of the sixth century BC

Five levels of participation

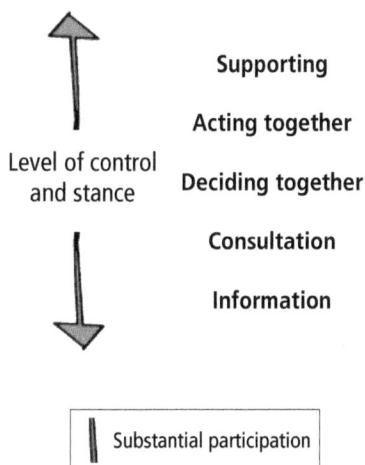

Supporting

Acting together

Level of control
and stance

Deciding together

Consultation

Information

Substantial participation

1. Commit to substantial participation

Let me introduce you to the idea of *substantial participation*. It covers the three upper levels of the 'ladder of participation', as shown below.

Level 5 – Supporting independent community initiatives.
Help people do what they want.

Level 4 – Acting together.
People with different interests decide together what is best, in partnerships.

Level 3 – Deciding together.
Encourage others to provide additional ideas and options; together decide the way forward.

Level 2 – Consultation.
Offer options and listen to feedback.

Level 1 – Information.
Tell people what you have planned.

2. Don't take the cooking stick...! Enter

The community must lead the way

Sanitation as an Empowerment Entry Point

The government programme to end open defecation consisted of building thousands of solid, free, western-style 'latrines'. Many years later the same latrines were still standing there, but no more had been built although local builders had been trained to do so. Why not? Because nobody had explained the benefits of sanitation and the villagers didn't find the point in investing in expensive latrines. Many proved unsustainable: people stopped using them when pits filled up, and many others were rather used for storage or even as temples.

In CLTS, communities are first selected and contacted. Then, the triggering Entry Point follows by stimulating a collective sense of disgust and shame as community members confront the facts of the health risk posed by mass open defecation: that they are ingesting (taking in) other people's excreta. So the goal is purely to help community members see for themselves the problem – then it's up to them to decide how to deal with it.

The facilitation team has several methodological tools, such as walks through areas of open defecation and unhygienic latrines, mapping of defecation areas, calculating daily 'contribution' of each household and money spent on medicine for related diseases such as diarrhoea. The pathway of faecal contamination is identified: flies to food to animals in contact with faeces to hands to food.

'Ignition' is the moment of collective realisation – that due to open defecation they are ingesting each others' faeces. Often strong arguments begin as to how to stop this situation.

> *... community members see for themselves the problem – then it's up to them to decide how to deal with it.*

Important concept: Entry point

The Entry Point is the moment at which you make your first contact with a community, in such a way that it stimulates community action. The underlying message is: 'We will be there, but you are the ones doing'.

The Community-Led Total Sanitation (CLTS) approach and the CARE Hunger approach are two examples of how Empowerment Entry Points are used.

Sanitation as an Empowerment Entry Point ...(cont)

At this point, the facilitator just listens. If asked what to do, she should answer that, as an outsider, she has little local knowledge and that they know much better what is best. If they believe latrines are too costly, the facilitator could simply tell them about low-cost latrines, without prescribing, and share experiences of other communities that have taken up total sanitation. If the community decides to stop open defecation, they should now look for their own alternatives.

Where ignition is successful, some actions are: sharing toilet options, facilitating an action plan and formation of community committee, and finding someone local to be the link person with suppliers of pans.

Where collective action does not emerge, some possible next steps are: thanking them for the detailed analysis and seeking their permission to leave, asking how many of them are going to defecate in the open tomorrow morning, fixing a date to return when others who may not be present can be there, and so on.

Abolishing hunger as an Empowerment Entry Point

Sanitation is not always an appropriate entry point, particularly in areas with periodic crises, such as hunger. Discussing hunger is used as the entry point by CARE Bangladesh, where seasonal hunger is widespread and distribution of food rations to the most needy may be the only option.

This intervention is then followed up by analyses of the causes of seasonal hunger with the poorest households, the findings of which enable them to consider collective strategies. These include using new spaces, such as road and canal sides, collectively cultivating food crops with the support of local experts, collectively securing more land or water from positive-minded local elites, growing cash crops, re-negotiating labour and contract arrangements and building up a reserve of food.

These strategies have helped people through the hunger period. The reserves have also saved poor farmers from taking loans from landlords during hunger periods. This subsequently allowed them to negotiate higher wages when landlords needed them to harvest fields of ripened rice. Within two agricultural seasons more than 1 500 agricultural day-labourers from fifteen communities were able to negotiate increased wages.

3. Smell what has been long cooking – don't bring your instant soup!

Start with what the communities know, have and want

If the entry point has worked and a community approaches us to support their own initiatives, what is then our role as NGO professionals? First of all, we should build a relationship of *trust* so that they know we will be there when they need us. It is also evident that we should know what they have been doing before, as life does not start with *our* Entry Points.

Idea 1. Spend time with people. Respect. Relax. Enjoy.

'My day' by Ha Lan, NGO fieldworker

A simple day for me, working in a community with an ethnic group, sometimes started with joining a drinking session of the community leaders, usually men. I understood that it was a local custom that a guest or a visitor should celebrate with them before further communications. Though it was very hard for a Vietnamese woman to drink alcohol, I still tried and could enjoy it.

On that day I came together with one staff member of the Women's Union of the province to do a small attendance survey before organising a language learning class for the adult women of the community. Most of the women were illiterate and led a life of hardship. It took us quite some time to reach the village, crossing a river and climbing to the top of a hill.

Yet, I chose to go in person rather than just send the attendance list, because I wanted to see and talk with the women, to learn what made them decide to enrol in this class. There were probably women who wanted to join in the class but faced barriers. If I went there, we might be able to encourage and support their participation.

Once we reached the village, it was already dark and there was no electricity in this area, so we worked with a fuel-lit lamp. I was so happy to see many women of young and middle age came to this meeting. I could not see every face around me clearly because of the dark, but I could feel how keen and how committed they were. They must have overcome the burden of their housework to take part in such a class. They sat at a distance from me and my Women's Union colleague; they were very shy with outsiders. We had to move close to them one by one, to ask their names; only then they would talk and share with us their reasons and feelings.

> We had to move close to them one by one, to ask their names; only then they would talk and share with us their reasons and feelings.

Important concept: Respect; Relax; Enjoy

Important concept: Community history

Idea 2. Learn about their culture and customs

Let them teach you, before you try to teach them. Imagine that you are on one side of a learning balance, and that for everything you say or contribute with, you need to have listened and taken from something else.

Tien and a project to improve nutrition in mountain villages

I am Tien, I work with the ethnic minority people in the mountain villages of Khanh Vinh, who live mainly by growing and selling cassava. When we suggested that they could grow a wider variety of food that the families could use to have better nutrition, at first they did not want to believe and learn to do that. So we stopped and spent time to listen to their ideas and priorities. Then we helped them to bring their cassava to market in a better way, so that they earned more for it and became less dependent on the usual middlemen.

After that, they began to trust us and to believe that we really cared about them and their welfare. Finally they were ready to accept advice about using the small area around their houses to grow a wide range of vegetables, for their own use, to improve their nutritional status.

Idea 3. Learn about their past

Learning from history creates collective memory and good trust between the community and the supporting organisation. It also enables organisations to have a stronger sense of their own identity and to better relate to, and support, other emerging organisations. Tools such as the River of Life, a time line, group discussions or the journalistic approach can be used.

'History through a journalistic approach' by Ha Lan, NGO fieldworker

My name is Ha Lan. In 2000, people with disability in Vinh Tu commune founded their own Disabled People's Organisation (DPO), with our support. It started out with just fifteen members, and generated only a few activities in its first few years. Then, rather sharply, in 2003 membership and budget grew rapidly. Members took over more responsibility for running the organisation, and the DPO's visibility in the community increased dramatically, with cultural and sports events and increasing participation in the commune's social and economic life.

In 2005, the Vinh Tu DPO was asked by the people with disabilities in other neighbouring communities to advise them how to establish and develop their own DPO. So we thought we first needed to learn from the history of the Vinh Tu DPO.

We introduced Vinh Tu DPO to a journalist to help document their 'learning history'. What had changed? What had led to the DPO's striking improvement? After a week of interviews a meeting of stakeholders went over the tentative conclusions. We all learned from the DPO's early days about the importance of organisational skills, and learning to make personal development plans that led to setting up small businesses and to improved health care. Key activities included exposure to role models in other similar organisations, extensive coaching, and organising community social events.

By learning in this way, the Vinh Tu DPO prepared itself to support the DPO from the neighbouring community.

Idea 4. Put questions, don't give solutions

Brazilian educator Paulo Freire underlined the need to see education (and we could add, development) as a dialogue. Mere mechanical memorisation (or orders and 'advice' in development) is not true learning – it is 'banking education'. If the situation does not permit such dialogue, then 'the structure must be changed'.

4. Helping the cooks…

Supporting natural leaders

Experience tells us that communities also learn from development workers – it's a two-way learning process. There are several issues around community leaders that communities demand and/or development workers feel are lacking. We need to encourage and support natural leaders in their roles of:

- Helping their communities identify and strengthen what they already know and can do
- Enabling their communities to see the gaps in capacity and helping them address these
- Supporting peer-learning and sharing between communities
- Helping their communities to access information for themselves from the outside
- Helping their communities to find the courage to engage with government and business.

The stories below describe how natural leaders are, and how they act. They are doers rather than talkers, are hard workers, articulate, committed, and are mobilisers with initiative. They share and are proud of what they do. They have the trust of their neighbours, standing with them, not above them.

Often natural leaders are not elected but are pushed forward by the people because they have proved themselves by what they do. These are the ones to be supported.

Important concept: Banking education

In 'banking education' the teacher (or development technician) deposits bits of information or knowledge in the minds of the learners (or communities) who are considered to be empty or ignorant. It is much like we deposit money into an empty bank account. Freire said this model made students (and communities) into passive objects to be acted upon by the teacher (technician). It conditioned them to accept the status quo of the dominant culture.

Important concept: Dialogue-based education

On the other hand, in 'dialogue-based education' the facilitator and learner (technician and community member) discuss and analyse their experiences, feelings and knowledge of the world together. The model explores problems or realities people find themselves in as something which can be transformed. It is the job of the facilitator to help the learners think critically, for themselves, about the situation. Freire called this *conscientisation*.

'We want to send two women of the community to represent us at the Groundnuts Marketing Fair,' Babacar said in the monthly meeting. 'How shall we select them?'

'But two women are not enough,' said Atta Sene, one of the community leaders. 'Can we send more?'

'No, we don't have enough budget, so only two can go,' Babacar replied firmly.

Babacar is a good example of the empowerment of local community leaders. Almost ten years ago, his village selected him as a facilitator to map community needs, as part of a participatory rural appraisal. He became an excellent facilitator, using the Reflect methodology, and learned other skills like writing, organising meetings, monitoring and evaluation, project management and organising exchange visits. He held different posts and eventually became the President of COCOGEP, the local community organisation.

What impressed me was how he linked village learning and international events. For example, he organised a local event with specially-created content on women's rights for International Women's Day on 8 March. He created his own content by combining questions and feedback of the community with information from papers and newsletters. He also introduced small-scale credit and saving schemes – not supported by donors, and therefore with more chance of sustainability.

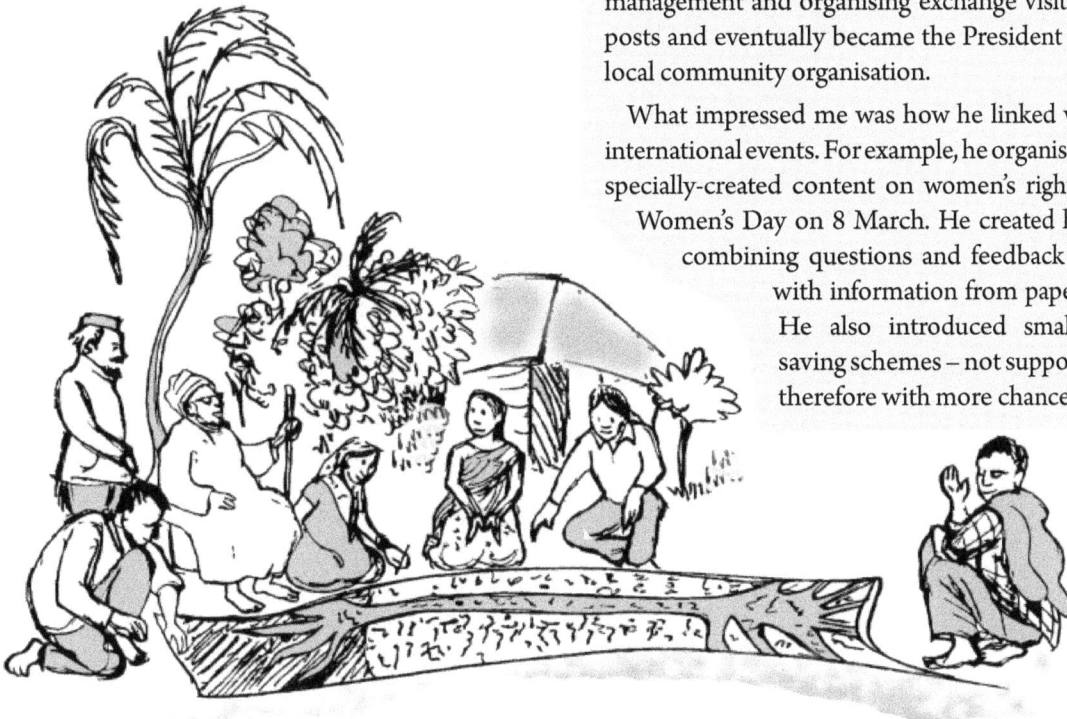

Fisherwoman Fátima: strength as the answer to hardship

I remember fisherwoman Fátima growing as a leader... She's quiet and reflective, with that inner calm that leaves you breathless. Her respect for others, innate. Her departure point, the group. I see her eyebrows pondering all the issues discussed. And I hear the words she pronounces sharply. Like an untiring ant, she gets things done slowly and steadily, smiling satisfied after a meeting; already planning for the next one. She invites me to her boat and shows me how to fish. She is proud of what she does. I experience things for the very first time: the deep loneliness on the open sea, the strenuous weight of the biggest fish, the frequent dizziness and stomach-aches, the unfair prices at the harbour. Fátima's life is a challenging one. I admire her strength as the only answer to hardship.

5. We can make the soup, but we need your saucepan!

Contributing with actions to demand rights: co-creating

Join a group of development workers and don't be surprised if the topic of the government's role in communities and social change gets everybody's attention, and raises diverse and passionate perspectives. Some argue for a community development approach with no state support, because the state cannot be relied upon. Others are critical of this and want to mobilise communities to gain their constitutional rights from the state. Their colleagues counter: a rights-based approach may mobilise communities, but once rights are won there is frequently a demobilisation, with the state taking credit for delivery and shaping the development agenda back to its own political priorities. And so the argument continues…

But is this an 'either-or' situation? Consider the work of Shack Dwellers International and the housing movements they support, where the best of both approaches have been combined.

Community mobilisation and learning

Shack Dwellers International – Recently, approaches to social change have begun emerging that move beyond simplistic needs or rights-based approaches, in some ways combining the best of these into something more effective and sustainable. Horizontal Learning is key to their effectiveness.

Shack Dwellers International (SDI) exists in over 30 countries, representing an integration of the two approaches. Self-responsibility or self-help is a foundation for the mobilisation needed to claim rights and draw the state into being a co-producer of services, rather than as deliverer of development. SDI's impressive gains have the attention of many actors involved in social change. Their practice has the following core process.

Important concepts:

Needs-Based Approach;
Rights-Based Approach;
Needs-for-Rights Approach

'Leaders who do not act dialogically, but insist on imposing their decisions, do not organise the people – they manipulate them. They do not liberate, nor are they liberated: they oppress.'

Paulo Freire

Step 1: From self-help comes self-reliance

Unorganised peri-urban shack dwellers (mostly women) are encouraged to form simple, street-based, daily savings-and-loan groups or associations. This is learned through horizontal exchange processes with existing, experienced associations of shackdwellers. These become the nucleus of community organisation and later mobilisation, rooted in an issue that is very immediate to people: ready cash. Through this process people are taking more responsibility for their own change, more conscious of what they can do for themselves, with each other.

Step 2: Community-to-community solidarity

Through Horizontal Learning exchanges, the different groups or associations build relationships of trust, connecting their organisations to larger Federations, enabling them to joining their savings and to gain access to bigger pools of capital. In the process they build the potential to act in solidarity when approaching the State.

Step 3: Self-research, self-knowledge

From this, supported by other communities, movements and NGOs with experience, communities can embark on 'enumeration' processes, a kind of horizontal research, where literate youth are trained to collect and collate data about each household, to help the community to develop an accurate picture of itself. This is shared and developed as a community-building process and enables them to approach the State with solid facts and figures.

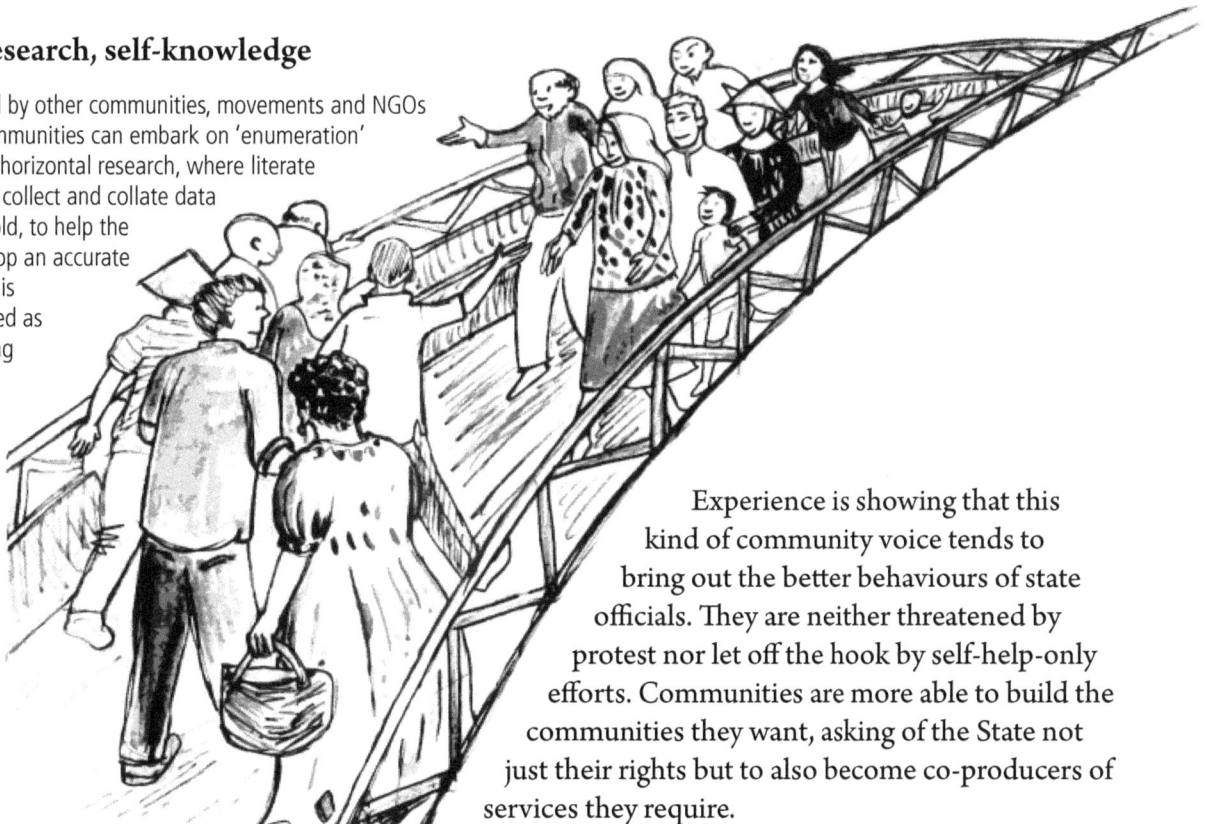

Step 4: Community visioning

Now 'enumerated' and with a better sense of who they are and what their real challenges are, they start looking at the future. Through "house modelling" they develop ideas and plans for the kinds of houses and communities they want to live in. This both unites and prepares them to engage with the State on the basis of visions and plans that they have created and own.

Step 5: Engaging the state in co-creation

The State is approached to meet with them. In effect the communities are now able to say to the state: 'This is what we can do for ourselves. We know who we are and what our real situation is. We have developed our own plans for the future. What can you do, as our government, and how can we help you do it?'

Experience is showing that this kind of community voice tends to bring out the better behaviours of state officials. They are neither threatened by protest nor let off the hook by self-help-only efforts. Communities are more able to build the communities they want, asking of the State not just their rights but to also become co-producers of services they require.

6. Cooking tools?
Only useful if the cooks are good!

Tools must be used by professionals with the right attitude.

How does your practice measure up? Have a look at this table and (honestly) judge where your practice lies.

Basic key attitudes and behaviours

DON'T	DO
Educate, lecture or tell people what to do	Facilitate people's own appraisal
Tell people what is good and bad	Let people analyse and realise for themselves
Push for, or demand action	Facilitate to promote self-mobilisation
Be in charge	Stand back, leave it to local leaders
Interrupt	Listen attentively
Favour the better off or more powerful members via seating or allowing them to interrupt or dominate	Facilitate taking into account power relations, speaking time, seating arrangements
Overlook emerging natural leaders	Appreciate those who take a lead and engage
Overlook women, children, those who often get left out	Always encourage women and the poorer sections of the community to participate
Overlook people who come forward to help	Appreciate community members' offers to help poorer members
Be too humble or too polite	Be bold yet cautious
Arrange a day, time and place convenient to meet for *you*	Ask people when is the most convenient day, time and place for them to meet
Cater to the 'dependency mentality' by feeling sorry for people or promising materials	Start with what they know, have, do and want

Source: Adapted from the CLTS handbook

Always encourage women and the poorer sections of the community to participate

The big challenge in using any participatory methodologies is in how we use them – not in the fact that we use them. They should be seen as a *catalyst* rather than a *substitute for debate*. The tools should never become an end in themselves. If power relations and good attitudes are ignored, there is the danger that they will be used in manipulative and damaging ways. Only with a deep awareness of power at all times, and power at all levels, can participatory processes be used effectively.

Case study – Reflect

Reflect is an approach to collective learning and social change. Using the Reflect approach, people sit together in Circles (groups), analyse different problems and find solutions – Action Points. Techniques such as drawing, drama, songs, dance, writing, speaking, numbers and visuals, for example calendars, maps and matrices, are used. These tools enhance people's capacity to think about their lives more actively and to collectively organise to engage with the world. The action could be to take initiative and do something for themselves, or to claim their rights.

... enhance people's capacity to think about their lives more actively and to collectively organise to engage with the world.

A. Engaging Reflect with communities

1. Getting started –
How to identify communities to work with

A community is chosen based on the results of research mapping those communities who receive less support, who have fewer development partners and who are the poorest in the country. After sharing the results, we agree with communities to do a PRA to identify the true needs. The challenges are huge but very objective – it's obvious that we cannot solve all problems.

Challenges: Some local governments or politicians may try to convince you to work with other communities. Firmly defend your strategy and your beliefs.

We now hold *community consultations* to see whether they want to try Reflect. Our theory of change is that communities have to transform their own lives. At a meeting we explain the approach and what it requires. At first communities think that we are just playing, not really thinking straight, because they don't believe they have many skills, and so far no external bodies have ever trusted them to run their own development programmes.

Challenges: We have to convince them that it is possible, but that they have to map their own needs. They have to learn horizontally from each other and sometimes vertically from experts, including learning some vital skills, like planning.

2. Identification of Community Facilitators

Communities propose their own facilitators but the choice must be confirmed by us before any training, because Reflect trainings are very expensive. Conditions of this type must be met: the facilitator has to be from the community, have experience in facilitating, usually has to agree to be a volunteer, be accepted in the community, speak the local language, be ready to learn, have level four or equivalent in high school and be able to write.

Challenges: some people may try to influence you to take their relatives as facilitators, but be firm. It is essential for the external organisation to be part of recruiting, in order to help communities to find the right facilitators. This is not to make the choice for communities, but to ensure there is clarity about what is needed for success.

3. Training

Training of facilitators is ten days in class and five days practical in the community, and it aims to use, and add value to, local knowledge. Experienced facilitators can later become trainers. Facilitators learn PRA tools and how to help people to use them to discuss and solve a problem. They learn how to hold a Circle discussion, how to create an Action Plan plus how to introduce literacy and numeracy in the process. They will learn a lot of pedagogy, and facilitating tools such as energisers and stories.

Advice: Be sure the facilitators understand the process. Let them take initiative, promote Horizontal Learning, give stimulation, make it fun, plan field visits, and give helpful feedback.

4. Opening of Circles Ceremony

This ceremony includes the community members, leaders and chiefs, local government officials, and resource people from health, agriculture, fisheries, education and other volunteers. This big ceremony is important as the agreement of the whole community is needed for the opening of Circles. The Reflect steps are explained as well as the results expected. There is time for questions, and then the facilitator is officially installed.

Challenges: All leaders have to be present to legitimate this installation, and you need to ask for the support of the whole group.

5. Running Circles using Horizontal and Vertical Learning

The first meeting defines some fundamental conditions such as number and times of meetings, the language to be used and, in some instances, a committee is set up to do different tasks. The facilitator explains the importance of participation. By the end of the first session, members should realise that the Circle is their own to run.

Challenges: The facilitator should not teach but should push people to discuss, to deepen knowledge. She tries to prevent anyone disrupting or monopolising meetings. Balancing oral, written, visual (PRA) and numeric forms can be a challenge.

6. Refresher training, motivation and other capacity-building

Annual refresher training is needed for an approach like this, where something innovative is happening every day. Peer and collective learning plus frequent meetings are facilitated. Generally, the support organisation is approached after one or two years to ask for trainings, or information on a topic such as in ICT, literacy or language, or even about something like flu, according to needs. Facilitators should to be connected to what is happening globally, but should use their local knowledge and adapt information if they find it useful, for example, on the price of crops, or literacy. They ponder their role in enhancing development of their sectors within the community.

Facilitators also have to attend Reflect meetings at local, national and international level to share views, experiences, skills and new tools.

Challenges: Some facilitators hesitate to reveal all their capacity-building needs, some of which are expensive and have to be repeated. Non-Reflect facilitators in the community may feel too much is being invested and you will have to explain that the approach requires it.

7. Implementation of Action Points

An Action Point is the project the Circle defines as the solution to one problem, for example, malaria. The Circle defines the causes and the consequences and Reflects the solution step-by-step to arrive at an Action Plan, comprising Action Points. An Action Point may take days, weeks or months to implement. So, many Action Points form an Action Plan of annual community-driven identifications and prioritisations. When funding is needed, the Circle may need to prepare a written proposal, such as the example in the table.

Global objective	Specific objectives	Responsible people	Beneficiaries	Where	Budget	Deadline: begin and end	Indicators
Reduce the infection rate	Remove standing water, injection campaign	Chief of village, nurse, president of Circle	All the people of the village	In Ndorong village	$1 000	July–Oct	Reduce malaria cases from 60% to 10%

The facilitator facilitates the project cycle through to M&E.

Challenges: As a supporting organisation, you need to help them to achieve everything they want, be it funding or contact with an official.

8. Involving a resource person

Circles work and act with the rest of the community, and the world. The facilitator and the community may ask a resource person, such as a nurse, to a Circle session to share ideas. Thus, the Circle is a space where you have Vertical Learning, within the Horizontal Learning happening collectively. The resource person also learns, and you have Vertical Learning from the supporting organisations everyone is working with.

Challenges: Sometimes, the facilitator struggles to share learning so you have to ask questions in meetings, to find out problems and find solutions. Sometimes he or she needs a little push from you. Budgets can also be limiting when dealing with so many actions. Remember to discuss decisions with all members. You must help them to do fundraising, showing them how it is done.

9. Local community mobilisation, advocacy and campaigns – taking it to another level

When people agree to mobilise themselves by taking action to resolve problems we call it 'community social mobilisation'. In the case of Reflect, people are familiar with this idea, so it is easier for them to mobilise. For example, they might organise a rally or a big campaign to get women access to land. They will already be in networks and can define some rules for taking action. One community might begin; others join when they hear of work in a domain that interests them. The learning is around how to engage together towards solutions. These activities mostly deal with policy change and rights.

Challenges: Funds are needed to communicate, generally via community radios or weekly markets, and using leaflets, T-shirts and so on. Help is needed to contact journalists, and the different media. Training may be needed in ICT.

> ## QUESTIONS
> ### TO THINK ABOUT
>
> - Which concepts presented in the chapter have you found in the Reflect case study?
> - Where have you found examples of Vertical Learning? And Horizontal Learning?
> - How does this example help you in your context?

B. From community social mobilisation to social movements

1. Community mobilisation

When many communities unite on one issue, we have social mobilisation. The heart of the mobilisation is the network of many Circles, perhaps including rural and urban people. The mobilisation has to be significant to get the attention of the authorities or the government.

Challenges: The first challenge is finding funding, because sometimes the network is informal, with work done by volunteers. It can thus be difficult to get reports on time, and have activities done regularly. The second challenge is communication. Where there is no electricity and no ICT, communication is by telephone, which is expensive.

2. Social movements

Here there is the same aim, one interest, but it is at national or international level. An example is the movement of peasants in West Africa called Cadre de Concertation des Ruraux (CNCR) or Via Campesina in Latin America. These powerful movements can challenge, for example, trade frameworks, the debts of poor countries and can seek the attention of powerful countries such as the US, or challenge the World Bank and the International Monetary Fund.

Challenges: The head of one movement can be more influenced by one organisation than another, especially when donor funds are involved. Social movements can also influence the themes of the network, causing disaffected members to leave. Governance can be a challenge if one organisation has more members than another. Politicians may also try to use the movement for other interests.

From learning to social change – developing new kinds of leadership

Social change requires social action, mobilising people and their innate resourcefulness to tackle problems that cannot be tackled alone. But rushing from action to action, which satisfies the activist in us, often leads us into simplistic strategies and needless confrontation. This can worsen the situation, undermine relationships, destroy trust and lose the support of the people.

Enabling learning, especially Action Learning and Horizontal Learning, where people collectively take time to learn and think together, to work in a participative manner with their own real experience, helps to build more solid foundations for action.

But to enable learning we need to invest in facilitation skills, helping communities and organisations to find the right people to play creative facilitation roles, and then giving them support and training. In many ways this is where the new leadership lies, not in building one strong, charismatic, mobilising figurehead, but in enabling many natural leaders to come to the surface, people who want bring the best out of other people, who enable leadership in others and in so doing unlock many surprising capacities for social change.

CHAPTER 8

Horizontal Learning:

a sideways approach to change

Growing food together at school

Mrs Letela stood gazing through the cracked pane of her office window, watching the children in the dusty playground. 'How many have eaten today?' she wondered. 'How many of their parents' fields stand empty? How has it come to be that the children of farmers come to school hungry? I am going to have to do something.'

Now, six months later, she watched the children sitting with healthy, gleaming eyes over their plates of steaming food – food cooked by the domestic science students and grown by the parents in the school garden. She remembered the day that she had decided to take action. 'How long ago that seems now,' she smiled. 'It has been quite a journey!'

As principal of the local primary school she had contacted a regional NGO network which promoted small-scale vegetable gardening, combining their local farming methods with principles and methods of permaculture.

Word had spread quickly! Parents and teachers from other schools visited and asked if they could be shown the methods as well. The parents of Mrs Letela's school had become teachers of other parents. Soon 58 local district schools and communities had started similar initiatives and this spread further to 200 schools in other districts, now with the help of the government. Mrs Letela's school had also set up a small, part-time advice centre to put people in touch with each other, to share resources and give advice.

This inspiring story shows how something small and tangible can grow naturally into something with a huge impact for so many, at very little cost. It shows us how people can learn and act from their own and each other's experience as peers. This is a key principle in many successful development programmes. We call it 'Horizontal Learning'. In this chapter I will explain to you how it works.

Horizontal Learning

What is Horizontal Learning? Learning from our neighbours, elders and peers is Horizontal Learning. It is an ancient and natural practice that has enabled sharing and collaboration through the ages; through it economic, social, cultural, artistic, religious and recreational life come together for mutual benefit. In many ancient cultures people met other communities in markets and during rituals. Exchanges of both knowledge and goods happened, assisted and accompanied by cultural activities like storytelling, song and dance. These were not only to amuse, but also to spread and celebrate traditional values and knowledge needed to live. In West Africa it was also a practice to use *griots*, great storytellers who travelled between communities to memorise and teach the history, practices and legends of the people of the land.

But in many societies these traditions are in ruins, destroyed through colonisation and the subsequent introduction of vertical, formal schooling, health, religion, justice and economic systems. Local wisdom was labelled as backward, local rituals and values as superstitions and soon people no longer valued their own or their neighbours' knowledge. In the last hundred years the teacher, priest, doctor, lawyer, businessperson, government officer and the mass media have become the trusted sources of knowledge. Yet these vertical sources have failed millions, if not billions, by promising a better life yet, more often, bringing about sustained and deepening poverty.

The story of Mrs Letela is, however, just one example of how Horizontal Learning and knowledge-sharing are still relevant. There are many more stories like hers. People are learning again to trust their own and their neighbours' knowledge and what they can do for themselves and each other. Increasingly community organisations, NGOs and governments are becoming aware again of the power of local knowledge and the potential for Horizontal Learning to help communities to mobilise themselves, share their knowledge and also to collaborate to face common challenges.

What role has Horizontal Learning played in *your* life and practice? Probably a lot more than you realise, as I hope will be shown as I discuss how different forms of Horizontal Learning can make changes at larger scale in society.

Key principals and ideas of Horizontal Learning

Some key principals of Horizontal Learning are listed below.

- Horizontal Learning is learning from the experiences and ideas of others like you: your neighbours or other communities, fellow farmers, teachers, teenagers and so on.

- Horizontal Learning builds on your local knowledge that comes from your own real experience.

- Horizontal Learning enables people to feel good about their own experience and knowledge and more confident about their own ability to makes changes.

- Horizontal Learning grows relationships and solidarity, often stimulating and building good foundations for collaboration and social action.

How Horizontal Learning is different from capacity-building

Conventional capacity-building addresses gaps in the capacity of people and organisations. How and when these deficiencies are dealt with is generally decided by experts, managers, trainers and so on. This is where the basic assumption of Horizontal Learning is different: it looks at existing capacities at community level. What and how learning will take place is decided by the learners themselves.

In many instances peers are better at sharing and teaching than trainers or teachers. Why? Well, they speak from their own direct experience, often more simply and in the same language and with a better understanding of what it takes for someone, like themselves, to learn what they are sharing. Horizontal Learning is often two-way, which brings confidence and energy to the process. Watch farmers sharing their ideas with each other – the chances are they will have a fruitful and passionate discussion that would not be possible with a trainer or teacher.

But there is a place for trainers and teachers. They often have both experience and knowledge that have a critical place in learning and may bring more conceptual clarity than is available in the peer group. The parents/farmers in the story needed the expertise of the permaculture trainers, without which little may have developed. But this new knowledge was brought *after* their own knowledge and experience was collectively surfaced and validated by the trainers. In this case the expert knowledge expanded what they already knew, rather than ignored the existing knowledge, as so often happens. Capacity-building – or Vertical Learning – efforts could this way add value to a Horizontal Learning programme.

Different methods of Horizontal Learning

Peer-to-peer teaching and knowledge exchange

Farmer to farmer, children to parents

'We were so excited in the bus, like schoolchildren, singing all the time. Most of us had never been that far before,' one of the farmers explained. The bus full of farmers from Nkwanta, in the Volta Region in Ghana, was returning from an exchange visit to Salaga with farmer co-operatives there. She told me how interesting it was to hear directly from the other farmers, how they were able to learn to use a mobile phone to access the market prices of different crops like soya beans, groundnuts and yam, and to communicate with different district markets using text messages. 'We always know less than the traders, so we feel cheated. They had tried writing out the prices on the village notice board, but most farmers lived too far from that, so they always had outdated prices.' She explained further, 'But here we have seen that it could be different, that if we work together we can be in control and not the traders,' she said.

The Salaga farmers had explained how the first trainings were difficult, until the local NGO changed its approach. Their children are trained first, at school, and they then help their parents to learn how to use the mobile phone. Now the farmers get regular price updates and if a trader visits them to buy their harvest they can negotiate a better price. They said that they have used part of this extra money to send more of their children to school. Most farmers also did not have access to electricity and had to walk far and pay a lot to charge their phones. But now the co-operative has been able to buy shared solar chargers to overcome this challenge.

Sharing their experience with the Nkwanta farmers was also a good reflection for the farmers of Salaga, something they did not do very often. 'We would also like to make such a change in our own villages!' one farmer exclaimed.

Back in Nkwanta, the local NGO that had linked the farmers of the Volta Region with the farmers in Salaga had organised a feedback session with other members of the community who were not part of the exchange visit. They will now act on the learnings together.

What is striking about this story? Several ideas come to mind. Simple and inexpensive. Unlocking local resourcefulness. Low-cost exchange visits. Farmers could show other farmers what they were doing – not as experts but as neighbours. Both skills and confidence were built, bringing increased and more sustainable income to communities. Enabled further investment in their children. And how about children teaching their parents? Turning things upside down, unlocking a surprising resourcefulness. Teaching everyone a valuable lesson about learning and working together.

Horizontal Learning and community mobilisation

A story of rapid spontaneous developments

The NGO director in Cape Town was feeling a bit overwhelmed. The street-based daily-savings groups in the informal settlements were growing beyond what was originally envisaged. The whole thing had developed a life of its own in the three to four years of its existence. Scores of savings groups had formed, mushrooming all over the place, one group after another learning from established groups how to organise themselves. One motivation to set up the savings groups was as a counter to domestic violence but this was difficult to keep track of and impossible to measure without interfering, though the stories of the women's groups beating on their pots and pans, confronting wife-beaters, was a hopeful development.

Now the groups had joined with more assertive savings groups from out of town to form a movement, a federation, boosting the number of groups to over a hundred, which was exciting. They were negotiating with banks and donors to access more capital for housing development. Three groups from towns up the West Coast were applying to the government, as organisations, for lucrative fishing rights. What was the significance of this? It was not yet clear where it would lead and what would be asked of the NGO as practitioners. This was not in the original logframe. What would the donors say? How could the impact of these spontaneous developments be measured?

> *'... dynamic possibilities ... are unlocked when community groups start to share their skills...'*

What strikes me in this story are the dynamic possibilities that are unlocked when community groups start to share their skills and experience amongst each other, and then use these learning relationships to mobilise themselves into larger movements to engage creatively with society. The story in the previous chapter about the federations linked to the Shackdwellers International NGO demonstrates this as well. These are not just protest movements demanding their rights, although of course there is a place for this when injustices must be confronted. But this is not enough. In these stories we see people actively mobilising themselves. They are doing what they can for themselves and using the organisation that this requires to actively engage with banks and government, not just demanding their space but actually claiming it and working with it to better their own lives.

Using video to go beyond community-to-community exchange

Farmer-to-farmer video sharing of new methods

Most farmers in Ghana still use traditional farming methods, and reap one harvest after the rainy season. But some farmers have been experimenting with new methods, sometimes with the help of researchers and NGO extension workers. Most farmers, however, remain unaware of the results of these new methods – so have no reason to change their old methods. A local NGO has now filmed some of the farmers demonstrating the new methods. The choice of good practices was done in a participatory way by groups of farmers, researchers and extension officers. In the videos the various steps of the production process are shown, for example demonstrating a new method of planting for cow peas, a better sieving method for cassava and good practices of harvesting honey. The videos are used to initiate discussion, in the local language, with farmer groups. They show the good new practices being used in combination with the traditional practices.

Through the use of video local knowledge can be made visible, not only in the same community, but further afield. This self-image conveys the impression immediately that one's own knowledge is important and that it can be effectively communicated. For those who cannot read or write, video shows information in a way that people can understand and relate to. It also is enhancing traditional oral storytelling, making it easy to exchange good practices in a way communities will understand.

Videos can be shown to an even larger audience on the internet, for example on YouTube, where people share videos with each other all over the world. This is already changing the way individuals learn, but could also help you to share your local content beyond your own community. Have could you use video as a method of Horizontal Learning or knowledge sharing? Using video will be explained on the Barefoot Guide website.

Learning groups

Another important method of Horizontal Learning is learning in groups of like-minded people, for example farmers, teachers and health workers, to share experiences, challenges and solutions.

Designing, improving, sharing

One of the participating teachers explained their learning group like this: 'We meet each other every month on a Saturday. First we designed local teaching materials together, as part of the project we were all part of. But now we also start to share other materials. We discuss the challenges we encounter as teachers and we asked the more experienced teachers how they would go about it. We are improving our professional capacities and have formed a Teacher Learning Group. We are now not only doing this face to face, but are now able also to use email to continue with knowledge-sharing, even from a distance.'

Teachers from seven schools (both government and private) in different towns, in the Copperbelt Province in Zambia, formed a project to enhance the quality of teaching and teaching materials in all subjects. They were trained to use, and how to incorporate these new technologies into their teaching. But what really worked well to improve the quality of teaching was the network formed by the participating teachers. They still face difficulties, like the internet going down, but now can use both SMS and email to reach each other to confirm face to face meetings. It is a big improvement for most teachers that they are regularly able to communicate with each other.

We tend to relate to our peers more openly than to experts, and can learn in different ways as a result. Sitting next to a peer, on the same level, rather than below, we can connect more strongly and more freely. And this is not only at a head level, but at a heart level too; we engage more empathetically.

We ... use email to continue with knowledge-sharing, even from a distance.

QUESTION
TO THINK ABOUT

- Someone who has just learned something can often be a better teacher than an expert who has known it for years. Why do you think this is so?

Combined learning groups

One method I found very effective in raising awareness of HIV and Aids and encouraging people to change behaviour, is Stepping Stones.

Key to this method is the combination of four peer groups – older men, older women, younger men and younger women – from a community. Mostly they meet each other separately to create a safe, supportive space for talks about intimate issues. But they do periodically meet together to share insights.

STEPPING STONES

Stepping Stones and other participatory activities use a different approach from the methods used by many organisations. Before we started using participatory approaches, we used to transfer knowledge to our groups. Now they use their own knowledge and we learn from them. We used to give lectures, now we facilitate people to learn by doing themselves. When people do the role play on sexual encounters, each peer shows actual behaviour. Men and women of all ages now analyse their own situation, behaviour and its causes.

Assertiveness using 'I' statements

Men and women appreciated learning how to be assertive (rather than aggressive or passive) by using 'I' statements. Men use the 'I' statement to ask wives more politely to perform tasks for them. For example, in Uganda, young men now use this approach instead of demanding sex, and said that as a result girls have a greater sense of ownership of themselves. Women said practising these skills helped them to say no to unwanted sex and oppressive male behaviour, as well as to ask their partners for money or permission to travel. Women appear to have benefited most from increased assertiveness skills, saying that they have more confidence to stand by their decisions and to deal with difficult situations.

Having four different peer groups together you are able to learn with your own peers, but in the shared sessions also build relationships and trust with different groups in your community. This could be a good base for change in the personal, household or the community level.

Communities of Practice

In this chapter I have touched on Horizontal Learning at community or grassroots level. There are also other types of communities, like 'Communities of Practice', that can work at any level of society. Communities of Practice are groups that share a concern, a set of problems or a passion about a topic and who deepen their knowledge and expertise by interacting on an ongoing basis. These communities don't have to consist of peers only. They can cluster around an interest, such as the production of soya beans. Farmers, researchers, NGO workers and government extension officers could all bring their own expertise. They become peers, each bringing important pieces to the collective puzzle. In a Community of Practice it is not only about knowledge exchange, but also about making sense of and interpreting context and experience together, and through this creating new knowledge. It is this ability to use knowledge, reject it or improve upon it that makes Communities of Practice such powerful tools for encouraging real change.

Before the internet, Communities of Practice were restricted to defined geographic areas. Membership boundaries were clear and the influence of the community reached as far as the area covered. Today they can span a variety of contexts and geographies. New possibilities on the internet have brought new ways of collaboration and community engagement.

> *... this ability to use knowledge, reject it or improve upon it ... makes Communities of Practice such powerful tools*

THEMATIC LEARNING COMMUNITIES

A good example within my own organisation is the Thematic Learning Communities (TLCs) created to stimulate learning between the people working in the field and the sector specialists in the office. We have several face to face meetings together to share the practices in the field and to see if we can detect common trends and identify good practices. We also have a virtual email-based discussion group where we share articles and links to websites, and practices that are relevant for the sector. On our intranet we have created an archive where you can find stored information on the TLCs. This helps us to see how other team members are doing in other countries, it gives us ideas about good practices and it help us to learn from each other.

Supporting Horizontal Learning exchanges

As we have seen, there are many kinds of Horizontal Learning processes. But one of the most useful versions is simply for people from one community or organisation to visit another, whether for a day or two or three, to see and meet people and learn directly from each other. Very easy to organise and often inexpensive, these exchange visits can reduce isolation, build solidarity, cross-fertilise ideas and stimulate enormous learning, initiative and change.

Enabling communities to organise and facilitate their own inexpensive, fruitful and enjoyable Horizontal Learning exchanges with other groups, communities or organisations, so that they can do so again and again by themselves, may be the most empowering thing that an NGO or external practitioner ever does. The ability to thus connect with other communities or organisations is fundamental to sustainable social change.

It is possible that community leaders already know most of what is needed, but often they are not conscious or confident of their own knowledge and resourcefulness, or they may need to unlearn certain habits that undermine good processes. For example, someone may have learned to be overly formal in a way that hinders participation and may need some encouragement to enable community members to participate and even share the lead.

NGO practitioners are often used to being in control: setting up the programme, organising the transport, venue and food and then facilitating the process. But successful horizontal exchanges often need to be run very differently. Not only can people often do a lot more than NGOs realise, but they often have a better sense of what is really needed. Community members may not be as professionally organised as NGO practitioners but often they know what will and won't work better than anyone else. Help them to trust their own instincts, and if things don't go perfectly then this is an opportunity for people to learn how to do it better.

> *Horizontal Learning exchanges ... may be the most empowering thing that an NGO or external practitioner ever supports.*

Some tips towards successful exchanges

Before:

- Encourage people on both sides of the planned learning exchange to discuss what they hope to learn and what they can offer. What do they want to learn most? They could prepare questions, discuss who will ask them and how they will record the answers or ideas they gather. Who will report back to those who could not be part of the exchange?

- Exchanges usually work best if there are practical demonstrations. What do they need to take with or prepare?

- Exchanges are usually so much richer if there are also cultural exchanges. What songs, dances or stories could be shared? Can simple gifts be given?

- Where will people stay? First prize is home-stays so that participants can meet families and friends. Often most important things are shared over meals or by the fire late at night.

- Often the visitors expect to learn more from those they are visiting. Help those who are being visited to not see it as a one-way process but to be curious and eager to learn from their visitors.

During:

- It is important that people meet and share in ways that they most enjoy and feel comfortable with. They may prefer to meet very informally. Or they may want to structure the meetings their own way, either pre-planned or made up as they go along.

- The most successful exchanges are not facilitated by outsiders, because it is then more likely that participants discover their own best way of sharing and learning. This does not mean being absent for the first exchange or two – it is about being on the sidelines and being available if things get stuck.

- Often there is so much to be shared that it helps for the group to split up and go and see different things.

- Sometimes it really helps for participants to use a small notebook to capture their observations, thoughts and ideas.

- It may also help for the groups to meet at the end of the day to share observations and ideas.

Afterwards:

- The point of Horizontal Learning exchanges is not just to exchange and learn, but to do things differently. Translating learnings and ideas into action is key.

- Sharing what has been gathered with those who were not part of the exchange may be the first step.

Some final thoughts

... learning together was the foundation for the relationships that led to change initiatives.

After reading this chapter you might have further questions. What is my advice going forward? Encourage people to *learn together* before they work together, to share their experiences and knowledge. This means not only boosting each other's knowledge and skills in effective, inexpensive ways, but also learning about each other's lives, really seeing each other and trusting each other! In many of the examples I used, you could see that learning together was the foundation for the relationships that led to change initiatives: change of individuals, of communities, of society.

Many civil society organisations do struggle to scale up their activities. Bottom-up approaches like participative methods, local ownership and empowerment are difficult to combine on a large scale. So, many organisations are tempted to move into more top-down planning with a kind of blueprint as the only way.

Yet we know that this often gets stuck, losing ownership, creativity and sustainability. With Horizontal Learning approaches a different logic becomes possible, unlocking new energies and linkages and enabling people to self-organise in ways that no plan could engineer. But it requires that organisations which are used to conventional project controls, like NGOs and donors, have to let go of predictable plans and outcomes. It requires supporting people and communities to find their own self-control, and to grow this themselves, so that the initiatives belong to them. This changes the whole idea of control and accountability. Of course funding must still be properly managed, but not boxed into budget lines that undermine creative and flexible planning and implementation.

We can stimulate this by facilitating peer networks and letting things grow, perhaps even into social movements. As Learning Facilitators we have to give people the opportunity to find their own process. Always ask yourself: 'Who is participating in whose process?'

Always ask yourself: 'Who is participating in whose process?'

CHAPTER 9

The heart of change: stories of learning

Every human society is complex by nature. As development practitioners and as organisations working for social change, we are often parachuted into complex social realities. We need to understand how societies learn and how this learning drives social change. To understand the realities on the ground, and to be aware of the impact of our interventions, we need to have an open attitude and continually learn ourselves.

Hello! I'm Sunny and I'm a development practitioner.

And here is Mo, my good friend from back in high school days. He wasn't always my friend. In the first year I thought he was the 'I know everything already' type and generally avoided him. Later I got to see the entertaining side of his character when we were together in a team during a school summer camp in our third year. Mo was always ready to help out with cooking and washing the dishes and amused us with his jokes. We've seen each other fairly regularly over the years since then, and last time we met, I told Mo how excited I was about developing a guide on learning and social change. Mo was not impressed… He said:

"So you people are writing a guide about learning and social change? I can understand writing about social change, because it seems to me that's what development is all about. But learning? Don't you think that's a bit of a luxury? There are people dying out there and you write about *learning* and social change? You should write about *action* and social change. That would make a lot more sense! If you ask me, learning is the icing on the cake. You must be a strange bunch of practitioners to waste time and resources on such a thing!"

I was taken aback by Mo's rather rude reaction but replied:

"So you think learning is a luxury? It is not! Social change does not happen without learning. Wherever you find people, you find learning is driving social change. Learning is at the heart of social change!"

Mo remained unconvinced. He still tried to persuade me we should be working on a guide that centred on action rather than learning. We got into a discussion that went on and on. Eventually I suggested a break:

"What we need is an exploratory tour into the subject of learning and social change – that will make it clear."

Mo loves travelling. We found a tour operator – <u>Social Change Unlimited</u> – that organised tours for people with specific questions about social change. They agreed to develop a programme for us. Although it was expensive, I don't regret a cent of the money spent.

SOCIAL CHANGE UNLIMITED (SCU®) offers you a tour into

The Landscape of Learning & Social Change

Key Concepts Wonderland & Ocean of Practice
10 days of exploration and learning

Key Concepts Wonderland

A. Concepts related to learning

Day 1: Visit the House of Learning

You meet your guide for the trip into his house of learning. His experience as a volunteer teacher on the island of Iberu and his insightful stories will encourage you to explore the concepts of learning and apply them to what you see.

Day 2: Enter the Tunnel of Unlearning

You descend into the Tunnel of Unlearning. We have coined the term "unlearning" and given it a special space on your tour because it is a very important part of the learning process.

B. Concepts related to learning and social change

Days 3–7: Visit the Minawa people

You journey into the past to visit the Minawa people and spend time with different members of the community. You will see some changes taking place. The new concepts you have learned will help you reflect on what you see – and so make sense of context and the processes of learning and social change.

Ocean of Practice

Days 8–10: Sail on the Ocean of Practice

You board a clipper ship and sail the Ocean of Practice. You will hear a story of good practice and a story of poor practice. You will relax and reflect. With the aid of the key concepts you learnt during your trip through Key Concepts Wonderland, you will make sense of the two stories.

Day 11: Return home

PART I:

Key Concepts Wonderland

A. Concepts relating to learning

Day 1: Visit the House of Learning

Mo and I arrived, ready to learn, with notebooks in hand. We liked our guide at first glance. His soft eyebrows, friendly wrinkles, pleasant and deep voice drew us into his stories instantly. The stories introduced several concepts about learning, but the following stood out most of all.

The guide's story

"Many years ago two of my brothers and I were chatting on a wooden bench under a tree, complaining about the end of the summer holidays. We felt sorry for ourselves – the coming return to school would ruin our present happy lives.

That summer holiday had been the best ever. On the first day we started a club and named it 'The Handymen'. The shed in the garden was our retreat, where we drew up a list of rules and regulations. Full membership could only be achieved if we learned a set of skills by the end of the holidays. The skills included woodcarving, decoding a secret language, lighting fires without matches, cooking on a fire, bush hut construction, swimming in open water (very cold), climbing trees and, last but not least, sneaking into nearby houses under construction without being spotted by the workmen! Not a single day went by without us improving our skills. We continuously compared each other's achievements and celebrated progress.

We had learned our heads off that summer holiday – though we would never have thought to call it 'learning'. To us, learning equalled school and school equalled imposed lessons.

Many people go through their lives thinking learning only happens through organised trainings and classroom instruction. We need to 'unlearn' this and instead embrace true learning. When I grew older I came to realise that learning is not only about a school, a university or high-powered training.

After our guide had finished his story, it dawned upon us that the key principles of learning are not rocket science, but instead are already known to us all.

The 'Making Sense of Learning – Key Concepts' Box

1. Learning is a collective and social process, in which people jointly develop meaning, competence and identity. Learning helps people shape the environment in which they live. We learn together, and we learn from each other.

2. We learn in practice. Learning is based on people's own experiences and knowledge.

3. Learning leads to changes in people's behaviour. It is not only about knowing something but about doing something with that knowledge.

4. Learning only happens when the learning process matches the needs and the reality of the learner.

5. Learning requires a safe environment, in which people dare to speak up, to experiment and make mistakes.

6. Unlearning is an important part of the learning process.

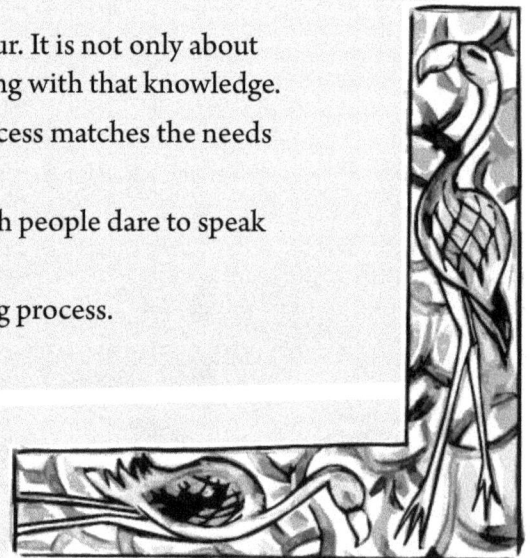

Day 2: Enter the Tunnel of Unlearning

After a good breakfast with strong tea Mo and I felt all ready to explore the Tunnel of Unlearning. We changed our clothes and wore miners' helmets with lamps on them so we'd be able to see something in this dark and scary space. Just when we were all ready to descend Mo hesitated, then stopped dead. He confessed he'd always been afraid of the dark, and we could read from his frightened face that he was just not ready for this trip. I was disappointed but the guide felt it was best to postpone. He took us for a walk in the beautiful countryside instead. 'Don't worry. You'll soon be ready to revisit this place,' he reassured Mo.

Like Mo, many people find unlearning hard. Yet, it is an important part of learning! You will find more about unlearning on page 139.

B. Concepts related to learning and social change

Days 3–7: Visit the Minawa people

The Minawa people live on Iberu Island. Mo and I set off in a wooden vessel full of local people (and their chickens!), who slept all over the floor. The trip took a whole day. I felt very seasick, but lucky Mo didn't seem to have much trouble. However, once I stepped out of the boat my sickness disappeared because the fresh, unpolluted air was so reviving.

Day 4: A glimpse of day-to-day village life

Our guide led us to a couple of huts that a group of Minawa had built as temporary shelters. He explained that Minawa society consisted of about five clans living in small groups, spread out over the island. He told us we would take part in the social life of the Minchassa clan for a day and handed us some of their local clothing. It was very simple – just some animal skins tied together – but still I admired the craftwork in it. I would not have been able to make it myself.

The women were all very friendly and did not exclude me in the least. After I'd gotten to know them a little bit they took me berry hunting. Well, not all of them; a couple of them stayed behind, some to keep an eye on the children, others to clean animal skins. The berry hunt was very interesting. There weren't many berries – just a few edible ones actually – but all were tasty and fresh. We also managed to find quite a number of carrot-like vegetables. The women seemed to appreciate my input, because they smiled at me, as if they wanted to say: 'Good job'.

When we returned to the village, the women cleaned the vegetables. Soon the men returned. They were all laughing; only Mo seemed a little disgruntled. Later I discovered he hadn't been able to keep up with the other men. They hadn't caught any animals but had met up with one of the other clans. Mo told me they had exchanged some beautiful shells for a small antelope.

Before leaving we had a wonderful meal of vegetable stew and a little roasted meat.

At the end of the day Mo and I met to compare notes about this society and its centuries-old way of life. We were a bit confused, because it was so different from our own. How could we make sense of our experiences?

Our guide said that what had really helped him to understand the context of Minawa society was a basic knowledge of living systems.

And, our guide was more than ready to share his knowledge with us. He gave us a beautiful box that contained the key concepts of social contexts. We worked with him to apply the concepts to what we had seen on Minawa

LIVING SYSTEMS

Mechanical systems are linear and work through cause and effect: X happens because of Y. For example, if a part of a car engine breaks the car stops going. The broken part can be identified and fixed or replaced, but only by a mechanic. The mechanic is not part of the car – he or she makes an intervention from outside. Outside forces can also damage the system beyond repair: a car cannot stop itself rusting. It also cannot mend itself.

A living system is different. It is a cycle and can self-organise. It can repair itself. It is evolving and regenerating. It can adapt to changes in the environment. The human body is constantly changing and reacting to the environment. All systems that involve living things, including humans, are living systems. So organisations and societies are living systems.

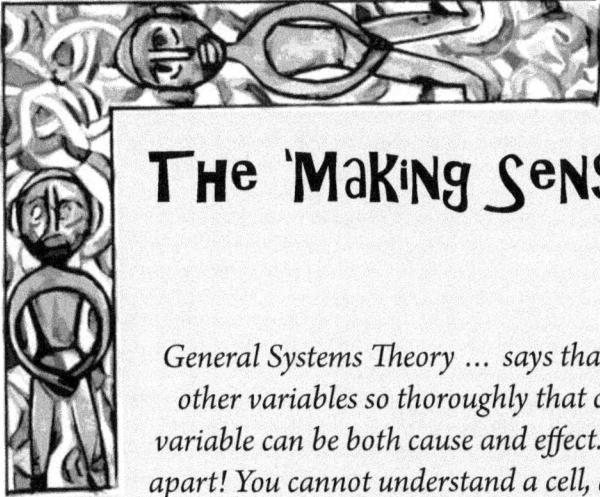

The 'Making Sense of Social Context' Box

General Systems Theory ... says that each variable in any system interacts with the other variables so thoroughly that cause and effect cannot be separated. A simple variable can be both cause and effect. Reality will not be still. And it cannot be taken apart! You cannot understand a cell, a rat, a brain structure, a family, a culture if you isolate it from its context. Relationship is everything.

Marilyn Ferguson

1. A living system continuously interacts with its environment.

A living system never operates on its own. It is not standing still, but is part of a larger, ever-changing environment interacting with other systems. The way different communities, non-governmental organisations (NGOs) and government departments interrelate in a country can be compared with the way different animals and plants interrelate in the jungle. Like different plants, trees and animals, different organisations and communities all have their different roles and functions in the system. Making one kind of animal extinct may have many consequences for the other species and may change the jungle system as a whole. Strengthening or weakening certain organisations or people in a country is also likely to have an impact on other people and organisations, in ways that are difficult to foresee.

2. The different parts of the system interrelate.
We cannot change one part without having an effect on other parts.

We know different parts interrelate but do not know exactly how. Therefore, we prefer to carry out small experiments, instead of making big changes on a large scale, immediately. Why? Because we cannot totally predict what the outcome of what we do – our intervention – will be. In our efforts to change a system we carefully pull on one string, affecting one part. If that does not work, we may pull another string. In other words: we continuously notice how our interventions in one or several parts affect the other parts of the system, and the system as a whole. When we see positive effects, we continue.

In Lake Victoria in Kenya the Nile perch, a large fish, was introduced in the 1930s. It was thought it would give fishers a better income and it would be more nutritious than the local Tilapia species. The Nile perch have now eaten most of the Tilapia and their numbers have attracted commercial trawler fishing. The result? Many communities around the lake can no longer get enough healthy food. The people who introduced the Nile perch were trying to help, but did not realise what the end result would be. They did not understand the ecosystem of the lake or predict that commercial fishing would destroy community fishing. Similarly, in some development projects the power of community leaders is boosted in a way that unbalances the traditional power sharing between different elders. Some leaders get more power and this can harm those parts of the community the leader does not like or represent.

3. **Any system is a set of parts that depend on each other and interact to form an integrated whole. Each part is a subsystem in itself or a part of the system.**

Every part of a living system is interrelated with every other part. We understand how an organic system like a human body functions by studying the different organs in their interrelationships. If we study each part on its own we can get such a simplified idea that we run the risk of not understanding the system as a whole. If we treat heart disease with a drug that damages the liver, we solve one problem only by creating another elsewhere – the system as a whole will still be damaged.

4. **A system is more than the sum of its parts.**

The way the parts relate defines the system. Living systems can only survive by keeping up a *certain balance between the parts*. If we strengthen or weaken one part, the whole system can change. The different relationships between parts of the system make it unique and define it. You will agree that the atmosphere in your family and in your office is defined by the different relationships between your family members and between your colleagues. When one person leaves, the whole family or office is affected. Relationships will change and develop until a new balance is created.

5. **Boundaries around systems are set by humans, not the systems themselves.**

As humans beings we are aware that everything is related to everything, but we set boundaries so that we can manage our lives more easily and feel safe. It is fine to simplify our lives like this. For example, a boundary around our families helps us love them and take care of them. We cannot take care of the whole world in the same way. However, we have to be aware that boundaries could have been set differently and need to be reset continuously. The fact that we have erected boundaries does not mean our simplification is reality.

Here is an example. In a water project the team leader decided that each hand pump would serve 30 homesteads. Then the team came across a water source that could serve 150 homesteads, if it could be connected to a water gravity system instead of to a simple hand pump. But the team leader would not change the preset boundaries, so the water gravity system could not be put in.

6. **In all systems, patterns of behaviour can be recognised.**

A pattern of behaviour, also often called a rhythm, can be found in all living systems. Recognising rhythm helps us to understand systems.

In my office, we meet every Monday morning as a team and discuss progress and issues. These meetings give me peace of mind and regularity in my work. The tree next to my house has a different rhythm too: in autumn it loses its leaves and in spring the leaves come back after a long, cold winter.

The concepts in the box helped Mo and me to revisit our notes. We thought about what we had seen like this:

Minawa society can be seen as a *system* with five clans who live together in different communities. Each community forms *a part* of overall Minawa Society. It would be interesting to find out more about the way in which these different clans, or *parts of the system, interrelate*. The concepts helped us to realise that the Minchassa clan might have a different role in society from other clans. For example, do only the Minchassa know where to find the shells they exchange for meat? We realised we had only seen a very small part of the society so far. We had set virtual *boundaries* around the Minchassa clan, because we could not get to know all clans at once. In one day we had only come to understand a little bit about the *subsystem* 'Minchassa clan'. That *subsystem* also has *different parts*: Mo now understood more about the men's daily life and I understood more about the women's daily life. We had seen *patterns* in their behaviours, with the men hunting and trading and the women gathering vegetables and fruits and cooking.

I felt good about our little exercise but Mo was anxious:

"Hello there! Are we still together? Maybe we made sense of the context of Minawa society, but Sunny, do you really use these concepts in your daily work? How? I don't get it."

I said, "Well, when I get involved in a development programme I always try to work with the team to make sense of the system we are working in. We do this on paper, or we create a virtual image on computer. We draw different parts of the system, show how they relate, and work out what the functions and roles of these parts are. This drawing helps us to ask relevant questions, and to then work with the people and communities to get an even better idea of the system. Only then we can work with them to see what change is needed. We constantly update our drawing as we get more knowledge about the way the system works, and the effects our projects have."

"Wow!" Said Mo, "I never thought the development work you did was so interesting. How do you guys cope with all these complex issues? Let's have a bite and some tea to get ready for tomorrow. I guess it will be at least as intensive as today."

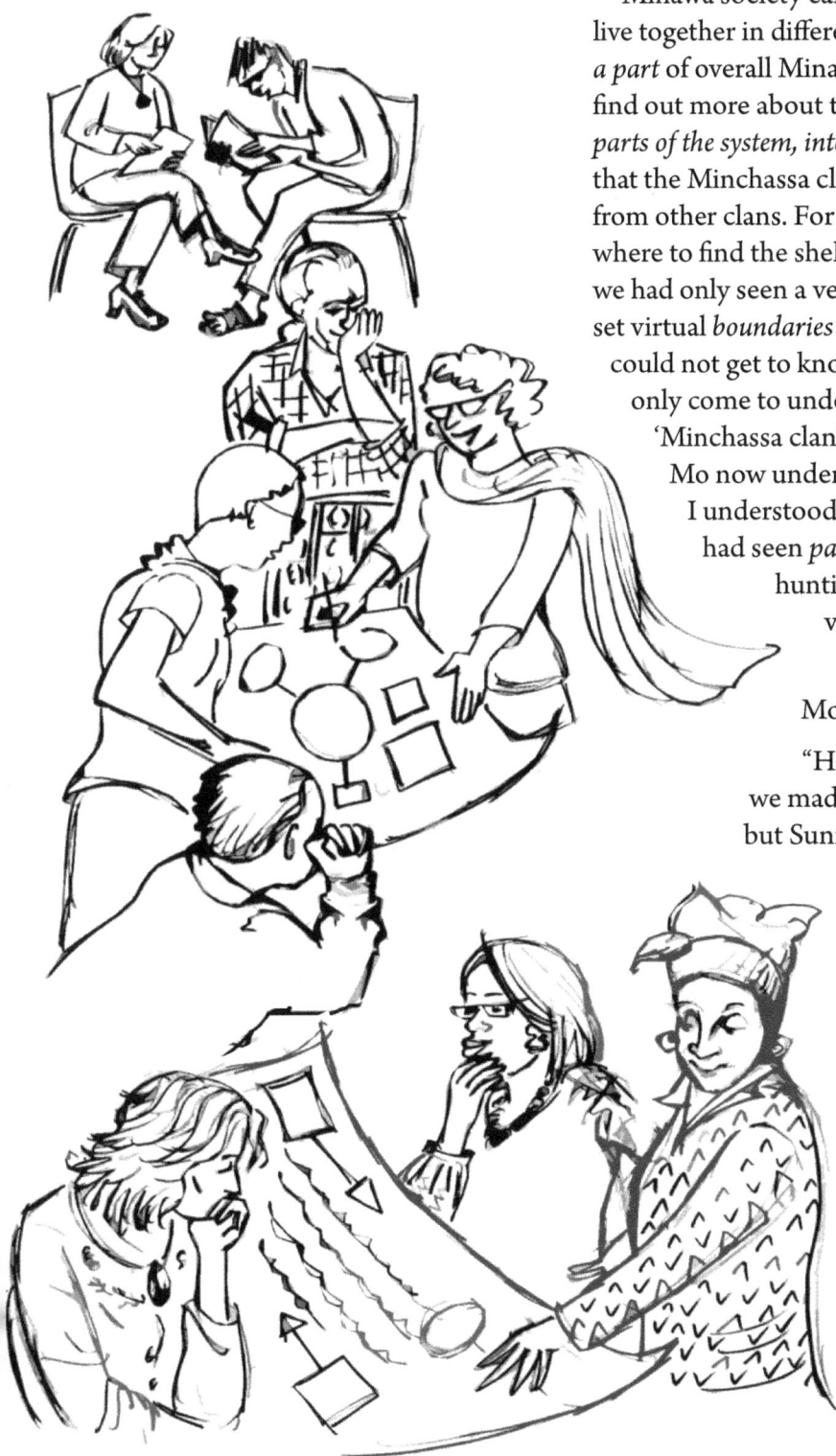

Day 5:

A glimpse into processes of learning and social change

Today we visited the leader of the Minchassa and he told us about something that recently caused a big change in his clan.

> "I'm sorry but I'm so busy organising a celebration that I don't have much time to talk to you. Why do I have to organise such a big celebration? Well, I have to entertain the other clan leaders and show them I have more resources.
>
> It's not easy to maintain my position as leader – there are plenty of others that want this job. To remain a leader I have to keep on proving that I have something extra, that I can provide more than the leaders of the other four clans.
>
> And guests, the key to my position currently is – chillies! My 'something extra' is my chilli-flavoured meat. Let me explain.
>
> One of my brother's sons is a really exceptional guy. While we were out on a hunting trip together he told me that he had been experimenting with growing chillies. He is very fond of chillies as they really add flavour to the meat. So he kept the seeds of the different kinds of chillies the women collected in the forests and started cultivating them.
>
> He discovered that some were hotter than others and that it was best to dry the seeds before planting. He also found it was best to plant them just before the rainy season started. He shared his findings with his good friend who became enthusiastic too, and wondered whether it would be possible to plant more of the seeds of the vegetables and fruits our women collect. As I am a rich man I can delegate hunting to the others. I decided to allow these boys to spend all their time on experimenting with seed planting. With time my homestead became known for its chillies. Imagine the possibilities!"

Mo tasted a chilli. He screamed that he was on fire and spat it out! You can imagine our embarrassment. I don't know how the teacher explained Mo's behaviour, but he did very well and I was incredibly relieved we got out of that hut unharmed.

Our guide told us to keep in mind that a social setting is always vibrant, never stagnant. It is a historical product of continuous social change. Social change is emerging everywhere, all the time. When we describe and analyse social settings, we should think of them as open-ended and fluid processes, without a beginning or end.

He then gave us another box full of ideas to help us understand the ongoing process of learning and social change in Minawa society.

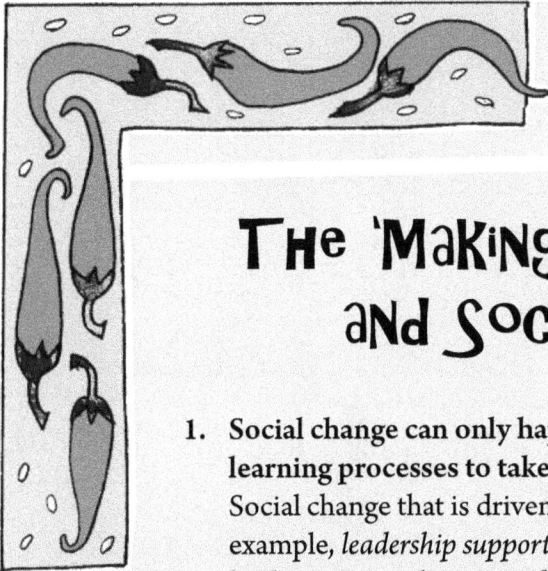

The 'Making Sense of Learning and Social Change' Box

1. **Social change can only happen when there are the right conditions for learning processes to take place.**
   Social change that is driven by learning needs *enabling conditions*. For example, *leadership support* is often a key condition needed for change. If leaders support learning, they allow experiments and do not mind if some mistakes are made. They create a safe environment for change.

2. **Drivers of change start changes and keep them going.**
   Where social change takes place, drivers of change can be seen. These are people or institutions that want to learn new things, and are ambitious and experienced enough to be confident about making changes.

3. **Social change emerges over time.**
   Social change does not happen suddenly – it happens *slowly*, or *emerges*. People take advantage of new learning opportunities and build on them to learn more.

4. **In processes of dramatic social change, tipping points can be recognised.**
   A tipping point is a moment in time when a lot of small changes and factors enabling change come together. These are stronger than all the forces trying to stop the change. Whole societies may change as a result of a tipping point.

5. **Feedback is very important in the process of social change.**
   As human beings we have very little information on whether what we are doing is useful. Other people must tell us whether this is so or not.

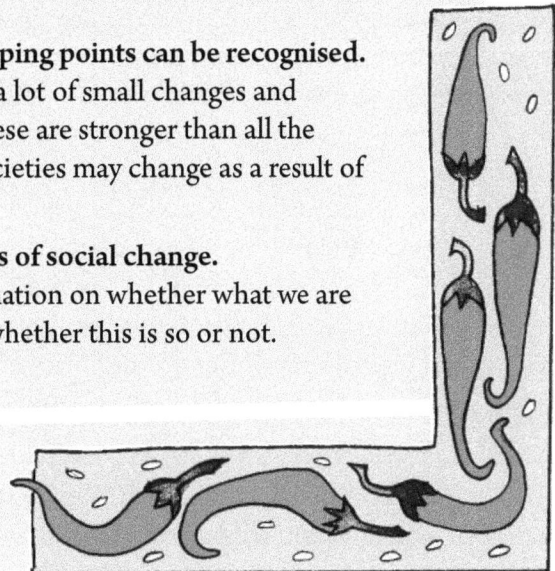

Mo and I realised that we had seen just how learning processes caused and supported *emerging change*. The e*nabling conditions* for domesticating chillies were those spots where the specific plants grow in the wild, the right soil and the *chance given by the leader* to a few youngsters to spend all their time growing chillies, rather than on hunting like their peers. The youngsters doing the experimenting seemed to enjoy a *safe environment*, in which they could speak up and in which they were *allowed to make mistakes*.

In this story the competitive leader was an *important driver of change*. The curious and experimenting youngsters were also *drivers of change*. The youngsters and leader took part in a *collective* and *social learning process*. Together they decided the new idea of growing chillies was a worthwhile thing to do, they learned the skills needed and soon chillies became part of what their clan was known for – part of their identity.

The leader would not have thought growing chillies was important if he hadn't listened to and learned from the *feedback* of the other leaders, who clearly showed they liked spicy meat. In this way, the leader realised that growing chillies could increase his status.

In Minawa society the *tipping point* that would transform it to an agricultural society has not been reached yet. People still live as hunters and gatherers. However, we have learned from other societies that the cultivation of plants does eventually lead to change to an agricultural lifestyle.

Mo asked, "Sunny, could you again give me a clue as to how these concepts help you in your daily work?"

I answered that when I get involved in a development programme I want to know which people and organisations are already experimenting to change the system they live in. Whenever there are clear problems or opportunities, you find people and organisations who are already working with them. Development practitioners can only make sustainable, positive contributions by supporting those who are already making efforts. So, as a development worker I need to find out who the drivers of change are and how I can strengthen the conditions they need for change to happen. If I don't work that way, my efforts will never be sustainable and, even worse, they may do damage rather than good. To be effective I have to continuously learn about learning processes that are taking place in the system I am working with.

Mo and I both felt pretty sad to be leaving the Minchassa clan as we had become attached to some of the people. As a farewell we were invited to the party of the clan leader – and ate lots of delicious spicy meat!

Overall, Mo and I were very pleased with our trip through Key Concepts Wonderland but we were also looking forward to our sailing trip on The Ocean of Practice.

PART I:

Ocean of Practice

Sail on the Ocean of Practice

Well Sunny, I am really looking forward to our sailing trip. I'm starting to realise how close this social change through learning is, both to your heart and your work. But, I'd really like to get more into the practical side of the matter.

I'm also happy we're about to sail. I'm sure we'll hear a story about good practice. Unfortunately, things go wrong out there as well, so we're going to hear a story about poor practice too. Let's see if the lessons we learned about social settings, social change and learning help us to reflect on these stories.

On our sailing ship we met Maria and Martin, both development practitioners. They were very happy to share their stories.

Maria's story

"I was 23 and had just finished my studies when I was hired by a donor to work with a European engineering firm. I was to look into the community management side of a low cost, on-site sanitation programme in the city of Madiristan. After a year I felt I had been accepted by the team and worked with on-site sanitary systems in different slum areas of the city. I liked the Madiran senior consultant who came from a city in the south. She was a strong personality, twenty years older than me. The team leader was a Dutch engineer, also much older than me. He was suspicious of my role at the start of the project. He wondered why social scientists needed to be involved in a 'technical' project and did not even bother to hide his mistrust.

However, one day the consultant and I went to the team leader's office to report on progress. We told him how six different areas in the city had been selected, how offices had been established together with local Community Based Organisations (CBOs) in the areas and how local men and women had been trained to build low cost latrines and provide hygiene education. He was amazed at what could be achieved by working with the community. In the end our half-hour meeting ran on for three hours, and from then on, he was much more sympathetic to our ideas.

Then, one of the female employees had a new idea. She knew from her own experience how difficult it was for women to be able to work outside the home, and thought of inviting the parents, brothers and sisters of all female employees in the programme to a high tea in one of the hotels. We all liked her idea and organised the event.

I was so moved to see the parents, especially the mothers! They came in their best, hand-embroidered clothes, and most of them had never seen the inside of a hotel before. Seeing the pride on their faces when we asked their daughters to tell about their work was so precious.

Inspired by this, we organised women's meetings in the communities. Because of these meetings, the demand for female schooling grew. The local consultant happened to have experience of girls' home schools and we encouraged her to apply the girls' home school idea in our work areas.

The popularity of the schools grew by word of mouth promotion among women in the areas and the number of girls in the home schools increased tremendously. As home schools were not an official part of the contract with the donor, our team did not talk about it with them much. As their popularity grew, however, we decided to discuss this unplanned development, and the donor agreed to set aside some special funding for this purpose."

Mo interrupted… "Sounds good, but how did all this continue after you had gone? What happened when the money ran out?"

"Well, when we were running our programme, we had taken a trip to meet NGOs working in water and sanitation in other parts of the country. We met one locally funded NGO and other NGOs that had also started work in areas like hygiene, health and low cost building. When, after several years, our programme ended, we asked for a one year transition grant for the local team in our agency to set up its own organisation. A board with influential politicians, a few scientists and practitioners was formed. Although many of the staff had not been involved in the original project, the new organisation's principles and approach didn't change. They were firmly rooted in the learning from the project. Now, fifteen years later, the organisation has around 100 employees and works in four different provinces in humanitarian aid, women's education, water, sanitation, health and hygiene."

Mo and I both liked Maria's story a lot. He tried to apply our concepts to her story and I was impressed with his newly-acquired skills!

Mo said… "The good relationship with the team leader and the donor meant the team could grasp the worthwhile opportunity that *emerged*: a project in girl's education. The visit to other NGOs inspired them to start looking further, beyond sanitation. Their constant process of *feedback* and adaptation meant they brought about real social change, instead of sticking rigidly to the project document. They clearly saw the *system* in which they worked as an *open-ended* one and *continuously reflected on patterns of behaviour* they found in communities. They worked with *existing drivers of change*: people rooted in the communities and local experts who had proved eager to develop their communities and who had the required skills and 'buy in' to make a difference."

"You're spot on Mo, you are spot on. I like the way you apply the concepts we just learned."

"Thanks Sunny. I thought you would never give me a compliment! And what are your reflections and observations? "

"To me, the story shows that there are *different paths you can travel to arrive at social change*. We saw how a programme that was run in an Islamic country succeeded in getting girls to school. And it was not because formal, regular schools were imposed – that would have caused problems in these conservative communities because the girls might have come into contact with men outside the family. Rather it succeeded *by connecting* to the ambitions of older, literate girls to teach the smaller ones. Older girls could set up classrooms in their own houses and fulfil their dreams. At the same time, parents allowed small girls to go as there was no chance of contact with men.. So the programme team *connected* to the parents' fears as well."

Meanwhile, Martin had listened closely to Maria's story. Now, he looked a bit sad as he told his own, but he told it so vividly we were captivated.

Martin's story

"It was a bright Sunday morning and I was on my way to Makassa. My friend Bertram, who was employed as an engineer in a city water supply programme, had been kind enough to invite me for lunch and tell me about his project.

While sitting in the car enjoying the beautiful tea estate view, I thought of the difficult water supply situation of the slum in the city where I live. My gardener, Sibu, lives in one of these slum areas. As I visit every now and then, and take tea with him almost every evening, I know a bit about the living conditions there.

The first time I saw young children playing in an open drain, my instinct was to take them out and tell them to go home – but home was probably a nearby two by three metre mud shack and a mother who was too busy to keep an eye on them. No wonder Sibu didn't want to move his family to this particular slum, even though it is nearer to my home, where he works.

In the slum where Sibu lives, there are municipal pipe connections and water kiosks. Most of these kiosks, Sibu told me, are illegally run under the protection of some political leaders. Sibu doesn't care whether a water kiosk is legal or not, as long as he can buy the water. However, water bought in the water kiosks is not clean. In the rainy season, when latrines flood, dirty water seeps into the leaking water supply pipes, contaminating it. Plus, about 40 per cent of the water flowing to Sibu's slum is lost due to leakages.

I work in a rural water supply programme, on spring protection and dams. I was interested to hear about Bertram's project, because I know that water problems in an urban municipality are a lot more difficult to solve. Villagers can manage their water system. But in the municipality, a new or repaired system needs to connect to the overall chaotic water supply system of the city. This causes lots of technical and managerial issues that cannot be solved easily."

I met Bertram six months ago. He was very enthusiastic about a management formula that he and his European NGO had come up with. He said they had found a way to solve the water supply problems in the city once and for all.

While we were sitting on the verandah drinking coffee, Bertram told me about the formula and what happened when they applied it.

This seemed simple! I asked him how it had gone.

Bertram said, 'We went ahead like crazy. The meters were perfect and we rented a beautiful building near the municipal hall for the water firm. Look at the graphs of costs and returns for the first few months.'

The charts really did show incredible progress!

Bertram continued, 'But then it all started to go wrong. I'm not clear why but the meter controllers who tried to get defaulters to pay were jailed three months into the project. Not long after that the municipality closed the firm down and took back municipal control.'

'Do you know whether illegal kiosks were operating in this area?' I asked.

Bertram shook his head, saying 'Might have been…'

'If they were, then for sure those who were making money from them would not have been impressed with your new formula.'

Bertram agreed.

'So, what now?' I asked.

'I don't know. This is a real blow to me,' Bertram replied, shaking his head. 'The donor has asked me to try the same formula in the provincial capital of Nyacha. I have no option but to move there next month.'

This time, Mo asked me to reflect on the story using the concepts we had learned. Here goes… It is clear the donor and team leader were so sure that their technical formula was suitable that they did not feel the need to learn from communities what the true situation really was. They did not think of the water and sanitation supply problems as being part of an *open system*. If they had done so, they would have known how people felt about the illegal water kiosks. When developing a 'problem-solving formula', they could have interviewed the residents, the municipality and some local politicians and *learned from them* about reasons for the existing problems. They did not know about possible *existing drivers of change*. They did not even know whether there were changes emerging that they might have been able to connect to.

Briefly, the formula was this:

- Pipes are leaking so they are repaired by project staff.

- Water meters don't work so the whole area is supplied with new meters.

- The municipality does not have the staff to maintain the water system. Therefore, a commercial firm is set up and water engineers from the municipality are attached to it. A business plan is made and the firm finds out it could make lots of money, quickly. Even after subtracting investment and maintenance costs, profits can be made within two years.

What strikes me most in this story really is the complete *lack of a learning attitude*. The team leader and donor thought they already had the knowledge needed to solve the problems, and this blinded them to the reality on the ground. Even when developments turned against them, they did not learn from their mistakes. Instead of *reflecting and learning*, and then *unlearning* their old practice, they moved into a new place to again use the approach that had failed.

Throughout the rest of the cruise we heard many stories, some of which you'll come across later in this book. We realised that the concepts we now knew could be applied to all of them, and could help us to learn from others' experiences.

On the last night Mo told me how much he had enjoyed my company and, guess what, he asked me to marry him! You may be surprised, but I wasn't completely surprised, as during the journey we'd become closer. I realised that our views weren't as far apart as they had been at the beginning of our journey. I was thrilled to say *yes*! After all, he may be different from me but I think we complement each other very well. And who would not like a husband as handsome and funny as Mo? But, I can't end this story with the words, '… and they lived happily ever after' as I cannot foresee how it will all turn out. We have learned from this journey though. We'll trust the process and deal with emerging issues. I am sure we'll be fine, as long as we both take our marriage as a continuous process of learning – and, of course, *un*learning!

Mo added "It's not easy to say goodbye, but I'm sure we will meet again. And for you, the journey is not over. There are so many more landscapes to discover and admire in this barefoot guide. Have a good trip and thank you so much for taking an interest in our exploratory tour into Key Concepts Wonderland and the Ocean of Practice."

CHAPTER 10

Unlearning:
letting go for a change

Story

The children of the land no longer bow their heads as the elders pass. The women no longer listen to their men and obey them. The traditional healer's son died of a strange disease. The local clinic has endless lines of patients. No one goes to the healer for help any more!

At the community meetings at the end of every month the people no longer discuss development issues in the community or how to raise fees for children who have been admitted to university or high school. The monthly cultural dances are no longer taking place. Something strange is happening. A lot of time is spent arranging funerals. Sons and daughters of the land who went to town to make a living for their families in the village are coming back home in coffins. One weekend Jack is in a funeral committee and the next there is a funeral committee making arrangements for Jack.

The Council of Elders and the medicine men held a meeting to discuss the state of the community. Many questions were asked: Why are there so many deaths? Why are children being born and in a short while both the mother and child are dead? Why is it that in some villages there are no strong, young people but only grandmothers and their grandchildren? What is happening? They all agreed that there is an curse in the land. The Gods are angry! What could they do?

A respected son of the land called a meeting to address the mass deaths in the community. On the day of his arrival the village was excited. Their son had come to make an important announcement. He stood up and said that there was no abomination. People were dying of a new disease called HIV and Aids and if no measures were taken the entire land would be swept of its sons and daughters.

'What can we do?' they asked him.

'One of the ways to reduce the risk is male circumcision,' he replied. The entire gathering wept and mourned. In this land people were initiated into adulthood using other means. Circumcision was an abomination. It was a taboo!

'Let us die instead of being circumcised! Who has paid you to come and finish us? You son of the soil, may your days be few in this world,' the elders cried.

People left the gathering cursing the respected son of the land. They did nothing and they and their children continued to die.

In desperation, the elders called the respected son of the land to a secret meeting. They saw the danger of losing more people. They had consulted the Gods of the land who told them that the power to change the situation was in their hands.

They agreed to circumcision after a lot of soul searching: What if we all die because of allowing a strange culture in our midst? If the young men die during the circumcision what will we tell the community? How do you circumcise a married man? Do we also need to be circumcised? What if the girls of the land refuse to marry the circumcised men?

Some elders even left the Council for fear of retribution from the Gods. Others left because they felt the community was being led astray. One old man in the community committed suicide. He refused to live to see the change that was coming.

But the Gods had said that the answer was in the hands of the elders. They realised that staying the same was not possible. Something must change. They agreed to allow twenty young men to be circumcised to see if this was a way of saving the community.

We cannot learn our way out of a crisis but rather have to unlearn our way through it. It is important to bring to light and face the reason for the crisis or problem. Underlying patterns of behaviour should be surfaced to reveal the beliefs, values and assumptions of the community. Surfacing and dealing with doubt, fear and resentment will enable us to test our will to address the crisis. Once the will is there, we can begin to see the change we want to make.

Some situations cannot be solved though learning new behaviours alone. They require letting go of deep beliefs, attitudes and assumptions that are important to us but have ceased to be useful to us, and may even be the cause of the crisis.

Unlearn? Forget?

Should I forget all that I have learned and known? Does unlearning mean that what I know and have done in the past is wrong? The answer is *no*!

Unlearning does not require me to toss out all my accumulated experiences. Rather it asks me to become open to different ways of getting things done. I should not assume that the way I have learned to be will be the right way for me forever.

What is unlearning?

Unlearning requires an effort of will. The path to unlearning is marked with anxiety, embarrassment and loneliness. We may have to admit to others that we were wrong and make difficult choices that may at first be unpopular. Unlearning involves a conscious confrontation of the past and an uncovering of our deepest beliefs. It requires us to look at how the things we hold dear may be hindering us from facing the future. We must accept the frightening fact of not having answers, of being in-between ideas, of acting in the face of the unknown. In this way unlearning prepares the ground for a deeper kind of learning.

From our past experience we learn rhythms of working and acting that we know help us to deal with our world. We also develop habits of reacting to or dealing with situations, or even learn how to avoid them. These rhythms and habits are so familiar to us that we are no longer conscious of them. When forced to become conscious of them, we find ourselves deeply attached to them and resistant to change. The challenge is to understand why we are so unwilling to leave our comfort zone, even when we know that what has served us well in the past is no longer working for us.

I find that it is important for me to unlearn some of the 'truths' that have made me successful in the past, so that I can be more effective and successful in the future. This involves unlearning the habitual, unconscious ways of seeing and the benchmarks I bring to situations and relationships. I have to learn to see things for what they are, not what they remind me of or what I want them to become.

It is through deliberately developing consciousness of my rhythms and habits that I can begin to free myself from the power that my own past and will exerts on my ability to 'arrive empty' into a situation.

Unlearning involves honesty and courage and so enables us to be more honest and more courageous. Sometimes it boils down to facing our own blame and guilt and forgiving ourselves. For example, our refusal to accept that we need to change in order to address changes in the world may have caused harm, to ourselves and others.

Inner reflection and meditation, perhaps with the help of a colleague or with an outside facilitator, is extremely helpful. Unlearning does not have to take place when we are alone. Within most cultures there are processes that help people to do inner work, both individually and as a group.

> *Some situations cannot be solved though learning new behaviours alone.*

"The illiterate of the 21st century will not be those who cannot read & write but those who cannot learn, unlearn and relearn"
Alvin Toffler

Replacing assumptions, old beliefs and values is uncomfortable. We should not do it lightly. Unlearning is not just about choosing change but choosing change that will lead to deep, positive differences. It is about keeping what still works for us and getting rid of what is no longer useful.

There is a struggle to unlearn but when it does take place freed energy is released. There is a feeling of lightness when we shed the weight of ideas and beliefs that can no longer help us. We can now soar to greater heights.

SISIN: Organisations unlearn too

Paulo had worked in SISIN for the last twenty years. He was proud of the work he had done. No one else in his region had good practice like them. Since SISIN had started, funding had been easy to come by, and the organisation had operated like an island because of the expertise it had. But times changed. Donors started to ask SISIN who its partners were and how it was going to collaborate. Funding agencies started giving their money to consortia of organisations rather than individual organisations. Still SISIN put in individual applications as it felt that its successful approach would be watered down if it had to work with others.

Paulo became worried, but it was difficult for him and the rest of the staff to let go of the belief that they were most effective when they worked alone. The monthly meetings became places of disagreement. Every morning when Paulo prepared to go to work he developed severe headaches. As the longest-serving member of staff, he began to talk to the other members of staff, urging them to look critically at their practice.

This was painful and, for a while, the atmosphere in the organisation became strained and difficult. The organisation now was vulnerable, but eventually he got the staff on board.

What of the practice? They came to recognise that, far from strengthening their practice by working alone, they were in danger of cutting themselves off from learning from others' experiences. By building relationships they were able to enrich their practice. It was not always easy and it took time but they were surprised to find how many others thought as they did, and were doing interesting and exciting things. Suddenly they were overwhelmed with requests for assistance from the donor community and other partners in the region.

Who unlearns?

Unlearning occurs at all levels of human organisation: individual, organisational and societal. None of these levels are exclusive. Unlearning at a personal level will inevitably carry the process into the workplace and into communities and connect with change that is emerging. Similarly, organisational unlearning means that individuals within the organisation have to confront their own habits and rhythms and ways of thinking and begin to unlearn.

Resistance to unlearning

Fear

Even when I am unhappy, I would rather choose to keep things the way they are. Stability does not require me to be vulnerable, to admit I need to change. I am afraid of admitting I was wrong, of losing power, of giving up the habits and rhythms that have been my safety net for many years. Fear of the unknown often keeps me from seeking the very change I desire. It is because of fear that leaders have been able to rule for decades while oppressed peoples remain silent to injustice. It is the reason why companies' growth stagnates in the face of evolving markets. It is why people choose to live safely, rather than live their dreams.

In many circumstances, what I know blocks what is emerging. I see what is emerging as a threat. I associate my learning with my beliefs and identity, so I may become defensive and try to protect how and what I know rather than look at it closely. Resistance becomes the natural response to any threat I encounter. In the face of this, I find myself in a scary spot because I am stretched beyond my comfort zone and am challenged to my core.

I have choices to make here. Do I become available to new understanding, or do I sit back and enjoy my comfort? Do I withdraw into denial of what I am afraid to face? I could also diverge from the main topic and use intellectual arguments to justify my current state, and be dismissive to ensure that the situation remains just as it is.

It is important that unlearning takes place in a supportive environment. Facilitators and counsellors can help individuals and groups to face their fear and feel that they are supported when they start to make transformative changes to their practice. Peer groups, such as action learning circles, can support each other.

Doubt

Am I taking the right step? Am I the right person to take this action? Why don't I just leave it for others? What will people think of me? What if I take this step and it fails?

Self-doubt creates contradiction within me. This is painful. I know that I ought to take action and move on but I have questions. I find it useful to share my doubts. Others have gone through the same thing and have been able to find answers. I find my burden lighter. Unlearning requires faith – faith in oneself and faith that if it can work for others it can also work for me.

Self- hatred and resentment

I come from a community that believes women are liabilities, problems, and men are assets, useful. With seven daughters, my father had to struggle to keep us in school and fight the way the community thought of him. It was always drilled into me by my aunties and uncles that it did not matter how much schooling I had, I was still a woman and my work would be to cook for a man. The words I heard spoken to my mother gravely injured my self-esteem. I could not speak in public. I did not believe in myself. I hated myself and often was alone. Why was I a woman? Why couldn't my mother have boys? How could people speak of my mother as if she were solely responsible for having daughters rather than sons? How could God allow this?

Several years later in the journey of my life I was a single parent still living in the same community. I had accepted that I was inferior. I struggled to accept single parenthood and bring up the children. Despite reading self-help books and attending motivation workshops, I hated myself and resented my community. I could never forgive these people for what they had said about my mother and my sisters. They didn't deserve to be forgiven!

I later met a woman who had been through the same thing as I had but had won the fight against herself. In a very religious way she took me through the Bible and taught me how women are valuable. She showed me that women had made important contributions in the history of the world.

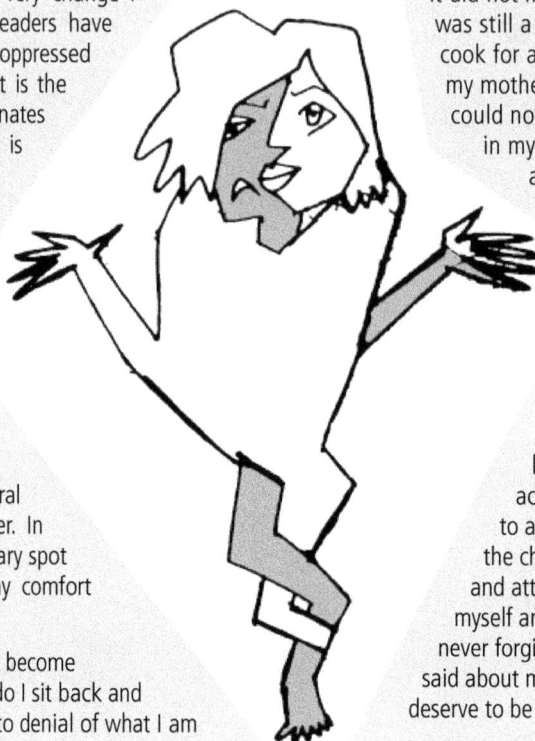

So women are valuable? They are important? Florence Nightingale saved dying soldiers? Then it can only happen to others and not me! I hated myself… did not have confidence. How could I move forward?

It took a lot of patience and guidance from my friend to help me love myself again. Often I cried and still I hid from crowds. I had to unlearn what had been drilled into me for years and had now become part of my identity. In unlearning I have been able to confront the belief that a woman from my community does not build a house for herself. I now have a lovely house overlooking the lake and several single women have bought land around my home and have built their own houses.

Unlearning requires love – love of oneself firstly and then of others.

So why make the effort to take the road less travelled?

There is no progress without struggle. Making the decision to unlearn requires making a conscious decision to work towards change that is transformational. While many of us working towards social change are all too familiar with our individual struggles, we have not incorporated unlearning practices into our organisational processes. So we carry on using stale strategies and duplicate interventions that undermine our impact. When we release our dependence on assumptions and beliefs we allow ourselves to be open to possibilities.

Unlearning promotes innovation by releasing people from the confines of particular ideas or ways of being so that they can think freely and creatively.

While the first success may be attributed to beginner's luck, it is the people, organisations and communities which actively choose to unlearn, when necessary, that have recurring success. They are they are always addressing the present situation in an open way, not trying to recreate the past or pretend things haven't changed.

CHAPTER 11

In the Sea of Change

Understanding your context

Environments are not passive wrappings, but rather, active processes which are invisible. The ground rules, pervasive structure and over-all patterns of environments elude easy perception.

Marshall McLuhan and Quentin Fiore

Staying relevant in a changing context

We are a coalition of NGOs and CBOs that support community development initiatives. In the last five years many of the NGOs have stopped making use of our capacity development services – they no longer find the training courses we offer relevant. However, they remain connected to the coalition through campaigns against mining activity on land that belongs to communities.

In contrast, many smaller CBOs continue to need the capacity-building support we offer to strengthen their management committees, which are required if they are to qualify for the annual subsidy from the provincial government. This is not what we originally set out to do.

We have always been funded by foreign donors but the last fifteen years have seen many donors withdraw from the country. For the last five years we have struggled to sustain ourselves financially and we have been forced to disband our volunteer programme. While we enjoy a healthy relationship with the provincial government, our relationship with local municipalities has been difficult. The Coalition has been fighting to access land owned by municipalities for our agricultural livelihoods programmes. This has been a long struggle with few gains and some of the communities have simply given up. People have lost hope. What are we missing? What could we have done differently? What do we do now?

QUESTION
TO THINK ABOUT

- How would you answer the questions the coalition are asking?

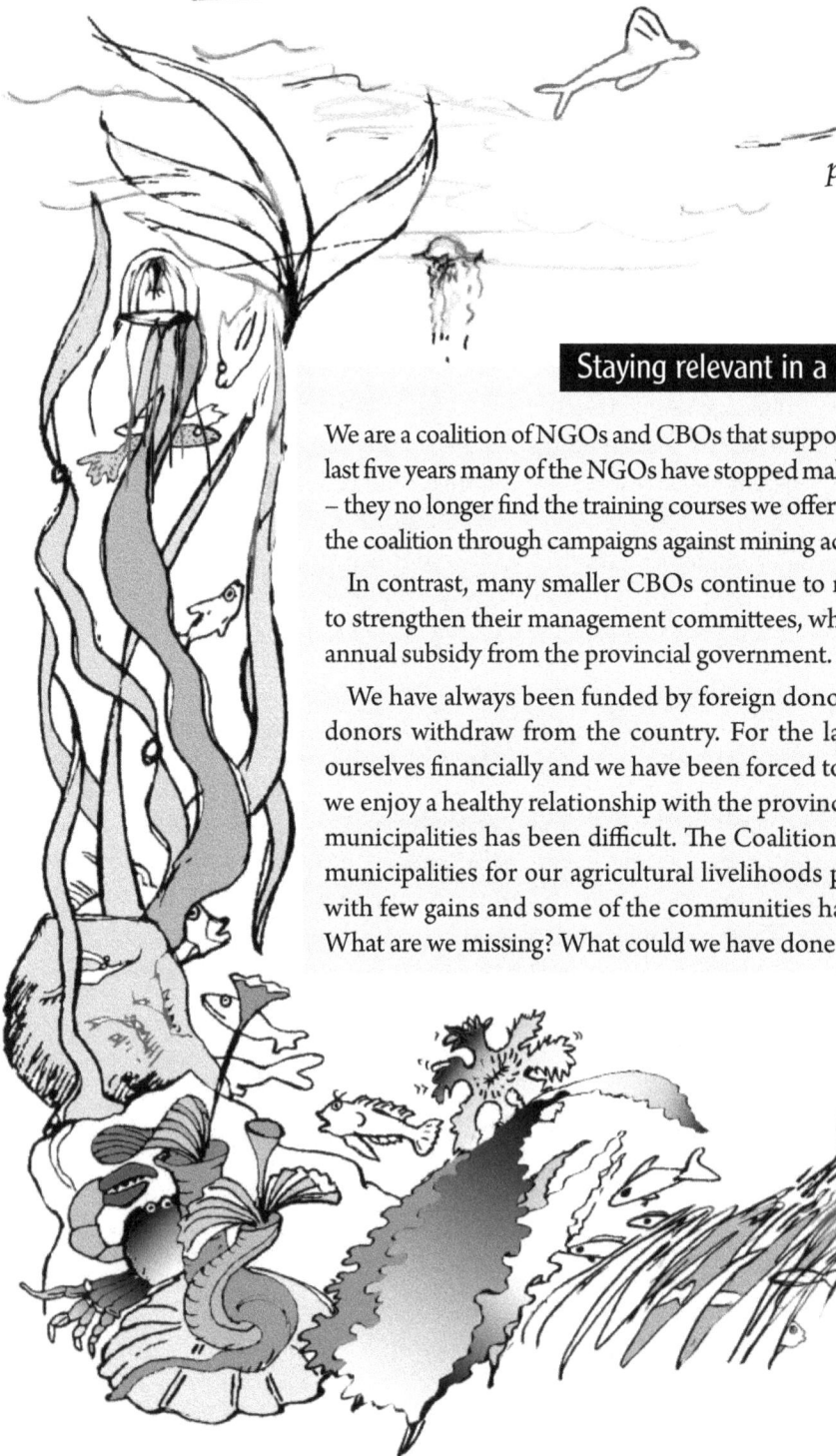

Different dimensions of context

The stories of all organisations unfold in a context. The way they work and learn is shaped by this context. There is a continuous interplay between the true purpose of an organisation and the needs it meets in the context. When organisations fail to notice and respond to changes in the context, they can become irrelevant.

This does not mean that your organisation has to respond to every change out there, but you have to be awake to the many possibilities and threats emerging. The key question you have to continually ask is whether the changing contextual reality is asking for the re-shaping of the purpose of your organisation.

This is a learning challenge primarily, learning from the past, learning about the present reality and learning from emerging future trends.

What are the dimensions of "context" to pay attention to?

Learning and the political dimension

The political dimension of context takes account of power. This exists in both formal, institutionalised power relations and forms and informal power relations and forms. And so we must consider such things as the policy and legislative framework through which governments engage with their citizens, including the different institutions, values and rules which govern the conditions in which organisations act and learn as well as the unwritten laws, the cultural rules that govern and determine the real politics, despite the formal laws and policies.

Political context is not only something we operate under, but also something to work into: the various arenas of the political context are often both the target of social change organisations as well the constraints under which they operate. In struggling for one right others that constrain that struggle must often be pursued. This reveals a complex terrain, with moving goal posts and unexpected challenges – all the more reason to factor contextual understanding into learning, indeed into "learning our way there."

Most organisations are expected to meet certain local requirements and obey policies and regulations guiding how they may operate. For example, organisations are expected to register with the authorities as legal entities before they can offer services, ostensibly to ensure accountability, particularly financial, but often, we suspect, as a mechanism of bureaucratic control, for its own sake.

In repressive contexts, where values of freedom, participation, equality and transparency do not inform how things work, learning can be continually blocked, threatened and undermined in numerous ways, in particular by fear, lack of trust, and the difficulties of being transparently honest and open. The space where organisations can operate may be limited; it is often a struggle to assert themselves in such contexts. When organisations do assert themselves, it can spell trouble for them. Of course, many civil society organisations are set to disturb the status quo and accept the risks and limitations, learning to work around them. Indeed, remarkable creativity and the deepest learnings often emerge in the most difficult contexts, but not accidentally. That Mandela's prison was called "The University of Robben Island" was no loose idea, but a deliberate strategy to counter the purpose of political imprisonment.

The political context is increasingly international. All of us also have experience of how changes in the political realities of northern-based donors can impact organisations and development programmes in southern countries. For example, the shift towards climate change as a priority area has resulted in a sudden reduction in funding for organisations working for social change in the HIV and Aids sector.

Learning and the economic dimension

The economic dimension includes the different economic systems and processes through which people are able to earn income and enjoy a livelihood. Most "development" work is aimed at addressing economic issues, understanding "poverty" as a largely local economic challenge. Increasing attention is being paid by donors and government to stimulating local economy, linking local business to global business. But is this an accurate or helpful understanding of the reality and the challenges facing communities living in poverty? What are the possibilities and dangers of an overly economic understanding of poverty and one that locates the primary challenge at a local level?

QUESTION
TO THINK ABOUT

• To what extent are the funding conditions and requirements of donor agencies a part of the political dimension described here? What does this ask of your organisation?

> *Power lives and is experienced through relationships.*

Certainly change that is authentic must grow out of local initiative, but in the context of rampant globalisation and climate change, are we not "building sand-castles at low-tide"? How do we pay attention to the local and the global so that sustainable gains can be made?

The larger, national and global economic systems and conditions influence organisations internally. The economic crises that began in some countries in 2008 affected funding flows to organisations working for social change right down to grassroots level. How can social change initiatives insulate themselves from economic shifts so that they are not so dependent on the prosperity and generosity of those who, in the larger scheme of things, are part of very problem they are trying to address?

There are no easy or given answers to these questions. More than ever we need to reflect on these questions.

The relational dimension

The "relational dimension" is a useful lens, which includes relationships an organisation has with communities, networking partners, funding agencies, volunteers who help us reach out to communities, and different levels of government. Relationships between organisations are different at different stages of the organisation's development. Our relationships with others are not free of tensions, but these tensions bring an interesting dynamic to our engagement with them.

While your organisation might enjoy a healthy relationship with a cadre of volunteers, its relationship with government might be at an early stage. A relationship with a particular government department that was difficult in the beginning has possibly developed into a strong, healthy one. Relationships are not static: they change and transform over time. More importantly, we have to bear in mind that power lives and is experienced through relationships.

Power dynamics, and how these play themselves out, form an important dimension of the context. Learning for social change emphasises a relational approach which requires an analysis of the power relationships across the various layers of the context – from local, through national to global. It is important for organisations to notice and understand the power dynamics that can hold back and undermine learning and social change efforts.

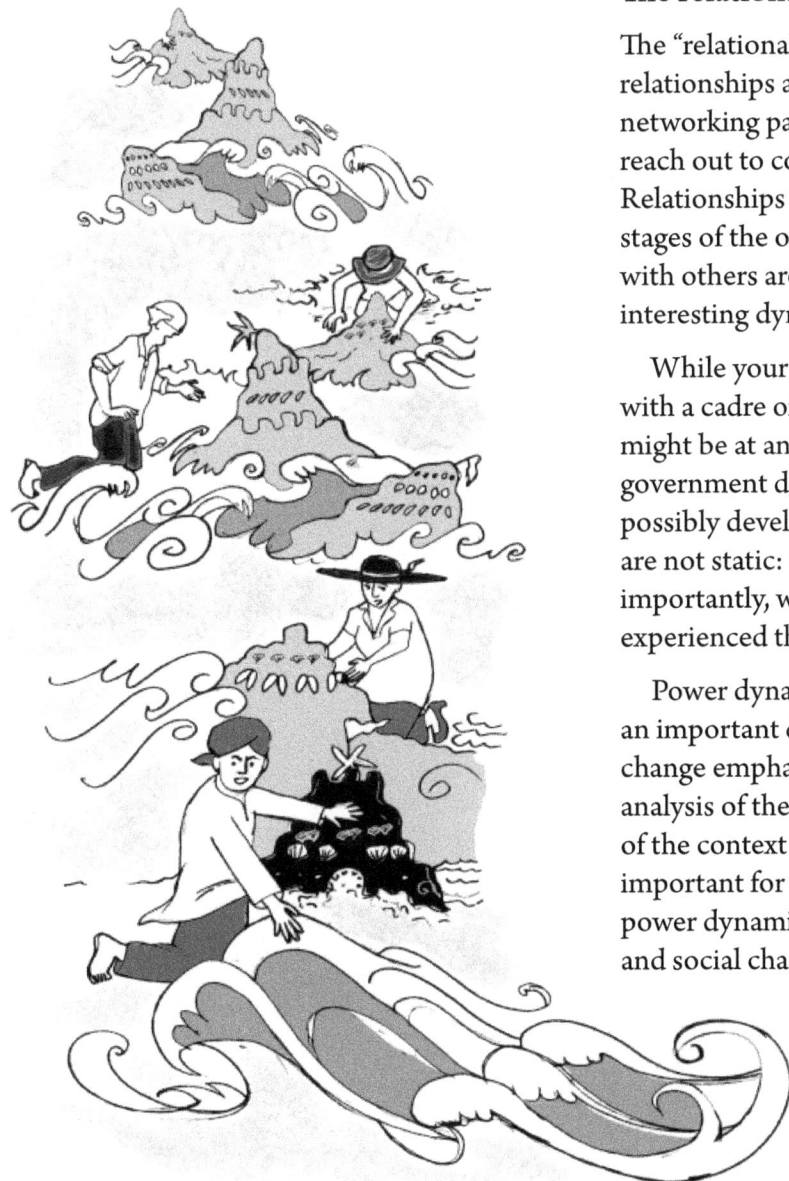

In many instances the power dynamics shape the relationship. All of us are familiar with the power dynamics in the relationship between donor agencies and recipient organisations and how they play themselves out. As recipient organisations we tend to become subservient, obeying without questioning. We see donor organisations as having all the power. We tend to downplay our own power. As a result, we seldom challenge what donor agencies impose on our organisations.

We also know that when the power dynamics are not surfaced and engaged with, toxic tensions in the relationship can be the result. It is important to be aware that effective, sustainable social change requires that relationships of unequal power be transformed. The unequal power relations between an organisation and other actors have to be overcome in order to facilitate learning and social change, as both means and ends. Not only do they perpetuate inequality – they can prevent collaboration, co-operation and sustainable social change because they limit the potential and actions of people and organisations. Yet, a collaborative learning process itself, if held and facilitated skilfully and humanly, can contribute much to laying a foundation for cooperation, for working together creatively.

The social dimension

The social dimension includes the people, organisations and institutions that influence the work of your organisation and are, in turn, influenced by it. It is important for you to know the different social actors and to understand how they influence your organisation and how you in turn influence them. You also have to focus on who does what, who knows what, who decides what and who frames the social change agenda. What is your organisation's relationship to the different actors? Do you feel more, or less, powerful in relation to them? Do they influence the work of your organisation positively or negatively?

The social dimension includes the histories and cultures of the communities your organisation works with, and the processes through which these communities learn. It also includes issues to do with the 'politics' of learning and knowledge. For many of us these are difficult issues to engage with. In some contexts, learning can be used to assimilate people into the dominant way of thinking. There are also instances when it is used to propagate particular viewpoints rather than exposing people to varied viewpoints and letting them choose for themselves.

> *The social dimension includes the histories and cultures of the communities your organisation works with, and the processes through which these communities learn.*

For effective, sustainable social change, understanding the different ways in which people organise is critical. When people organise themselves, this helps to focus collective, interdependent power. This can be seen in community-based social movements where people organise around issues of common interest and shared struggles. The way in which people organise contributes to creating movement, and change happens where there is movement. How people are used to organising themselves thus forms an important part of the context to be taken account of and worked with.

The various social problems are an important element of the social dimension, and shape social change efforts. We do not have to be reminded of how HIV and Aids have redefined the landscape in which organisations work – for many it has introduced a sense of urgency. In the worst affected countries, even those organisations that do not provide directly related services responded to this reality by developing internal policies to deal with the social impact of HIV and Aids.

From the above exploration, you will be aware that context is the often-unnoticed background that influences the realities of organisations. It affects our organisational change and learning processes, and at the same time we have to deal with it through our learning processes, continually waking ourselves up to changing realities. In a world that is demanding more instant action and delivery, more fast-food takeaway outputs and outcomes, how can we pursue a reflective, action learning approach, needed all the more to understand and respond thoughtfully to the growing complexities of change? This book has a lot of focus on learning approach and method, but unless we have the courage to insist on the space to learn, to really take the time to understand the context we are facing and what we are doing in it, we face the danger of always reacting to others and pursuing whimsical work that never quite achieves anything.

The complex and dynamic nature of context

The social change context includes a diverse group of people, organisations and institutions who represent diverse needs, expectations, positions, perspectives, interests and habits. Diversity enriches organisations but also adds complexity.

Not only is context complex, it is also dynamic, and this poses challenges for organisations. Because the context changes continually, new and different realities are created all the time. Many organisations and communities find that what was true last year may no longer be true in the present environment.

And many experience the context as changing much faster than the pace at which they can effect change. While organisations cannot respond and adapt to all changes, they cannot afford to ignore changes that may render them irrelevant. For your organisation to remain a relevant and active participant in social change, it has to be responsive, flexible and agile.

> " *Many organisations and communities find that what was true last year may no longer be true in the present environment.* "

The challenge of staying flexible and agile

Although the context is crucial for our learning, we guard against being pulled in many different directions. We fear being separated, divorced from or drifting from our purpose. At the same time, we guard against focusing too narrowly on what we do as this can lead to alienation from the needs and expectations of the context – it can equally disconnect us from the social realities. The biggest challenge for us is ensuring we remain flexible and agile. It is not easy for us to keep up with the changing realities. We find that it is not easy to live in the now and be awake to what is happening inside and around us all the time. We used to conduct needs assessments in communities … we realised that by the time we had finished compiling the report, things had changed completely and communities had moved on!

The complexity and dynamism of the context can also be attributed to the fact that social change requires the active participation of many different actors, plus many factors, forces and perspectives need to be taken into consideration. There is engagement at local, national, global, interpersonal and inter-organisational levels. These interactions happen across a web of relationships, and so outcomes cannot easily be predetermined or predicted.

For example, when your organisation engages actively with the communities it supports, such engagement could be at different levels. Some of the field staff could be engaging with volunteers at the same time as negotiations are conducted with community leaders around implementation of a new programme. While this is happening, you are also consulting

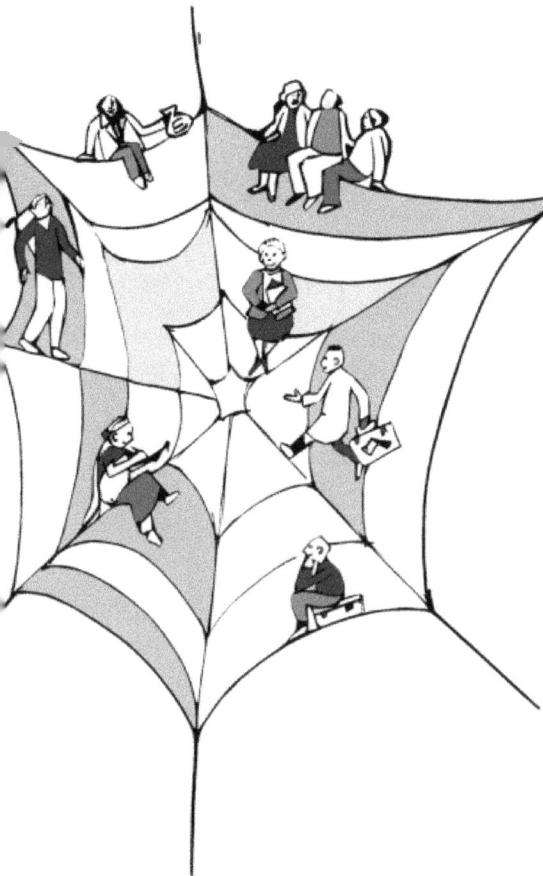

with the government department that will become involved in the programme, and talking to project officers from the donor agency to request funding support. More and more, organisations have to hold and manage relationships with competing demands and expectations.

So how does the complex and dynamic nature of the context affect organisations? Many of us find ourselves in situations where the approaches, methodologies, strategies and ways of engaging that used to provide solutions are no longer appropriate. They have become outdated and we can no longer rely on them to bring about meaningful change. The current context of social change calls for strategies, approaches and methodologies that will enable organisations to navigate uncertainty and change. In addition, community and organisational processes are unpredictable. Engaging with them is about working with uncertainty – working into the unknown.

The dynamism of the context also means that we experience how decisions, changes or events at one level can affect our actions, functioning and learning at another level. The interconnectedness between our own organisation and events at a global or national level means we experience their impact or influence in our work. The economic crisis mentioned in the previous section is a good example of this.

Sometimes events at a local level can have devastating effects on the functioning of organisations. For example, when a community takes civil action against a local municipality, it can have serious effects on the programmes of organisations.

Noticing and making sense of changing contexts

Describing the context is not enough

In my organisation I am not sure we have processes for noticing and making sense of the changing contexts that are deeply integrated into our practice – this happens intuitively. We have a strategic process every three years and this coincides with our funding cycles. As part of this, we undertake a contextual scan that helps us identify the changes and trends. However, we do not engage rigorously with what is surfaced by the scan. The director of our organisation writes the funding proposal and further develops the piece on 'context' and, unless I happen to read the funding proposal, I seldom get to read what is contained in the section on 'context'. We do have informal conversations about the things that are changing in the context and how these affect our work … these get most of us excited. But we do not do much in terms of exploring the implications of such changes for our work. The one thing that concerns us all deeply is how difficult it has become to secure funding, but we have not really stopped to engage with this and explore the implications for the organisation more deeply. This we see as the work of our director.

Our organisations face many dilemmas in our attempts to respond to and deal with the ever-changing contextual realities. How we respond to these is critical.

Most organisations work in complex social contexts and it takes time to get to know such complexity. However, the dominant culture in many contexts tends to demand quick fixes or ready-made solutions and there is pressure to demonstrate tangible, visible results. Consequently, very little time is invested in trying to read, notice and make sense of the complex changes in the context that have a bearing on our work and actions.

Many of us find it overwhelming to engage with the complexity of the context – it is difficult to work out. Often we realise that we do not have the abilities, mechanisms nor processes to get to grips with the changing situation. For many organisations, reading and making sense of our contexts is an event; it is not seen as an important process that should be part of our reflective learning practices and processes.

How organisations respond to context

So, what do most organisations do? We reduce an important learning process to a quick environmental scan, through which we generate a great deal of information or data that we seldom make sense of or use to inform our work and practice. For many organisations the three-year funding proposal is based on a three-yearly reading of a very complex, unpredictable, uncertain context. After the environmental scan has been conducted we cement the context in time. We ignore its dynamism and turn it into something that is predictable. We use the information we have gathered to shape our programmes for the next three years and we set them in a context that we treat as static, as unchanging.

Challenging contexts that undermine our work

What do we do as organisations when the contexts in which we work promote values and principles that go completely against the values and principles that underpin and guide our work? Do we compromise or stand firm in our conviction? In many contexts there are strong forces, trends and changes that can undermine our work.

Competition over resources is a force that defines our contexts very strongly. We see organisations scrambling for resources all the time, competing even with those they are meant to be collaborating with. This is especially prevalent in the current funding climate where the conditions and requirements of donor organisations redefine the landscape all the time.

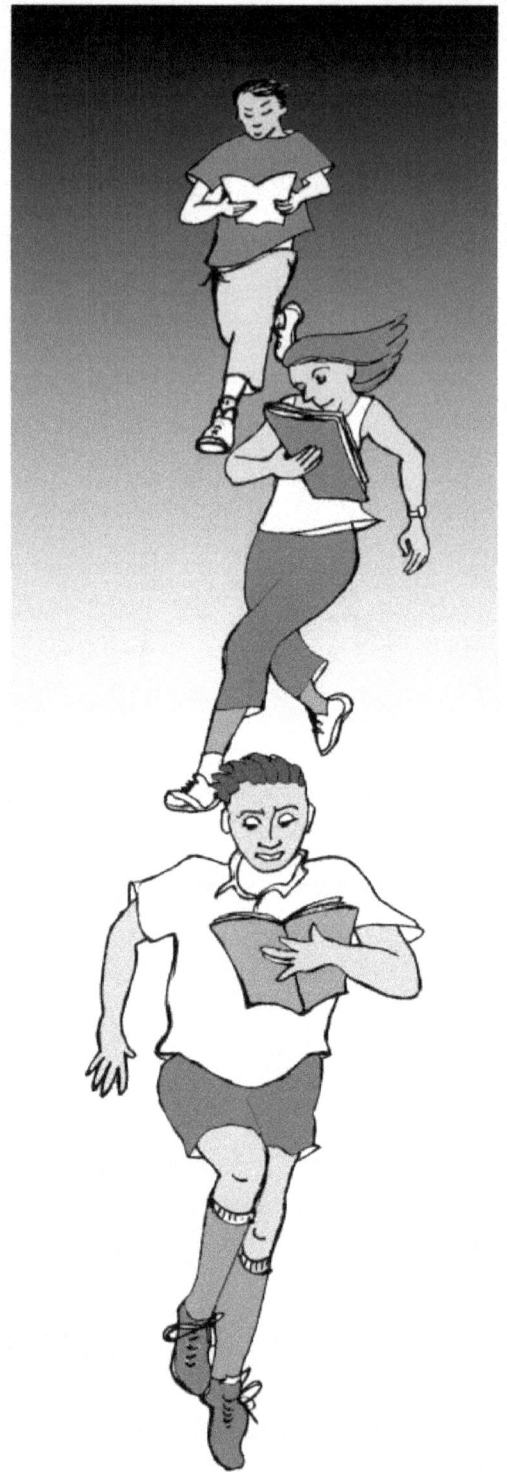

QUESTION
TO THINK ABOUT

• How would your organisation deal with such a dilemma?

QUESTION
TO THINK ABOUT

• How does your organisation involve those closest to the social problems in determining the solutions, when the context is one where their voices tend to be ignored?

While the context forces organisations to compete for limited resources, we know that effective, sustainable social change processes require innovative collaboration among the different social actors. In our attempts to respond to the context, we find ourselves getting drawn into competition over resources. Such action sends our organisations into survivalist mode and threatens to prevent us from pursuing our organisational purpose with integrity, determination and commitment.

Organisations also face a dilemma in instances where social change is not part of the agenda of those it engages with. I am reminded of working with an organisation where the donor was mainly interested in projects that could be replicated and be used to demonstrate tangible results. It did not matter that these did not contribute to transformative processes of positive, sustainable change in the lives of people. The organisation was clearly faced with a dilemma. Should it focus on replication of the project or invest energy in working on transformative processes that contribute to changing people's lives?

A challenge facing many organisations is how to help donor agencies learn about effective social change, and about the importance of learning. We are aware that resources play a critical role in learning for social change. Those who control the resources tend to dictate the agenda. This often not only has to do with the issues that get addressed but also the pace at which change processes unfold. We are familiar with the pressure to show results.

We cannot deny that donor agencies have come to have a huge influence on the learning practices of organisations and communities. Their support can make learning possible. However, donor-imposed constraints can affect organisational learning processes negatively. The insistence that resources be spent on programme work can sometimes mean fewer resources are available for learning. It is common for reflective learning practices to be seen as time-consuming and taking practitioners away from their work. Learning is not seen as important work.

Another dilemma that we face as practitioners and organisations is building learning processes that are genuinely inclusive when the contexts in which we work are characterised by exclusion and marginalisation. The desire to be inclusive lives strongly in all of us. It is a driving force in our work. Yet, the world over, 'gurus' and 'experts' are revered. They are looked to for solutions. This often happens at the expense of marginalising those closest to the problems.

Adapting to changing context

In order to stay alive and relevant within a complex and dynamic context, our organisations have to embrace reading, noticing and making sense of complex dynamics and changes that affect their ability to do the work and learn effectively. It is, however, not sufficient for an organisation to understand its context. This has to be accompanied by the right attitude, appropriate strategies, approaches and methodologies. The way your organisation locates itself within its context will determine how it relates to the dynamics and complexities of its context.

The challenge for organisations is to develop and identify processes for reading, noticing and making sense of the context in its full complexity and wholeness. We have to develop abilities that will enable us to engage with the context meaningfully – we have to develop what Matthew R. Kutz calls 'contextual intelligence'. This is a competency that refers to the ability an organisation has to transform data into useful information and this information into knowledge and then, most importantly, to assimilate such knowledge into practice.

This means that organisations should not stop at reading and noticing the changing context. Organisations need to constantly adapt to the changes in order to improve actions and practice. Organisations need sense-making processes to help transform information or data into critical learning and knowledge. While some organisations have clear, conscious and structured sense-making processes, for others it happens intuitively.

Not that there is anything wrong with doing this intuitively. It is common in pioneering organisations where reflective learning processes are informal, unconscious and intuitive. Organisations in the pioneering phase read their context through sensing, observing and listening. These are important abilities and in many of our organisations we can sense these changes even before we rationally analyse them. However, we need to make sure we acknowledge and discuss this intuitive learning and respond to it effectively.

For organisations in the rational phase, (see *Barefoot Guide 1* Chapter 4, Phases of Organisations) processes and mechanisms of sense-making need to be integrated into reflective learning practices and processes. This can take place through an ongoing process of questioning, observing, listening and sensing which is followed by adjusting strategies and tactics, adapting, improving and rethinking practice and actions.

There are many organisations with learning rhythms and practices through which regular reflection and learning happens. This gives engagement with the context life! The organisations are able to identify the change, and explore its implications for their work and practice. This leads to deeper insights, increased awareness and improved action and practice in the organisation – thinking ability is expanded. Such sense-making processes mean the true purpose of the organisation and its actions in its context are in harmony.

An organisation that learns from changing context

In my organisation we have different processes through which we gather information and make sense of the changing context. In our annual strategic review process we reflect on our strategy, identify what works and what needs to be improved. During this process we conduct an in-depth reading of the context by bringing in external people with knowledge in areas that have bearing on our work and practice. Together with them we explore the implications for our organisation. In addition, we have monthly 'practice development' sessions where we focus on specific aspects of our practice. During these sessions we also focus on context and collectively explore the changes influencing our work and practice. In addition, we identify relevant reading materials and use the content to look at what is coming out for us and how it can influence our practice. We have a Practice Co-ordinator, whose role is to manage our continuous learning about our practice and explore how we can improve on it on an ongoing basis. She helps to create a summary of the contextual issues and changes.

QUESTIONS
TO THINK ABOUT

- Whose voice and learning drives your organisation's sense-making processes?

- What organisational spaces have you created to honour all voices?

- What existing activities and practices provide opportunity for collective sense-making?

In many organisations the process of reading, noticing and making sense of changes in the context is one that is undertaken alone – it is commonly part of the organisational strategic planning or review processes. Most organisations conduct an environmental or contextual scan. I think you will agree with me that, although the process can generate a great deal of excitement and energy, it often turns into an information-gathering exercise.

The product of such an exercise is usually a matrix with information. How many organisations actually draw on and use this information afterwards? Once the energy and excitement have dissipated, organisations realise that the matrix in no way captures the complexity of the context. The environmental scan is an important tool – but only if what comes out of it remains alive in the subsequent decision-making processes of the organisation.

Sometimes the environmental scan is done by an external consultant who collects the information and analyses it. The sense-making is contracted out. You can imagine who learns most from this process.

Increasingly we see organisations using collective learning processes, such as seminars and multi-stakeholder dialogue sessions, to gain insight. These allow for creative ways of reading, noticing and making sense of the context. They create a platform for a diversity of perspectives, understandings, ideas, experiences and questions to be shared, exchanged, explored and engaged with. They help to create a holistic picture of the changing environment and open up an opportunity for organisations to bring communities, networking partners, donors, government and other role players into their sense-making processes. By involving others beyond the organisation, the conversation is enriched and a more comprehensive picture of the complex context is developed.

By involving others beyond the organisation, the conversation is enriched and a more comprehensive picture of the complex context is developed.

Context influences learning

The context in which organisations operate can be conducive to, or undermine, learning. How the context does these things is determined by the dominant culture, which refers to the beliefs, values, principles and thinking that inform and shape how things happen in that particular context.

Where a learning orientation and culture is appreciated, encouraged, valued and supported, learning practices are seen as central to the ongoing change and transformation of people, organisations and even the broader society. Learning is seen as important for helping to develop creative responses to social problems and challenges. Its value in enabling adaptation to the ever-changing context is recognised. Actively-learning people and organisations nurture a creative response to the changing context.

Further, a context that is conducive to learning allows the difficult questions to be asked. Learning requires a safe space for people to speak up, ask questions that make us uncomfortable, and to make mistakes without fear of reproach.

People and organisations are viewed as active participants in social change efforts and they are helped to cultivate capacities, competences and capabilities that are in tune with creative social change processes. Learning is recognised and appreciated for what it contributes to the expansion of the imagination of people – it enables them to explore possibilities.

… a context that is conducive to learning allows the difficult questions to be asked.

QUESTIONS
TO THINK ABOUT

- In your context are people allowed to admit that they do not have all the answers to the problems they are facing?

- What ways of knowing are recognised, valued and honoured in your context?

In contexts that idolise experts and gurus, being open and honest about not knowing things, about making mistakes, is not encouraged. In contexts that undermine learning there is a tendency to treat knowledge as a commodity held by a few, and ignore knowledge that is created through other means. Often, the knowledge of local communities and marginal groups, that has been developed from experience, is ignored.

Learning for social change requires that the learning needs of all the different role players be taken into consideration, including marginal groups. If this does not happen the social change agenda can be undermined. The challenge is to create a context that is inclusive and can create space for the diversity of needs, interests and aspirations.

In a context that supports learning, people are encouraged to develop solutions that address inequality and discrimination. Such solutions:

- lead to change in the underlying social problems

- are arrived at through conscious learning

- are not imposed from outside the situation

- seek to bring about changes in attitudes, behaviours, policies, laws and the institutions whose actions and policies affect the living conditions of people and communities.

Finally, note that in some instances learning new behaviours is not enough. Some situations require a change in beliefs, new values and attitudes!

Conclusion

Organisations can both respond to context and influence context. They need to learn in order to remain relevant and effective in the context in which they work. But they also need to work to change the context so that it is more conducive to the learning that allows social change to happen. Organisational learning is not an internal process. It is fundamentally linked to the external context in which the organisation works.

CHAPTER 12

Harvesting experience: learning how people learn

Learning from our experience – Action Learning

Our own real experiences are a rich resource from which we can, and do, learn. In social change work, learning from experience is called Action Learning. It is a natural change process, something we all do every day, but it makes sense to improve how we learn. In the first chapter we said that 'learning lies at the heart of social change'. Now let's expand that: *action* learning lies at the heart of social change.

To learn well from our experiences we need to develop skills which enable us to do this. It is not enough to just ask ourselves, 'What have we learned from this experience?' We need a more thorough approach that helps us to be more thoughtful, and that leads to deeper and more useful learning.

> *Real experiences are a rich resource from which we can, and do, learn.*

The story of Action Learning in Ghana Association of the Blind

Under a regional VSO Action Leaning Program, five learning sets were set up in the Ghana Association of the Blind (GAB). One was at board level, two at staff level in the head office and two at district level. There was initial introduction training by the VSO volunteers following the start-up workshop, plus a planning, monitoring and evaluation (PME) training and several meetings.

What has happened since ?

Colleagues now come up with day-to-day issues and reflect on them. Sitting together they are able to suggest solutions and make decisions. This is a big change. Before that a person took an issue home, brooded on it and it grew bigger. This led to staff dissatisfaction, resentment and apathy. Now people talk about commonly-experienced things at work and are able to make their own decisions. No longer is the Director, or someone else, turned to for solutions. By reflecting, listening and asking questions the staff recognises it has solutions itself. This is helping the organisation at all levels to become open, responsible and transparent.

The set holds the structure for critical reflection, but the principles learned in the set are more generally applied. Action Learning skills like listening and questioning are sharpened and applied in daily work. Now, when someone comes with an issue, whoever are around sit together, reflect, and come up with ideas and solutions.

For the first time it also became possible for staff and board to have a joint, fruitful annual reflection. Instead of the usual confrontational tone – 'This was planned. Why didn't it happen?' – it was a meeting without defense mechanisms; it was really reflecting.

Board members gained new insights and understood better their relationship to the professionals in the organisation. This learning began with reflecting on why some targets weren't met. Staff explained problems they experienced when board members walked in, 'dictating' what had to be done at that moment. The staff felt forced to stop current work and to pay attention to the board member. Result: the actual work wasn't done in time.

At the beginning there was some resistance to Action Learning, to leaving the comfort zone. The questioning was challenging. It was hard to not take it personally or to be afraid that it could be used against you at another moment. Several things helped to overcome the resistance: the initial training, the carefully-facilitated set meetings, the patient initiators who gave the process time. Then experience showed that it was safe to speak up, and showed the benefits of this approach. And now it works. People are more accommodating, are able to listen in a non-judgmental way. They listen and ask good questions, which is difficult, yet key.

The staff is also able to help the beneficiaries in another way: 'Instead of planning *for* them, we listen to their needs and provide or try to meet them at their point of need.' It makes working easier, knowing that people can find their own solutions. In Action Learning sets you listen to people, you hear them out. People have wonderful suggestions, listen to each other and contribute. It is becoming real teamwork.

Staff started with baselines in districts, and, sitting together to reflect on this information, they saw that districts have different needs. A staff member said, 'Before we had some supply-driven service (everybody needs empowerment), but now we saw some districts needed different things and we discussed what they really needed. So we planned various deliveries, dependent on the needs. And the districts are more happy with what we deliver. And that means that the relationships are improved'.

Four Kinds of Action Learning

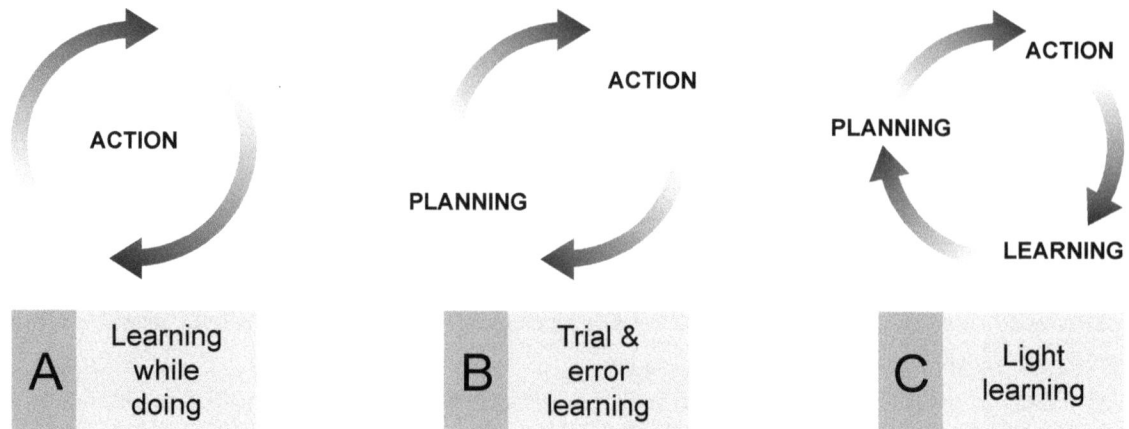

A — Learning while doing

B — Trial & error learning

C — Light learning

D — Deeper learning

We learn from experience in many different ways. Most often we **learn while doing** which is unconscious learning but effective for simple tasks. We also learn by **trial and error** where we try something and if it does not work we try something else, until we find a good solution. This is fine if we can afford a few failures. We also have **light learning** processes where we need to think a bit about what we have learned before acting again. But when things are more complex, where we cannot afford to make too many mistakes we need to spend more time reflecting to enable **deeper learnings** to emerge. This is the kind of action learning we focus on in this chapter.

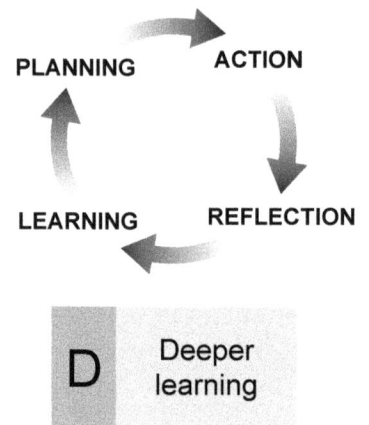

Experiential Learning

When we reflect we think deeply about something that has happened, and we discover what the experience means for us personally. At the same time, we develop skills of inquiry. We can then look at our experience in a new way – we reinterpret it. Making sense of experience in this way is what educational theorist Paulo Freire called 'critical reflection'. Experiential Learning is a method that includes this. An experience is reflected upon and then turned into concepts, which in turn become guidelines for new experiences.

There are many models of Experiential Learning, but the common theme is making sense of things (through reflection) and sorting things out for ourselves. In this Guide we use Action Learning as a form of Experiential Learning.

> *The pot has to simmer a bit – otherwise the learning can be shallow and obvious.*

Using the action learning cycle – things to watch for

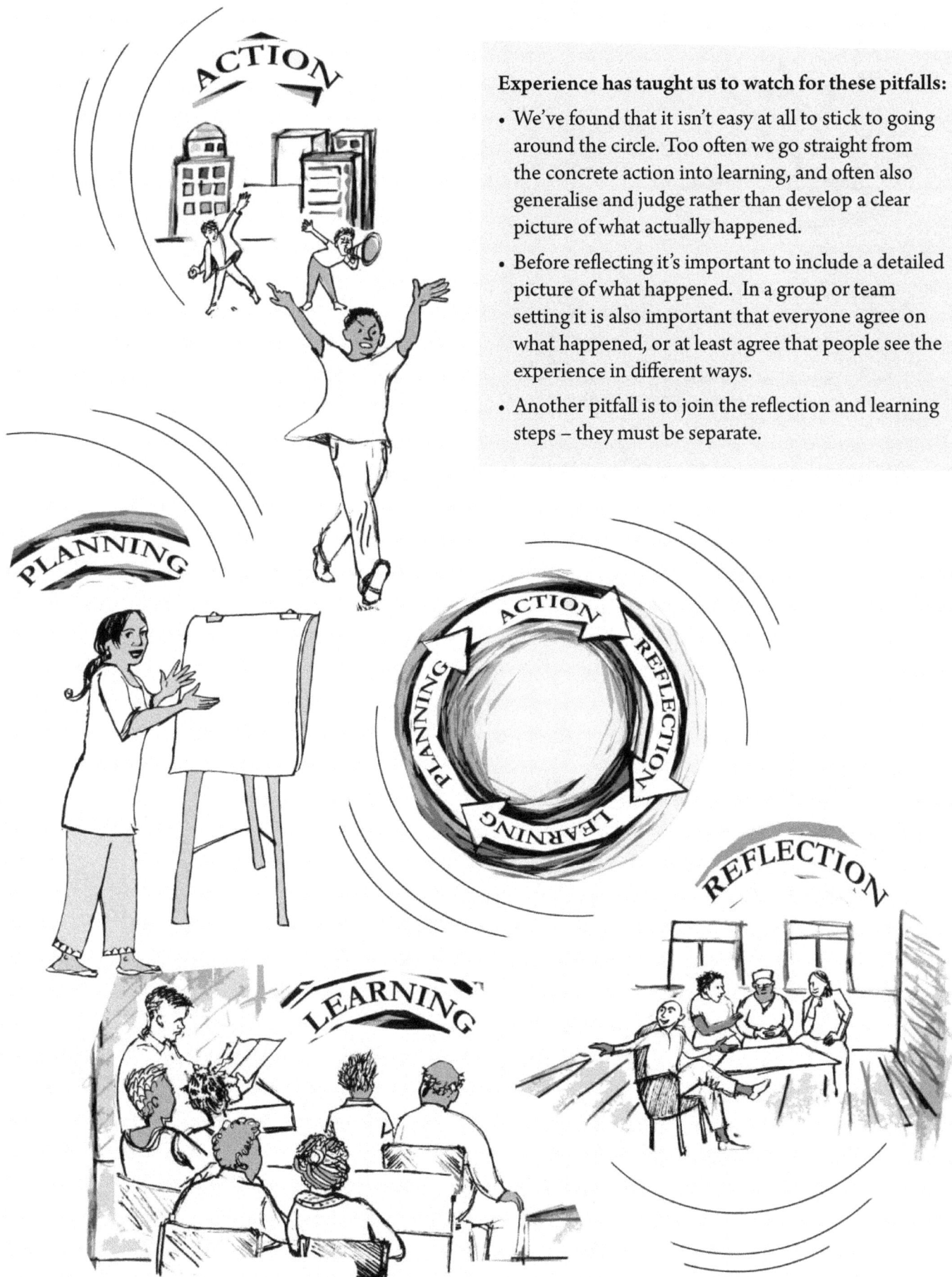

Experience has taught us to watch for these pitfalls:

- We've found that it isn't easy at all to stick to going around the circle. Too often we go straight from the concrete action into learning, and often also generalise and judge rather than develop a clear picture of what actually happened.

- Before reflecting it's important to include a detailed picture of what happened. In a group or team setting it is also important that everyone agree on what happened, or at least agree that people see the experience in different ways.

- Another pitfall is to join the reflection and learning steps – they must be separate.

We suggest these steps for using the Action Learning cycle:

Step 1. Action

The first step before reflection is to recall and describe what actually happened, in as much detail as possible. Some people call this 'collecting data'. (Avoid asking 'Why?' and possible learning at this stage.) Include the circumstances that led to the event, where it happened, who was involved, what was said and done and the outcomes, decisions made (or not made), conclusions reached, agreements, disagreements and so on. What were people feeling? What images do people have of what happened? You are mining the experience to find the 'what?'

One useful approach to collecting data is to write in two columns. In the left-hand column write down the story of what you could see happening, the events. This is the 'outer story'. Then in the right-hand column write down what was happening inside you and others: your thoughts, feelings and struggles, and what you observed was happening to the relationships between people. This is the 'inner story'. This way a deeper picture can emerge to then reflect on.

Step 2. Reflection

Now you all ask yourselves and each other what were the assumptions, beliefs, values and attitudes of the different people that might explain why they behaved like they did. For example, I might have decided that no one would be interested in my opinion. Whether they were interested or not, this explains why I did not speak up. Perhaps some of the people were only there for money or employment opportunities. This was what they valued, informed their attitude, and explains why they left as soon as they discovered there were no opportunities.

Ask 'What helped the process? What held it back?' Explore these simple-seeming questions.

Thinking back on the event, what were people's intentions? Why did people act as they did and what did they want to achieve? Evaluate the effectiveness of their actions and behaviour.

> *What were the different assumptions, beliefs, values and attitudes?*

Step 3. Learning

Describe what you have learned from the event. What do you know that was confirmed? What new questions have arisen? What could you have done differently to achieve a different outcome? Why would you want the outcome to be different? How could you act differently to achieve your intentions in similar situations in future?

Start making connections between what you are discovering and what you know or believe now. What theories, ideas or insights from your past did you, or could you have, applied?

Do your new learnings make you uncomfortable? Do they contradict what you know or believe? What do you have to let go of, *unlearn*, so that you can accept these new learnings?

How does what you have learned relate to other events in your life? What patterns, themes and similarities do you notice? What do you appreciate about what you did, and its impact? What have you learned from other people's actions and behaviour?

Step 4. Planning

How can you apply these learnings, and what will happen when you do? How will they fit in with your existing plans? What will you have to stop doing, or do less of? What will you have to start doing, or do more of? What blocks might stop you applying the learning? This is another place where you may surface what you need to unlearn.

Finally, what are your next steps in applying the new learning?

Applying the Action Learning cycle

Using the Action Learning cycle is both an attitude and a way of working. It is what is behind a learning culture, it is a practical approach to learning and it asks you to reflect and learn as a continual process.

To have this attitude requires us, and our organisations, to make choices and take steps:

- Firstly, there is the choice to adopt the state of a learner, the will to be a learner.
- Secondly, Action Learning must be part of existing, regular meetings.
- Thirdly, new time must be set aside, individually and organisationally, to work with Action Learning as a different way to improve what we do.

The learning facilitator can support this process, but she needs to have an understanding of how adults learn and how they can be supported in this.

... one day I realised that I did not really understand why I was doing what I did ...

Facilitating adult learners

Many of us have become learning facilitators without any formal training or qualifications. It just 'became part of our job'. If this is you, then the next paragraphs will help you to understand what is important for adult learners, why some people learn differently to others, what helps or blocks learning, what we can do to help them learn better and so on.

Some learning facilitators work with in-house staff; others offer outside training. We aim to give ideas and guidance to learning facilitators of both sites.

A journey in becoming an adult educator

I had spent ten years of my life in various NGOs training others. I had been on courses on Experiential Learning, leadership, designing and running educational events, personal growth and human relations. I was confident as a facilitator and could plan and present workshops. If asked, I described myself as a trainer, and I loved my work.

Then one day I realised that I did not really understand why I was doing what I did when I trained people. So, I decided to study adult education and slowly came to realise that what I had been doing was actually based on some important principles of how adults learn. As I grappled with these concepts I realised how restricted my view of training was, how I was not really that good at what I did. I lacked the understanding and ability to really promote learning in myself and others.

My style then changed from one of arrogance (I know) to a more inclusive one of seeing myself as a co-learner on a journey that could not be neatly packaged in a design.

Some key things about adults and learning

Firstly, adults never stop learning. Most learning does not come from a teacher or a book – it is a lifelong task. Some learning happens through formal courses, but most happens either less formally in workshops or informally through life experience, interactions with others and the world around us. Our intuitive (instinctive, untaught) side sometimes surprises us with new insights and ideas. Because we never stop learning, it makes sense to learn more consciously and effectively, so 'learning how to learn' is important for all adults.

Secondly, learning is a very personal process. We learn when we really want to learn and when we're ready to learn. Some learning is linked to our development as human beings, so we find that we need to learn particular things at particular times.

Thirdly, learning is more than just adding knowledge or a new skill – learning involves change. When we learn something we find that our way of viewing the world, our behaviour or our knowledge and skills may need to change. If the new learning contradicts the old, we may have to let go of past ideas and beliefs. For learning to make a difference in our lives, we have to make it our own and fit it into our existing knowledge and skills. This also means that learning takes time.

And lastly, when we are learning something we bring with us life experience, knowledge, skills, values and ways of being in the world. All are valuable resources to our learning and are the foundation on which we will build new learning.

If we understand these adult learning principles we can design learnings that have the impact we want. We also need to respect what each person brings and use this as the starting point for new learning. In our organisations these same principles apply for both group and individual learning.

Learning styles

We all learn differently

A description of a learning experience

We had asked participants of the upcoming learning to do the Kolb learning test to find out their individual learning styles. As facilitator, it seemed a good idea to take the test myself to refresh the experience, in the same way as health workers encouraging people to take HIV tests should have the experience themselves. The Internet is a rich source of Kolb learning tests: long ones, short ones. Curious to find out differences or whether (and how) the test results would vary, I completed eight of them. In between I experimented with different examples of learning experiences in the back of my mind. I took on different attitudes and moods when completing tests. It was striking to find out that whatever I tried, the Kolb test results were the same. I now have to believe that the results show how I prefer to learn: as an activist, by feeling and doing.

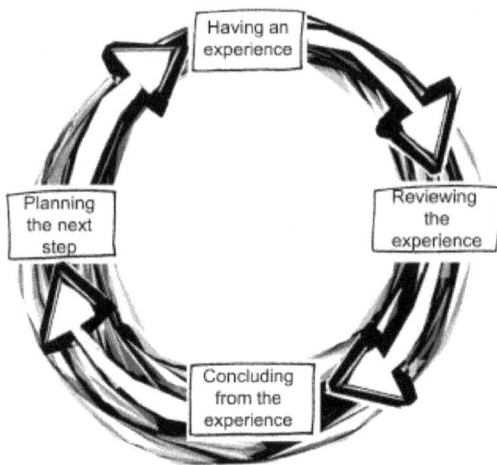

HONEY & MUMFORD'S LEARNING CYCLE

❝ *There are different 'learning styles'.* ❞

We're all unique, so it's no surprise that there are different learning styles or preferred ways of learning. Some prefer learning through 'doing' something: making a model of a village in the sand. Others love to 'reflect' on what happened: when Ms X said… the whole group… .

Others create a 'theory' of how things work: I've noticed that whenever there is a problem it is because… . Yet others may prefer to immediately plan how they can 'apply' what they have discovered: we could use that idea like this…

There are several ways learning styles are described. A well known model is Kolb's (see 'A learning experience'). Peter Honey and Alan Mumford build on Kolb's model to create this diagram using a simpler set of concepts. They mark the following styles:

- Having a concrete experience: *Activist*
- Reflecting on the experience: *Reflector*
- Concluding from the experience: *Theorist*
- Planning and experimenting: *Planner*

Activist

As an Activist, you involve yourself fully in new experiences. You enjoy the here and now, are open-minded and enthusiastic about anything new. Your philosophy is: 'I'll try anything once'. You throw caution to the wind, enjoy short term crises and tackle problems by brainstorming. You thrive on the challenge of new experiences but are bored with implementation. You involve yourself with others but can hog the limelight. *You learn by feeling and doing.*

Reflector

As a Reflector, you like to stand back, consider experiences and think about them from many different angles. You are happy collecting facts, both first-hand and from others, and prefer to chew them over before coming to any conclusion. Collecting and thinking through, analysing information is what counts, so you tend to put off reaching conclusions for as long as possible. Your philosophy is to be careful: 'Look before you leap'. In meetings you prefer to listen and get the drift of the discussion before making your own points. You have a slightly distant, tolerant, unruffled air. When you act, you try to see the wider picture, which includes the past as well as the present. *You learn by feeling and watching.*

Theorist

As a Theorist, you adapt and work what you see into complex but logical-sounding theories and opinions. You think problems through in a step by step way. You tend to be a perfectionist who won't rest easy until things are tidy and fit into your clear and rational scheme. You like to analyse and combine ideas into new theories. Your philosophy is: 'If it's logical it's good'. Questions you often ask are: Does it make sense? How does this fit with that? What are the things we must assume here? You tend to be clear-headed and analytical rather than going on your feelings or being ambiguous. You like certainty and feel uncomfortable with personal judgments, lateral thinking and anything flippant. *You learn by thinking and watching.*

Planner

As a Planner, you are keen on trying out ideas, theories and techniques to see if they work. You search out new ideas and take the first opportunity to try them out. You are the sort of person who returns from workshops brimming with new ideas to experiment with. You like to dive in and get on with things. You don't like beating around the bush and tend to be impatient with thinking, reflecting and open-ended discussions. You are a practical, down-to-earth person and respond to problems and opportunities as a challenge. Your philosophy is: 'If it works its good'. *You learn by thinking and doing.*

> *In any group there will be participants with different preferences for how they want to learn.*

Making sense of learning styles

As you read the four learning style descriptions did one, or possibly two, attract you? These are most likely your preferred learning styles. Why not challenge yourself to use some of your non-preferred learning styles and see how they help your development as a learner? For example, if you are a reflector think about what stops you from being a planner or an activist.

The key thing is to recognise that in any group there will be participants with different preferences for how they want to learn. We need to design our learning processes so as to engage all four learning styles. If only using one method (e.g. lectures), some participants (the theorists) will love it, but those who prefer doing (activists) or those who prefer applying (planners) will find it difficult to engage. We can strengthen each person's range of learning styles by catering for all four styles and so build individual and group capacity to learn.

While it might seem that some learners won't get involved unless it's their preferred learning style, this is not true. Using our preferred learning style makes the learning opportunity more engaging for us. However we are more likely to lose an 'I'm bored' attitude if we also try out 'non-preferred' learning styles.

A danger for facilitators is that our preferred learning style can influence our design. Being aware of our own style or styles helps us balance the learning opportunities we offer to others.

Each learning style has a place. The activists will like the role play, the reflectors the reflection. The theorists will like creating a theory about leadership, and the planners will work hard to apply what has emerged in a future action.

An example of using different learning styles

Teaching a group of learners about Leadership

Step 1. Active experience:
We introduce an exercise or task with different leadership roles. For example, we work in groups with each participant role-playing a different leadership role, such as inspiring, focusing and challenging.
(*See Barefoot Guide 1, pages 43–45*)

Step 2. Reflecting on the experience:
We reflect on what happened when these roles were used.

Step 3. Connecting with and building on theory:
We ask for additional ideas, comments and understandings of what happened and how this helps us understand leadership better.

Step 4. Experiment and apply:
Finally we look at how these ideas ('theories') can be applied.

QUESTIONS
TO THINK ABOUT

- When did the learning take place in this story?
- What does your answer say about your underlying assumptions about learning?

' *Learning…*
usually takes time. '

Learning as a process

Learning isn't something that just happens – it usually takes time. Just being told something does not necessarily lead to learning. It remains just a thought, unless we make it part of our lives. So how do we do that?

How do you learn to drive a car?

If you have learned to drive a car, this might sound familiar.

At first, under the eye of someone experienced, you learn about things like gears, clutch, brake and accelerator. You learn that to change gears you need to slowly let out the clutch while increasing pressure on the accelerator. For the first few times you do this too fast. The car leaps forward like a rocket and stalls! Eventually you get it right and can change gears quite smoothly.

Then comes the driving test. You're terrified you may fail. But no, you manage those gear changes just right, saying to yourself in your head: 'Slow out with the clutch and slow pushing down on the accelerator.'

After a few months of driving you no longer tell yourself, 'Slow out… push slowly down'. You seem to just do it. In fact as you drive today I doubt you even notice changing gears at all. This part of driving has become so integrated into your skill-set that you do it without thinking.

The four-step learning model explains learning as a process, and can be used to help plan learning

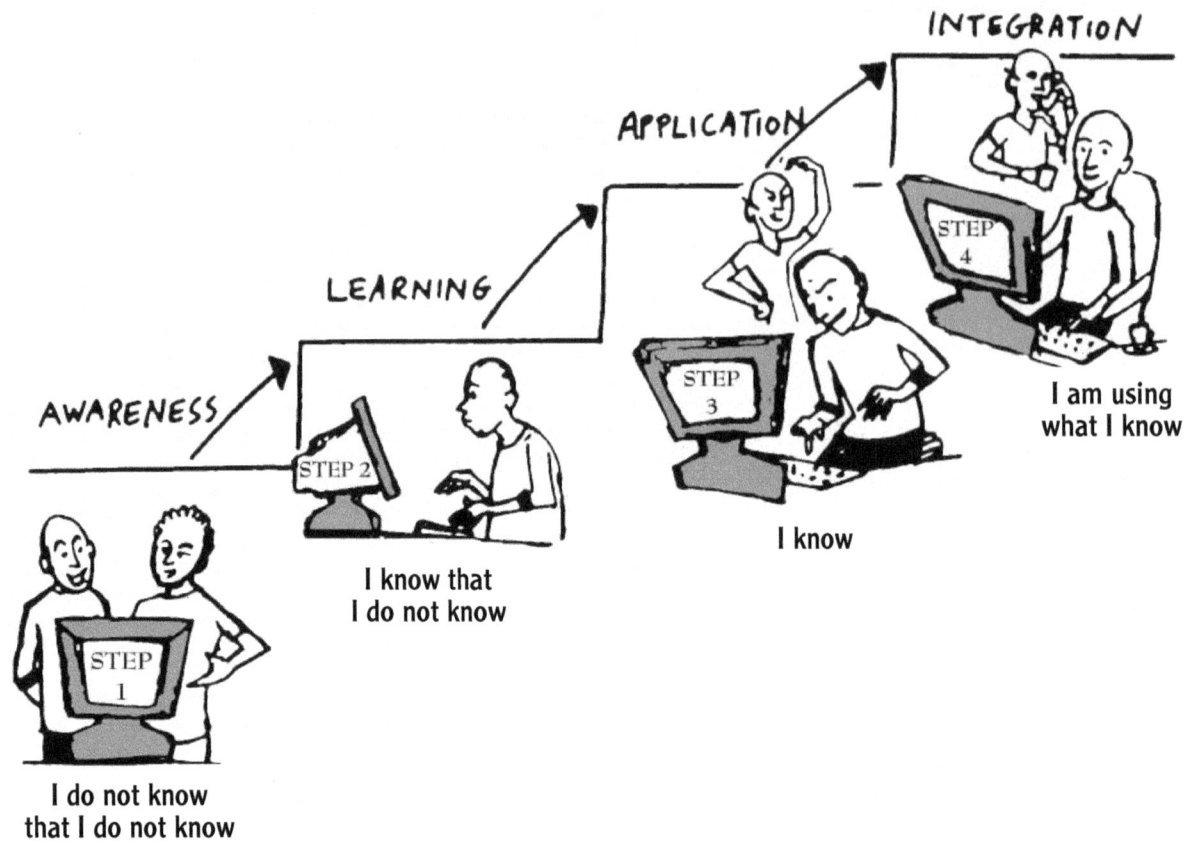

INTEGRATION

APPLICATION

LEARNING

AWARENESS

STEP 1

STEP 2

STEP 3

STEP 4

I do not know
that I do not know

I know that
I do not know

I know

I am using
what I know

Step 1. We become aware that there is something we don't know, that we want to know, for example, learning how to use a computer or furthering our knowledge about our community's history. Awareness comes through self-reflection or with the help of someone else and prompts us to move to Step 2.

Step 3. This begins with this sense of knowing, and we begin to apply this new knowledge or skill. We alter our behaviour, attitudes or relationships. This is sometimes the most difficult step, as applying what we have learned is not always easy in the real world. For example, we may decide to change a work pattern by not taking phone calls or interruptions in the mornings. However, this can cause conflict with other staff members. As we apply our learning, it also may feel unnatural and we have to continually think about what we are doing. For example, learner drivers have to consciously remember the steps for changing gears.

Step 2. We begin our learning and gain the knowledge or skill that we need. This could be through a range of learning opportunities, for example attending a computer training course, using the Internet or asking people about our community's history. As we move to Step 3 we often feel we have done some 'learning'. *We know!*

Step 4. After applying the learning repeatedly, it becomes integrated in our lives. We are using what we know spontaneously and naturally – it's part of our behaviour and lifestyle.

> *As we apply our learning, it also may feel unnatural and we have to continually think about what we are doing.*

Thinking about the four learning steps

This model suggests two key things for learning facilitators. Firstly, participants need to see the need to learn something – they must become aware that they do not know. This means that we must prepare participants for learning.

Secondly, it is at Step 4 that learning has truly taken place. People need to apply what they have learned, and integrate their learning into their own knowledge or skill-set. Processes must be designed to ensure the learning is applied in our programmes.

Preparing learners for learning – how?

Facilitators often comment: 'We can bring the horse to the river, we cannot force it to drink.' Unless learners really want to learn something they may not do so. Many people are sent on a workshop that they really don't want to attend, go through the motions of participating, say it was 'okay' and then carry on doing things as if nothing happened. We can help learners develop their intention through supporting them with questions like:

- What do you hope to learn from this workshop/session?

- What will you do to help achieve this learning?

- How will you know you have learned something?

As a learner it might help you to write a statement of what you want to learn and so contract with yourself how you will go about doing that. For example: 'I want to improve my minute-taking ability so that I can produce useful minutes that clarify exactly who will take what action.' This is sometimes called a 'learning contract'. (See our website www.barefootguide.org for more on Learning Contracts.)

Participants should also guard against sabotaging their own learning, for example by setting unrealistic goals, undermining their learning by criticising the facilitator or group, or finding fault with small things.

We also need to make sure learners are ready for the event. Do they have the required knowledge or skill? For example, an advanced computer course requires they already know the basics, or they will feel lost and will not be able to engage at the required level.

> *Write a clear statement of what you want to learn.*

> *We must prepare participants for learning.*

> *We ourselves need to develop skills and tools for our own learning journey.*

Reluctant learners

Have you ever come across a reluctant participant? I am sure you have. Sometimes people find themselves sent to a workshop and the only thing that gets them there is either a day off work or unwillingness to annoy the person who sent them.

Any sign of reluctance must be respected and worked with.

An example of reluctant learners

After attending a personal growth workshop that I had run, the Director of an NGO invited me to run the workshop for his staff, saying they would benefit from getting to know themselves and each other better.

The room we were to use had a flipchart and several tables with six chairs at each. The eighteen staff members came in and sat in the groups. I took them through my design, and gave exercises to be done individually and in pairs and groups. The tasks asked them to begin to see themselves as they really were, and how they came across to others.

As the workshop progressed, I noticed some silences and reluctance when I posed questions and then asked them to share in their groups, but I pushed on. After all, it was just the first session. It often takes participants a while to warm to this kind of process. But by the end of the session I realised there was a problem. The staff didn't want to share the personal questions – such as 'What are your ten best and ten worst qualities?' or 'What do you need most from others?' The questions pushed them into areas of sharing that they considered private and none of their colleagues' business.

In the final session of that first workshop we discussed this and agreed not to continue with the workshop over the following weeks.

It's a key aspect to address: are participants willing to engage with the workshop and its processes? We can check this at the beginning by asking about commitment to the workshop aims. Any sign of reluctance must be respected and worked with, to find out what is stopping them from engaging. This doesn't necessarily mean cancelling a workshop. It may be possible to redesign it, taking into account their feelings and resistances.

Learner responsibility

Being more aware of your own responsibility in a learning process makes you a more self-directed learner and equips you for life-long learning. This is important. Given the knowledge explosion there is always something new to learn or discover and we can't always be dependent on a teacher. While others can facilitate our learning journey, we ourselves need to develop skills and tools of our own. Understanding ourselves and our own preferred learning styles are skills we can develop.

QUESTIONS
TO THINK ABOUT

- What stopped this group from sharing at a deeper personal level?
- What comes up from your own context and experience?
- How can you as facilitator deal with such situations?

I have long believed that learners need to take more responsibility for their own learning, so when staff in our organisation asked for a workshop on Organisational Development (OD) I was determined to try something new with the group.

'Hi. Welcome to the workshop on Organisational Development. I believe that as adults, given your own experience as OD practitioners, you have important things to add to this workshop, so I want us to design and present this workshop together. We'll spend the first two sessions designing the course and then over the next ten sessions we can share the teaching.'

Shock, disbelief. 'But I came here to learn from you – to be taught.'

'Yes that's true. However, I can't begin to know as much about OD as all of you together.'

They were sceptical but agreed to give it a try. We worked for two sessions building the course content, planning and allocating roles and tasks. Out of this came a design where I taught only three sessions out of the ten and we invited in two guest lecturers for a further two. The remaining five were taught by the learners themselves. Not everyone led a session but all contributed and were highly committed to the design.

Overall it was a great success. The learners did more work than usual, particularly those who led a session and taught the remainder of us.

QUESTIONS
TO THINK ABOUT

- What are your thoughts and feelings when you read this story?
- What would you need as a facilitator to start working like this with a group?

By involving our learners from the start we encourage them to become partners with more ownership of both the content and process. They learn to become more self-directed as learners, moving from being dependent to being independent. There needs to be a desire and willingness, not only to learn, but also to plan one's own learning.

On the facilitator's part there needs to be willingness to share power over content and process. Many of us do not realise the power we hold. We can, however, break this invisible power relationship by talking openly about it. It is a real dilemma for us. Do we give all the responsibility to the learners? Do we share the responsibility? Or do we hold the control of the learning event tightly so that the learning design and process is run 'correctly'? Are we able to 'let go' of some areas – and rather share and develop the learners' capabilities?

However, the dilemma is that learners tend to want things delivered, and are often happy with the power exercised, even though they do not call it 'power'. Rather they see it as the facilitator's 'job'.

Tell me

One of the challenges we face as facilitators is that our participants often expect us to 'give' them all the knowledge or skills that they may need.

I was training a group of our fieldworkers about the use of groups and group dynamics. They were all experienced facilitators coming for further training. I set up the room with a semi-circle of chairs. The fieldworkers came in talking amongst themselves. I stood up at the front of the room and greeted them. From the smiles on their faces and the silence in the room I realised they were eager to learn. I started the workshop with some introductory remarks. I talked about the idea that there was a lot of experience and knowledge in the room, they were all experienced practitioners and therefore their contributions were also important to our learning process. Then I asked what they knew about group dynamics and what they wanted to learn.

Silence!

I looked at the group and they looked at me. It was clear that they were waiting for me to begin – to tell them. 'Do you use groups in your work?' I asked.

'Yes' some answered.

'So what are the problems you face?' I continued. A few problems emerged. 'How can you tackle these?'

Silence!

Even after a few exercises and group discussion it was clear that when it came to the 'theory' of how groups worked, they believed that I 'knew' and that they didn't. Therefore I must tell them everything.

> As we get to know what they bring it gives us starting points for any learning intervention.

Participants bring their experience, skills and theories of how things work to a learning experience. We can help them recognise and value all this as a rich resource. As we get to know what they bring it gives us starting points for any learning intervention. We can also draw on this during the learning process by making connections to what is happening in the event itself. This looping back helps make the connection between new knowledge or skills and what the participant already knows or is skilled in.

QUESTIONS
TO THINK ABOUT

- Have you as facilitator experienced this 'waiting to be told'? If so, what did you do?

- What could have been done to draw the participants' knowledge and experiences in more?

Where does theory and knowledge fit in?

Paulo Freire described most education as 'Banking Education'– learners just wait for the educator to 'deposit' the knowledge in their brains. This creates dependency. Unless we encourage our learners to actively create their own knowledge, through a process of reflection and awareness (he called this conscientisation), we keep our learners dependent. Participants must learn from their own experiences, learn how to use resources (both people and books) and then be helped to integrate new findings with what they already know.

Given the amount of knowledge and information in the world we need to learn how to make links between what we know (inside of us) and what is outside of us. It's about connecting these two sets of knowledge in ways that are useful. We need to limit the outside flow of knowledge if we are not to be overwhelmed.

Facilitators are also challenged on how best to share their knowledge so that learners can make it their own. We can show and tell, but we can also write as a way of sharing.

Writing to support learning

One of the ways to reflect and integrate our learning, and to share our knowledge, is through writing. We put down thoughts and ideas and play with them, develop them, clarify and ultimately see what is there. A tool we can use for process writing is 'learning journals'. They are a record and help us keep track of learning along the way. In a workshop, you can use a learning journal to identify questions you still have, things you have learned and ideas that need further exploration. (See our website www.barefootguide.org for more on learning journals.)

Ensure that learning is applied by the learner

We saw in the four-step learning model that it is only as we begin to apply the learning that it becomes integrated into our life. For example, a manager who goes on a workshop and learns some new strategies will need to integrate these into her already 'in use' managerial style. This may cause conflict requiring unlearning, or may enhance her managerial capability.

We can help participants and ourselves to apply our learning by asking:

1. What do we now know or what have we learned?
2. What are our first steps as we apply this new learning? What will we do or say?
3. What will support or block our learning being applied successfully?
4. How can we deal with these blocks?

Writing down the answers helps commit us to make the learning our own.

A key aspect in application will most likely be 'unlearning'. Unlearning is difficult, as the learning we need to let go of has become a habit, part of our way of being and acting in the world. As facilitators, we need to provide a safe space for participants to try out new learning and work through the pain of letting go the old. (See also Barefoot Guide 1, page 141, and U-process, page 112.)

CHAPTER 13

Mirror, Mirror:
knowing and changing yourself

I thought I already knew myself

It was my fourth job in life, I was in my mid-forties and thought of myself as quite grown-up, with plenty of life experience. I had just ended my first marriage after many years of exploring what was going on within me, and in my relationships. Now my organisation wanted me to go on a training in Human Dynamics, which is an approach to learning more about how people function, and differences between people. But I was not really interested. I felt that I knew myself well because I had been through several kinds of psychotherapy, both as a client and as a student. I didn't feel open to being confronted once again with my limitations and weaknesses.

But I had to go. Despite my misgivings, after half a day I was fully involved. It was a shock to identify myself with one of the personality dynamics (there are six different ones). Yet I was pleasantly surprised because I wasn't confronted with limitations and weaknesses, but with qualities and strengths. Instead I was given a different picture. Yes, this was me, with my drives, my way of communicating, my logic and my way of problem-solving. And I felt appreciated and valued.

Afterwards, co-operating with colleagues who were aware of their own, and my, personality dynamic was a great experience. Our revealed differences didn't lead to irritation; it encouraged fruitful dialogue. It was truly an experience of being valued only because of the person I am. And I learned never to say again, 'I know myself'! Yes, I knew myself to some extent. But a new way of looking also gave new insights. In future that can happen again; I am never too old to learn.

This chapter is about taking up the challenge for each of us to learn more about ourselves. Why should we do that? How does that contribute to learning and to social change? What route does the journey of self-knowledge and personal growth take? What can we use on that journey? I describe processes that happen in daily life, that you will easily recognise. I give you some suggestions and signposts. Some models are also good to use with others: friends, family, colleagues or community members.

To start this journey of self-knowledge, let's begin with some direct questions.

- **How do you describe yourself?**
- **And how do others describe you?**
- **Are these two descriptions different?**

QUESTION
TO THINK ABOUT

- How do you think people and society change?

QUESTION
TO THINK ABOUT

- Where does your own drive to learn and change come from?

Social change comes through individual change

People and groups are social beings. We each have a strong drive to belong to a group and to interact with others. We belong to families, communities, organisations. Things are changing in these systems all the time. Some people leave the system, some people enter; people themselves change and connections between people change. When an individual changes, the configuration of the system changes and it follows that this will, one way or another, influence the system. Exactly what impact the change has on your family, community or organisation, on their habits and ways of doing things, is another question.

It is clear that a system cannot change without individuals in it changing, and a number of people need to change to make a visible difference in that system. If you, and your neighbour or colleague don't change, nothing will happen.

Individual agency and personal leadership

Agency is about the individual: a person's action, will, intentionality, choice and freedom. It refers to the inborn capacity of each of us to act independently and to make our own free choices.

Personal leadership has nothing to do with a position or a title. It has to do with our attitude and how we see our role in life. It is the desire to take charge of our own life, being the captain of your own ship. It is strongly reflected in the catchphrase: 'Before I seek to change or motivate others I must first learn to change and motivate myself'.

Rediscovering our drive to learn

Learning – despite school teaching!

'We all know that children learn despite school teaching.'

I was astonished to hear this. It was the first meeting, on the first day, of my first job in the educational sector. A really experienced practitioner who had supported teachers and school teams for years said this. Others in the meeting nodded. He continued:

'When will we stop hindering their natural development by forcing our theories and systems on them?'

Self-awareness is the ability to know (facts) and understand (see the processes, work with the facts) oneself. It is thus connected to learning. Why is that so? A little child is not aware of him or herself and yet is naturally driven to learn and develop. Learning and developing happen when you support an enabling environment. Somehow, in growing up, we lose much of this natural drive and energy. For example, we are educated to not ask questions and to accept given answers. Or we are educated to give only the right answers and so we become shy and afraid to speak up. Or we are educated to behave like a 'real girl', not supposed to climb trees or to participate in a discussion, so we *unlearn* bringing our true voice.

As adults we have to again find the connection with our inborn drives to know, to develop and to improve. That is why we need self-awareness and self-reflection.

> As adults we have to again find the connection with our inborn drives to know, to develop and to improve.

QUESTION
TO THINK ABOUT

- What things inhibit your drive to learn and grow?

Drives and motivation

According to Coenraad van Houten in his 1999 book, *Awakening the Will: Principles and Processes in Adult Learning*, there are three primary 'drives' inside all human beings, drives that feed the learning process. These are the:

- **Drive for knowledge** – the continual need to understand ourselves and the world we live in.
- **Drive for development** – the basic force of our spirit which shapes and reshapes us as we grow.
- **Drive for improvement** – this stems from a deep inner sense that things could be done better, that we are on a path, not yet at the destination.

Talking about 'the force of our spirit' and 'a deep inner sense' connects to a kind of learning, other than school learning. It connects to our values, our beliefs, to the resources that keep us going and to what we see as our task in life.

The issue of motivating people to learn has to do with these kinds of questions. To express oneself and open up with others about drives, passion, values and vision is highly motivating. Cultures, education or personalities can be very diverse in a group, yet the members can at the same time find common ground in motivation and drives.

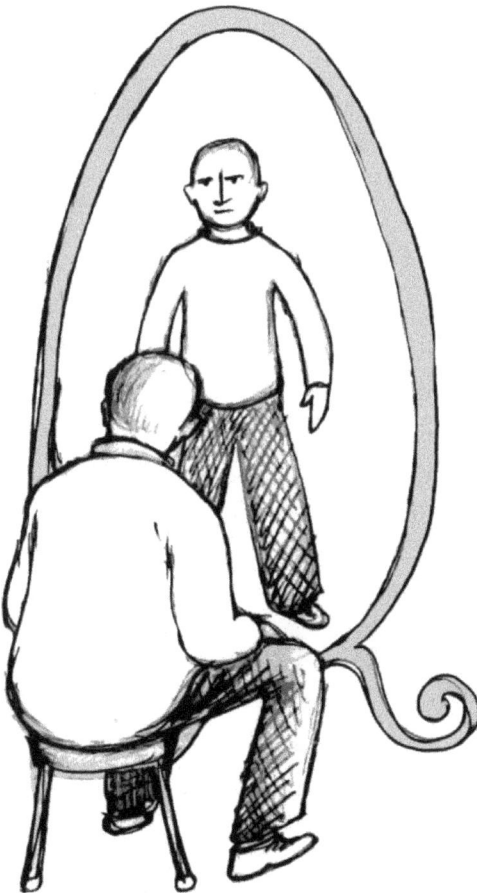

Deep listening to yourself

Barefoot Guide 1, page 30, speaks about listening to our heads (thoughts), hearts (feelings) and feet (will) together, and discusses the challenges of listening at the three levels.

Firstly, people all have their own ways of seeing the world and thinking about things. Be careful not to assume they see things the way you do. Secondly, listening to someone's true feelings gives you important clues about what really matters to them. And thirdly, listening at the level of will is where resistance to change is usually found and where the drive for change can be awakened. Helping people to listen to, and transform, their own will is one of the deepest challenges of change.

Deep listening to others is a highly-valued ability when working with people. But what does it mean in connection with you? What is 'deep listening to yourself'? It is about being aware of yourself as a whole person, with head, heart and feet. It means noticing what you *feel* about a certain situation or a certain person, but also noticing what your *thoughts* are too. What comes up first, your feelings or your thoughts, and what is the connection between the two? Once you are aware, how are you able to change your reaction?

And what about your impulse for *doing*? Do you know your will, what you really want, and is it easy for you to express what that is?

Thoughts and feelings – which changes which?

The answer to this question is that it seems to be easier to first change your thoughts, and your feelings then naturally change at the same time. It is quite amazing to experience changing your feelings and attitudes by *consciously* changing your thoughts, because we usually think this works the other way around. Yet, it is all about finding another way to look at things, how you tell the story. Which angle do you choose? Do you say the glass is half empty and you feel sad about that? Or do you say the glass is half full and you feel happy?

Another aspect connected to deep listening to yourself is the ability to become silent. To make space for your inner voice, or even your inner voices. The section below explains this further.

Diversity within yourself

If you are like most people, you experience never-ending discussions with yourself, in your mind, especially when you are supposed to make a choice. There is always a voice 'on the one hand' and a voice 'on the other hand' or even a third or a fourth voice. Each of us has a whole community of voices in our heads, often talking at the same time!

When you pay careful attention you can describe some voices. You understand that one voice is you being a 'good family member'. The other is you being the 'responsible volunteer'. And the third one is you being a 'playful child'. And we have many more. Most of us are more or less familiar with the father or mother voice: the severe conscience. More diverse are the voices of, for example, 'the brave fighter' or 'the jealous sister'. How you name the different voices is up to you – it is how you recognise the different parts within yourself. We have experienced that a lot of people recognise the 'little child' part of themselves. The little child that can be playful, but sometimes also scared, or panicking, or longing for comfort. Some theories about personal development call this 'the inner child'.

' Another aspect connected to deep listening ... is the ability to ... make space for your inner voice... '

Work with your diversity to stay energetic

When you have a discussion in your mind about taking a decision, and hear the different voices negotiating with each other, you are aware which voice wins the battle. The winner will mostly be the one that is dominant or has the most power. Other voices aren't able to come through. We aren't even aware of some of them. This might be the case with the inner-child-voice. Yet this voice is the one that can help you to stay energetic, to stay healthy and avoid a burnout. The inner-child-voice talks about freedom, about playing, about exploration, about need for sleep or being comforted and hugged.

When you are overloaded with tasks, work too hard, start to lose your enthusiasm for almost everything and you are ignoring your inner-child-voice you still have one rescuer. That is your physical body and the signals it sends. Actually, it is also a kind of voice. It is part of deep listening to recognise the signals of your body in its need for rest, relaxation, rhythm, food and so on. When you ignore both the inner-child-voice and the signals of your body, your body and mind will start to give you very strong signals, like bad headaches, lost concentration, constant tiredness, stumbling and having accidents. You are really far on your way to collapsing. Turn around and go back! Listen for the voices that need to be empowered – let them come through. It isn't that different from your work for social change; the only difference is that you work with the diversity within yourself instead of the diversity in society.

The path of self-knowledge

Facilitators have a double task in gaining self-knowledge. On the one hand they need to know about themselves and on the other hand they need to be able to help others towards self-knowledge. The facilitator herself is the most important instrument in her work and therefore should be a 'learning facilitator of learning'. She brings her personality, her temperament and her typical way of thinking, feeling, doing and interacting in her work. These things affect her work and the people she is working with, either in courses and workshops or in other processes she is involved in. She needs to be aware of who she is and how she affects others.

How can you gain more awareness of who you are, in the sense of new insights and gaining common language to express yourself and share with others what your typical characteristics are? What can you – as facilitator of learning – use in supporting people to gain more self-knowledge and self-awareness? There are many different ways and different frameworks to guide your exploration processes towards self-knowledge.

Meditation

We have talked about listening to oneself and mentioned 'becoming silent'. This touches upon meditation. Different spiritual schools practise different forms of meditation; you might find it in your own religious context.

Biography work

Another way of getting to know more about yourself is through biography work. Biography work means working with your own story, past, present and future. From this you can gain valuable insights into what has formed you, what your patterns of behaviour are and what future challenges and strengths you have to work with.

'This work is also about seeing and being seen. To be seen is a blessing, which engenders in us new strengths to listen to our deepest calling, the courage to search for what our heart seeks and the capacity to take responsibility for our own lifepath.'

Biographywork.org website

See "The Chapters of My Life Exercise" on the BFG1 website in the Resource Centre (Chapter 2 - Inside Out)

Using models on the path of self-knowledge

Observing yourself, noticing what your thoughts, your feelings and your doubts are, keeping a diary, and becoming aware of your own personal history are actually things we can do always, everywhere. We don't have to use tools, models or instruments to learn about ourselves.

However, models or tools can be of some help. Below, we suggest two models that we like, but there are many others that are also helpful.

One warning about models: using a model is like looking at a three-dimensional reality with the help of a two-dimensional instrument. A model is only a tool to look at reality and give a common language to talk about it – it isn't reality itself. If you find, for example, that your preferred learning style is 'Theorist' it doesn't mean that you have to identify yourself as: 'I am a Theorist'. It is even more dangerous when others define you by saying 'You are a Theorist'. Human beings don't like to be put into boxes. So let's not use models to do that, but rather to give direction to growth and development. Now that I have discovered that I tend to learn in the way of a 'Theorist', I can challenge myself by looking for and using other learning styles, and so enrich the ways I act.

And when you find out from someone else that she learns in the way of an 'Activist', you can put out a friendly challenge and support her to use other styles. Never criticise, or fix on her a certain characteristic; it does not invite learning and mostly causes resistance.

A good model is useful not for its answers but when it helps us to ask ourselves better *questions*. Models are dangerous if we use them to give us *answers* – every situation in life is unique and a model cannot possibly give answers to all questions!

In the context of this Guide about learning, the model of *learning styles* is probably one of the first things to look at. In Chapter 12, *How do we learn?* you can find a description of several learning styles.

The *Barefoot Guide 1*, page 36, gives the model of the 'Four Temperaments' with background, further description and ideas of how to work with this model.

Below we introduce to you the models of Human Dynamics and Core Qualities.

> ❝ *A good model is useful not for its answers but when it helps us to ask ourselves better questions.* ❞

Managing diversity – Human Dynamics

All around, you can observe that people behave in very diverse ways. Some make contact easily and tell personal stories; others will look for a quiet corner at a meeting and will leaf through the pages of the material at hand. When a question is asked in a conversation or meeting, one person will think and frown while the other starts talking right away, and forms his reaction in the process of talking. Differences can also be seen at work. While one colleague says little during staff meetings yet afterwards wants to ask questions about a decision that's already been made, another colleague is noticing who is comfortable and at ease, busy watching carefully if everyone has had something to drink. Another colleague, uninvited, starts to speak. He asks a few questions out loud, then in the same breath presents four ideas for a new project, leaving everyone else confused. Some executives are valued for their pleasant and supportive conversations, but their plans are never realised. Other executives write clear policy plans and synopses of the annual plans, but they blunder when it comes to communicative skills. Some executives can express their view on work in impressive ways, but they fail to persuade others.

Sandra Seagal and David Horne discovered that there are fundamental differences between people that can be explained using a set of universal behavioural features and patterns. They call their model Human Dynamics.

The model refers to three principles that are present in each human being. These are the *mental* (rational, thinking) principle, the *emotional* (sensitive, relational) principle and the *physical* (practical, acting) principle.

Sandra Seagul

David Horne

HUMAN DYNAMICS
HUMAN DYNAMICS
HUMAN DYNAMICS
HUMAN DYNAMICS

This model is connected to the Threefold Human Being, as described in the Barefoot Guide 1, page 29

The theory of Human Dynamics proposes that each person has one principle that is dominant and which relates to the way the person experiences their environment and how they process information.

- People with a dominant mental principle process information in a linear and logical way. They feel comfortable being alone, don't often express their feelings, come to clarity by thinking and prefer to talk about meaningful issues.

- People with a dominant emotional principle process information in an associative way. They love to interact with people, to brainstorm new ideas, to sort out their thoughts or to share all kinds of personal experiences.

- People with a dominant physical principle process information in a systemic way. They feel a strong connection to the group they belong to. They come to clarity and solutions by viewing all different aspects of an issue and connecting it to a specific and practical goal. They like doing things with other people.

What are the benefits of using this model?

Knowledge of Human Dynamics can be useful for the interaction in a team. It offers insights into the way in which co-operation takes place between the team members with different personality dynamics. Differences in the speed of information-processing during a staff meeting become clear. You alter your communication and meeting habits.

It also increases your motivation to tackle competencies that have not yet been fully developed. Personal challenges can become clearer, once a person becomes aware of their own personality dynamic. When an executive, for example, is conscious of their personality dynamic, that knowledge may lead to more subtle, but essential, changes in leadership style.

Human Dynamics can play a significant role in helping people in a learning process. It gives direction to setting up a rich and differentiated learning environment, where it is possible to include specific needs of the different personality dynamics.

Finally Human Dynamics is useful for examining the interaction between the dynamic of a facilitator and participants of a training or a course. An emotionally-centred facilitator may find it incomprehensible that a mentally-centred participant wants to be alone, and may try to prevent it. A physically-centred trainer can be amazed and even annoyed about the need of an emotionally-centred participant to discuss everything during a training session.

More about this model can be found on the *Barefoot Guide* website.

Core Qualities

Core Qualities is a model created by Daniel Ofman. He believes that every person has a few core qualities – qualities that have always been part of you but that you are hardly aware of. For you this quality is so self-evident that you think that everyone has it or should be able to show it. Core qualities are, for example: patience, persistence, caring, decisiveness and flexibility.

Strengthening core qualities is called empowerment and this can be done by using the 'core quadrant'. The quadrant has four concepts: qualities, pitfalls, challenges and allergies.

The *pitfall* is when the quality is 'too much of a good thing'. When the positive quality goes too far, the strength turns into weakness. For example, 'flexible' becomes 'inconsistent'. But note that on the other hand, behind every 'negative' pitfall you can find a positive quality!

The core quality and the *challenge* are complementary. The point here is that your core quality is always dominant. The way to avoid this situation – stepping into your pitfall – is to develop a complementary quality that gives balance. What is the positive opposite of the pitfall? Being inconsistent is negative; the positive opposite is being organised. So when your core quality is 'flexibility' and you develop 'being organised', you can *avoid* being inconsistent.

The *allergy* is the negative opposite of the core quality. It is called allergy because it is 'too much' of your challenge. For example, when seeing this in your colleague, you feel 'allergic' to his behaviour. With your core quality of flexibility, you detest (are 'allergic' to) rigid people. It is difficult for you to collaborate with such a person. However this person presents you with a bit 'too much' of the quality – being organised – that you need yourself. This is, indeed, your challenge.

So the core quadrant in this situation looks like this:

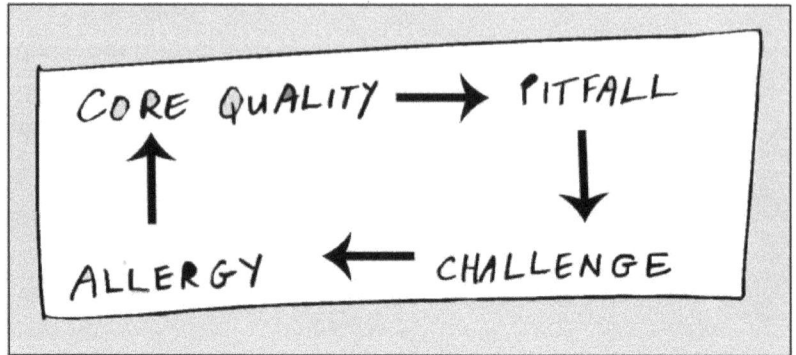

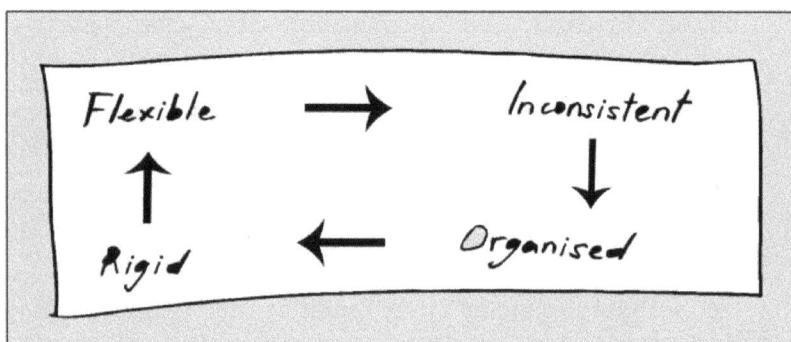

But, note that 'rigid' is, of course, your colleague's pitfall – too much of a positive quality. So the quadrant representing both of you is linked in this way:

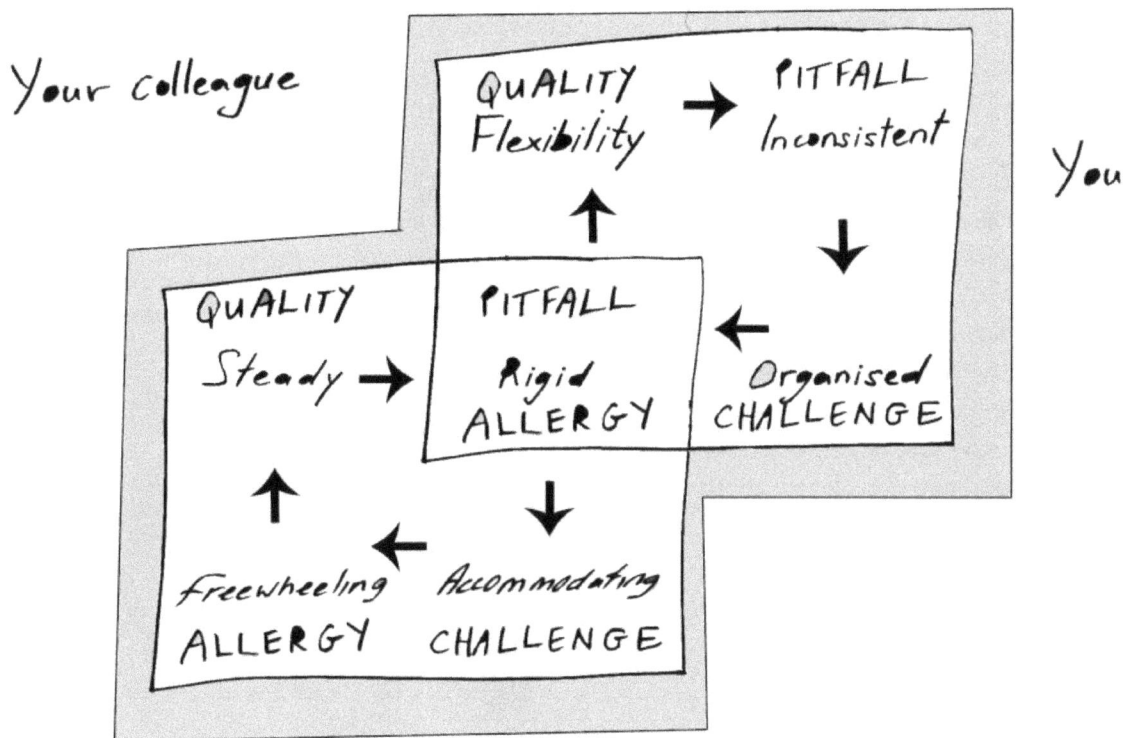

Your colleague

QUALITY
Flexibility → PITFALL
Inconsistent

You

QUALITY
Steady → PITFALL
Rigid
ALLERGY

Organised
CHALLENGE

Freewheeling
ALLERGY

Accommodating
CHALLENGE

In teams and other situations of co-operation, working with linked quadrants like this helps you to look behind the vexing behaviour of your partner and see that there is also a positive quality – in fact the quality that you have to strengthen. You have complementary qualities and can learn from each other.

How can you work with this model?

You may start by identifying your strengths (core qualities), working them out using the pitfall, the challenge and allergy, as in the example. You can also start with a challenge, reasoning back to your pitfall, and recognise the quality behind it.

Or ask friends, family or colleagues about your weaknesses (pitfalls). They are probably able to mention a few. Work back from pitfall to quality and then discover your challenge and allergy.

Are you immensely bothered by a colleague? Discover the quality behind what bothers you and what you can learn from that. You can find a challenge, pitfall and quality of yourself.

I recommend taking time with colleagues to draw up core quadrants and openly discuss allergies. This allows you to increase your level of collaboration.

You can watch Daniel Ofman himself explain the use of quadrants – Google "Daniel Ofman core qualities video"

Self-knowledge can be a collaborative process

Learning more about yourself can be difficult to do on your own. Although sometimes quite painful, being confronted by others can help you to become more aware of your behaviour, and its impact on others. People always do give you feedback, in one way or another. This is often not in clear, spoken words, but in the way they behave. They start to ignore you for example – a very clear signal of negative feedback. The problem is that you do not hear or notice the exact behaviour that was rejected, so you don't know what to change, unless you ask. Asking for feedback is a good method to learn more of yourself. Your blind spot, what you don't know about yourself, becomes smaller. The bonus is that when you combine increased self-knowledge with sharing more about yourself, others learn more about you.

Arja's friend experiences collaborative self-knowledge

A friend of mine wasn't aware of his talent to make sculptures (it was unknown to himself and to others). Shortly after his retirement he looked for something nice to do and attended a starters course on making sculptures. In this course he discovered his talent in this area (it became a private knowledge). He showed his creativity to others (brought it from private to public) and people told him they really liked what he made (they gave feedback). Nowadays he runs a shop in town, that is meanwhile his atelier (gallery), and he sells his sculptures.

When I am really absorbed in a subject or discussion, I am often acting and reacting in an impulsive way, not very fine-tuned to the other people. I tend to focus more on content than on personal issues. In different situations three colleagues let me know that they really didn't like such blunt reactions. That it actually shocked them or made them feel stupid or rejected. So by their feedback I knew that this behaviour wasn't pleasant for others, but I struggled to understand how to cope with this. I don't want to feel obliged to be nice and friendly. I come to my work to do a job, not to make friends. And I thought my colleagues should get used to my way of doing and then it would be all right. But the question was: what did I need to bring to build fruitful relationships in the context of my work? Indeed it is not about becoming friends – although it is nice when a friendship emerges. Working relationships have surprising similarities with family relationships. I have neither chosen my family nor my colleagues; I can't choose to drop them (in a work context unless I want to leave the job) and I don't like each of them equally. A striking aspect in family relations is that whatever one of your relatives will do or say, you are loyal till the end. You cannot drop your relatives, because you have blood ties. That is what we probably could bring more into work relationships. There are no blood ties, but we are tied in serving a common goal in the job. And we need to be loyal and supportive to each other. That doesn't mean avoiding giving honest feedback. Honest feedback builds open relationships. And what I learned finally in order to lessen my blunt behaviour is that it is too much of the quality of being strict. And I found my challenge in courteousness, which I now try to practise daily.

CHAPTER 14

Writing to learn – learning to write

Not everybody loves writing. But I do. Some people know what they think before they write. Not me. I love writing because it helps me separate myself from the blur of my busy life. I love writing because it helps me to see myself in the crowd and to hear my own voice above the babble of competing voices. I love writing because it helps me figure out what I think and feel, helps me peel away the husk, and reach in to where I am most alive.

Usually I write when I am alone, when the house is empty, or everyone else is asleep. I write memoir and poems. I write bits and pieces that I throw straight into the bin and I also write snippets that may grow up into a book someday. Sometimes I write on demand: 'Mamma, write a poem about the big bed,' says my daughter, and I do. I read these poems to my most appreciative audiences who laugh raucously at themselves and at me and always ask for more. 'Write about the time we had a fight in the shoe shop, Mamma…'

I also write at work, about work. I write about topics I'm researching, conferences I've attended, about projects I want to do, and projects I've done. I write about my practice and about the six months just past. I write about my colleagues and the colours of the carpet under the table in our meeting room. I write to find out more about myself and my topic and the relationship between the two. And I try to ground even this kind of writing in my own experience of whatever topic I am writing about.

What's in this chapter?

I describe some of the thinking behind my approach to writing and offer some practical tips to help you write to explore, enquire and learn.

I also outline the phases of writing, when writing for others. I hope this will be helpful to those interested in writing papers, articles, stories – even poems – intended to contribute to other people's learning as well as your own.

Writing to learn

Writing has become so central to how I *make sense* of what is going on in my life and my work as a development practitioner that I often ask myself, 'How will I know what I think until I see what I write?' Writing to learn, or writing to find out, is quite different to sitting down to record what we already know, what somebody else has said, or what we have read somewhere. When writing to learn we have to adopt the attitude of an explorer. We must be willing to take risks, to journey into the unknown and to discover new things, or discover things anew. In this approach, writing is a kind of *inquiry* process.

Writing helps us to *reflect* deeply on our experiences, personal and professional. Through writing, our return to the experience is much more vivid because we add detail to what we remember. By describing the characters involved, the setting, the process *and* the feelings of it all – including our own feelings – we bring it alive again.

When we stop to make sense of a particular experience, or time in our life, or phase of a project, writing helps to unpack, let go … and let come. By this I mean allowing ourselves to be *surprised* by what we write. It is easy to tell and re-tell our experience from the safety of the familiar point of view – even when telling it to ourselves. Repeating the same version of an experience or event confirms our beliefs and reinforces our position. But it also closes us down to seeing things in different ways. Writing to learn requires us to take risks, to make ourselves vulnerable, to be uncertain, playful, creative, and even uncomfortable at times.

First thoughts

One way to do this is to pay attention to our first thoughts. First thoughts are literally those thoughts we think of first. First thoughts flash through our mind and are then quickly rejected by all the norms we have internalised, the rules about what we can and can't think, feel or say. Natalie Goldberg, in her 1986 book *Writing Down The Bones*, says, 'First thoughts are those thoughts your mind actually sees and feels, not what it *thinks* it should see and feel.'

Writing this way helps us bypass the clever, safe or expected answers – the answers we think others want to hear. It helps us to go behind the correct, polite or public version to find our own *voice* and our own authority. It helps us to bypass cautious writing.

NATALIE GOLDBERG

Different perspectives

Another way to write about our experiences is from different perspectives. For example, try writing a totally different opinion to your own on something that matters to you. Write convincingly, as if you really believe in what you are writing. Or write about something that happened from another person in the story's point of view. Choose someone that was part of your experience, or make up a character. Imagine you are them. Write a dialogue with one of the characters in your story – perhaps it's a difficult colleague, or a powerful person in the community you work with, or an elder you'd like to seek counsel from. 'Talk' directly with them. Tell them what it is you really want to say and then give them a chance to talk back to you, as if it were a real conversation. Talk to each other about a situation that disturbs, puzzles or delights you; a situation or experience you want to learn from.

Authority on a topic is often seen as belonging to the experts and the academics. It's easy to be put off writing about something because there's a voice asking: 'What do *you* know about it?' But there is also the kind of authority that belongs with the practitioner. The 'knowledge-of-the-doers'. And by writing to learn, we can tap that source of knowledge, making it more available to ourselves, and then perhaps also to others.

Often, when I pose these exercises in a writing workshop, people respond by saying: 'Oh, but I really don't know what she would say.' Or, 'Gosh, I don't really know what I want to ask!' Write to find out. Somebody else might object, saying, 'But if I make it up, then it's not real. It's just invented, or imaginary.' And I reply: 'Does it matter?'

You are not a minute-taker taking minutes of a meeting, or a court record keeper whose records are used in making judgement and passing sentence. You are not publishing an article or betraying confidences. You are a writer writing to explore, to find out, to learn.

The basic principle in this approach to writing is to write to discover what you think and how you feel. This is totally contrary to the 'think first then write' approach you were probably taught at school. How can you learn to write this other way? Here are a few tools and practical tips drawn from my own writing journey.

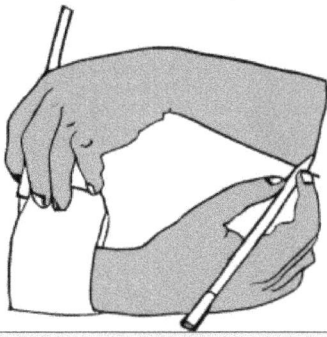

'Attempting to create distinction between fact and fiction is a waste of time with regards to reflective practice. Any writing is writing from the practitioner's depth of experience, knowledge and skill. This experience, knowledge and skill is as true as you can get: in the way a straight line is true.'

Gillie Bolton

Learning to write

Free writing: a basic tool

I have found free writing to be my most useful writing tool. Free writing is a simple writing technique which involves writing without stopping for a set amount of time. To begin with, write for five or six minutes, and later, after some practice, you can go on for fifteen to twenty minutes at a time. When free writing, you are not in control – your pen or pencil is. Let your pen decide what it wants to write and follow its lead: think of it as a *magic pen*. When free writing, keep your hand moving, and don't stop. This helps writing become the thought process.

Usually we like to know what we are going to write before we start writing. We want to have it all figured out in our heads. With free writing we listen out for what we are meant to write and, in a way, let our writing write through us. Free writing helps us write down our first thoughts, before we can stop ourselves by saying, 'Oh that is so ridiculous'. It helps us override the inner critic who criticises everything we write as rubbish and stops us writing even before we have begun.

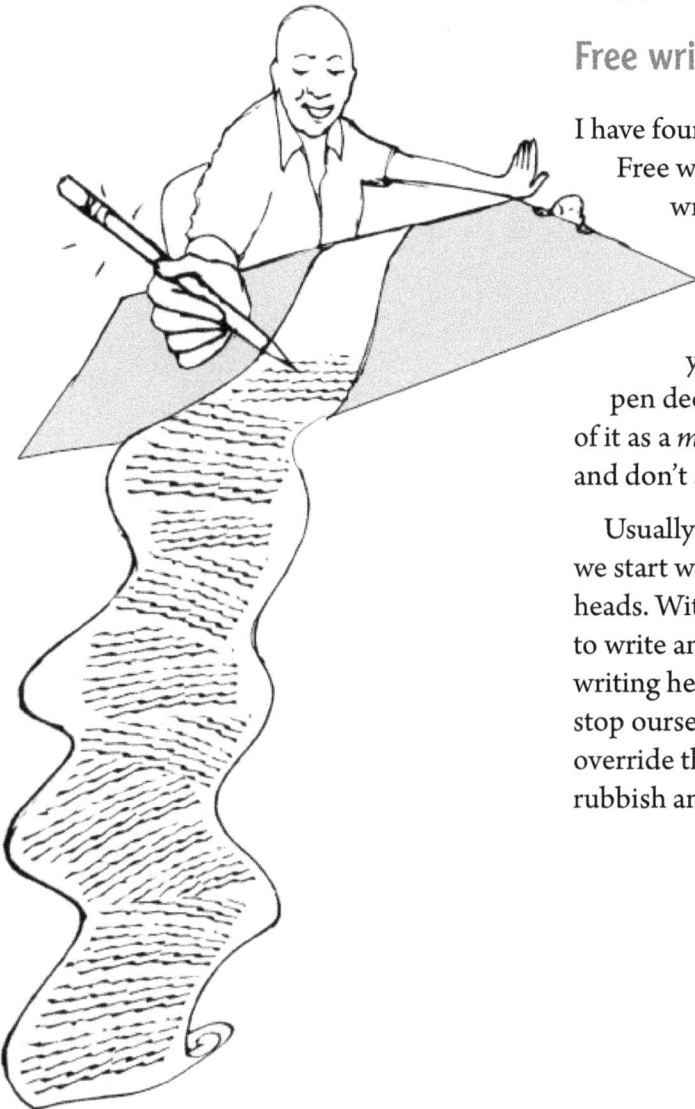

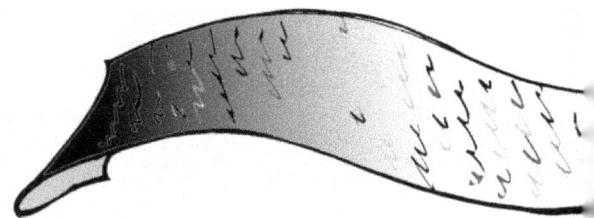

When free writing, write *by hand*. It will route your writing through your heart! Try it for yourself – somehow there is a more personal connection with your writing than when writing on a computer. Writing by hand also helps keep you from worrying about spelling and grammar mistakes – no automatic spelling or grammar check to light up your page and distract you with those red and green squiggles!

Once you are done free writing, take a few minutes to read over what you have written and to underline words, phrases or sentences that you like in colour pencil. This helps you to develop an appreciative eye. Also look for and underline what unsettles or disturbs you. There is often something important there. You may want to write more on one of the words, phrases or sentences you underlined. Do so, or save them as prompts for future free writing.

Free writing with a prompt

Free writing can be open (sometimes called a writing 'spree' or stream of consciousness writing) or it can be focused by using a prompt. A prompt is a short phrase or question which sets you off in a particular direction – even if you land up going on a detour! Three prompts I enjoy are:

- Today I …

- I remember …

- I see …

You can also choose a particular topic or theme that you want to learn more about as your prompt. By free writing on a topic, you can uncover what you *intuitively* know about it, what you 'know-you-know' about it, what you think about it and how you feel about it. Free-write on a real life experience, a specific example of the topic rather than a broad, generalised description. Don't write about 'ownership' or 'participation' or 'learning' in general. Write about your experience of ownership, participation, or learning. Take a specific example as your starting point.

> By free writing on a topic, you can uncover what you intuitively know about it…

When I began to work more closely with colleagues within my own organisation, issues around relationships and collaboration became more pronounced. I found it really useful to explore what was going on by free writing about it. Much later, I was asked to write a paper on collaboration for a client organisation and found these pieces I had written, purely for my own learning, helpful in identifying key themes to pursue.

Before learning about free writing I would spend way too much time deciding which example, which incident, which moment to choose as my starting point. Say for example the task was to write about a significant event … I would sometimes panic and go blank. (I don't think anything significant has ever happened in my life! I really only have a very boring and insignificant life.) Or I would torment myself trying to figure out which was the most significant, the most worthy, the most interesting and so on. I would make a hundred false starts, skipping from one event to another and then give up, defeated. With free writing the agony of choice is avoided and feeling blank is an advantage: with free writing you really have to let go and follow your pen.

Free writing without a prompt

Free writing without a prompt is a great way to begin a writing session. It helps to get the creative flow going, and provides an opportunity to write down all the stuff which is cluttering up your head and preoccupying your mind. In short, it helps you to be present and attentive in your writing. Whether I am writing by myself, or running a writing workshop, I often begin with a six minute free writing spree. Once you are done, you take a few minutes to read over what you have written and underline what you like. You may be amazed by what you find: a theme emerging, an important question to face or perhaps even the glimpse of an answer. You may, however, find that nothing but mixed-up nonsense comes out. Or perhaps a long to-do list. It is all fine – better out on the page than taking up space in your mind.

Writing for others

Exploratory writing is hugely valuable for people wanting to learn. But there is a second chapter to my story on writing. This chapter is about writing for others, about conveying what we have learned in a way that is useful to them and has *effect* on them. In this chapter, the main character (you) is now the guide, rather than the explorer, and in this new role, you have additional skills to acquire and work to do.

Sometimes, when I am in the middle of an article, somebody will ask why I am writing about it at all when the libraries and the internet are so full of information already. It's always a bit of a discouraging question – yet it's true. We live in an age of information overload, more information that we can possibly handle. But a lot of it is just that: information. When I write, I try to avoid cold, clinical, depersonalised writing. I try to write with voice, to share a bit of who I am and the sense I have made of the experience or information I am writing about. In this way my writing is more likely to engage the reader, to speak to her imagination, intellect, heart and will.

My first writing assignments as a development practitioner were fund raising proposals and donor reports. How I wish I had known about free writing back then! And I bet the donors would have appreciated documents that weren't dense with dull motivations, dry accounts of who did what when, sickly sweet success stories – and of course all the jargon and development-speak of the day. I undoubtedly wrote in beige.

Free writing helps us find our voice. Writing with voice quite simply means putting yourself into your writing. So often we write in 'beige'. A beige voice could be anybody's. It lacks individuality. It is stilted. Wooden. Dead. Poet and writer Seamus Heaney said writing with voice 'means that you can get your feelings into your own words and that your words have a feeling of you about them.'

Donors

Here are some examples of more colourful writing taken from two different organisations' reports.

Reporting with stories

The aim of Cape Flats Nature in South Africa is to build good practice in sustainable management of the City of Cape Town's nature areas, in a way that benefits the surrounding communities, particularly townships where incomes are low and living conditions poor. As a pioneering partnership project, Cape Flats Nature wanted to stir up and then distil ideas among conservators, planners, officials, activists and community leaders. They also needed to account to their partners, donors and community members. They decided, instead of a report, to write a booklet that included a number of very short stories. Here are two stories based on long and detailed field reports.

Feathered friends

Holiday programme. Flocks of bored youth looking for entertainment. Calls of excitement. Bird monitoring is a scientific task. Results must be reliable. Everyone and no-one wants to be involved. Long term. Only five volunteers serve as bird monitors. But they too migrate. The monitoring group grinds to a halt before take off even happens. Another year, another group, another bird club, this one in full flight. Track down the missing monitors, bring the groups together, more training, on-going support, endless encouragement. Watch them fly.

Going shopping 1

It's about six. Getting dark. I send the kids out. For potatoes. Or cabbage. Or bread. They come back, big eyes, empty hands. Hungry. We search in all the usual places. Five Rand. Enough for something from Sparkies Corner Café. It will take me half the time if I use the path across the veld.

Going shopping 2

The people using the path are just going shopping.
They are just not interested, have no idea about biodiversity.
And they are a fire hazard.
The path definitely has to be rerouted.
But the community reps have specifically asked to keep it. We're supposed to be attracting these people into nature conservation, not shutting them out.

Going shopping 3

Why did you change your mind?
I read that newspaper story.
……..?
About the girl who got mugged going shopping.
It could have happened anywhere.
We had another meeting with all the stakeholders: we decided to keep it open access.

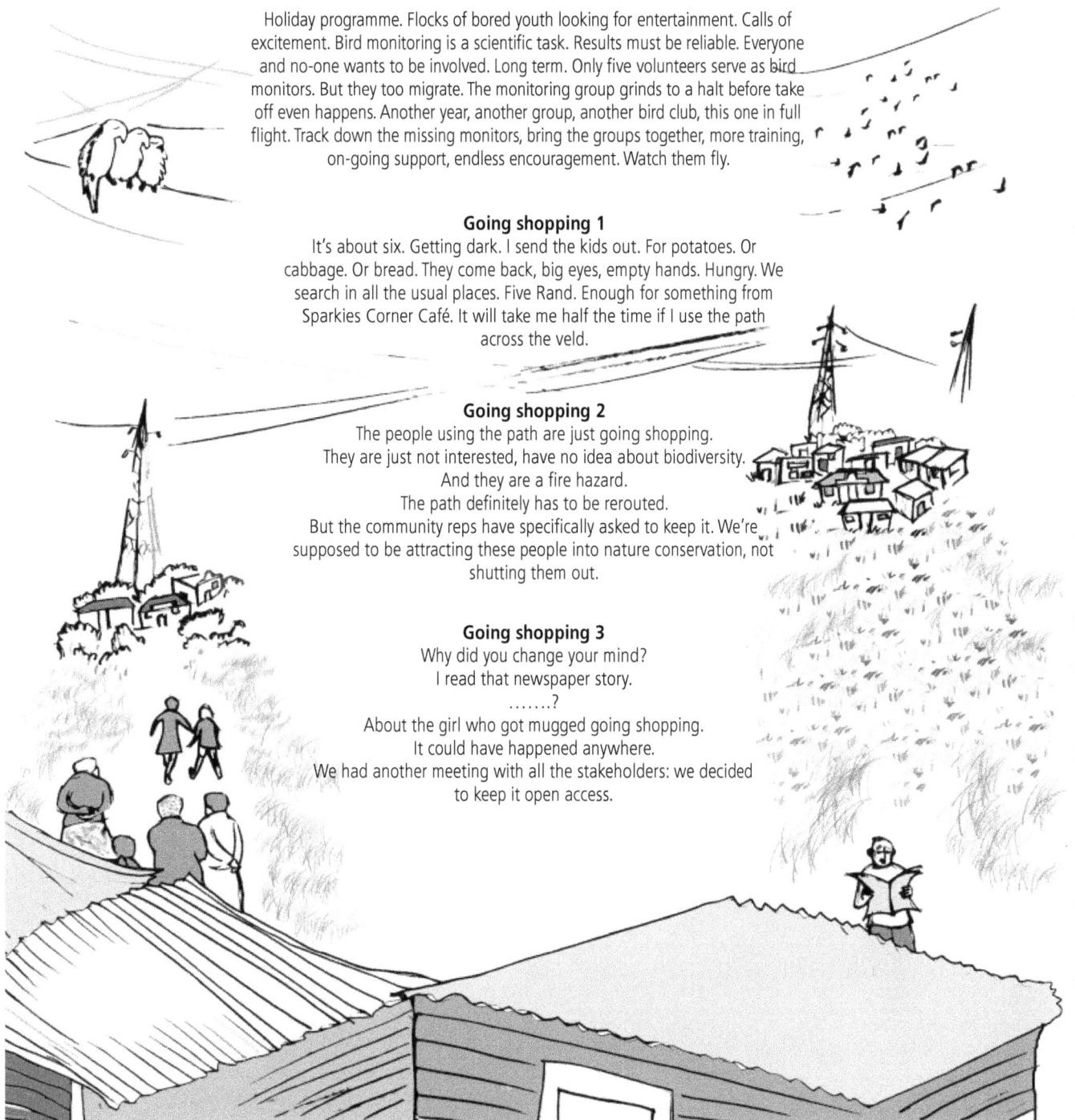

WWW.BAREFOOTGUIDE.ORG

Telling the organisation's story

The Environmental Monitoring Group hadn't written an annual report for six years. Yes, they had accounted to donors and met all those requirements, but they really wanted to account to *all* those they were connected with. They wanted to share a little of who they were as an organisation and what they had learned. The staff collaborated on the task, commissioned a writing workshop and help in pulling all their material together.

What do you do?

What do you do?
Many things at the same time

Today you are here, tomorrow you are there
Most days I am supposed to be everywhere
This meeting and that meeting
This person and that person

What do you do?
Many things at the same time

This document and that document
This website and that website
This email and that email
This book and that book

What do you do?
Many things at the same time

This call and that call
This workshop and that workshop
This conference and that conference
This seminar and that seminar

What do you do?
Many things at the same time

This EIA and that EIA
This training and that training
This funder and that funder
This injustice and that injustice

What do you do?

By Thabang Ngcozela

I'm sitting on the ground, in the cool shade of a tree in a village in rural Uganda. Next to me is a young woman, beautiful in her best floral dress. Then an older woman joins us. There is a clear tension between them that I can feel but don't understand. There are children all around. Godfrey, my guide and translator, explains to them that we are here to listen to their story, and that we would like to take photographs. 'I have been here before,' I said, 'and I took photos then.' That was five years ago. I tell them how I have used those pictures at conferences and workshops – to try to show how stupid and insensitive educated 'decision-makers' can be, to show how worthless a policy paper is when it is not translated into a language people can understand, to show the difference between good intentions and the dismal failure of their actual implementation.

I am sitting on the ground, under a tree. The young woman next to me has three children. She is the second wife, sharing one house. Now I understand the tension between her and the older woman. They begin to talk. 'When the American company built the resettlement village they said we would only get one new house per family, no matter how many of our houses were flooded by the dam. But what is a family? Is it a man and his many wives or is it a woman with her many children?'

I had extended my stay in Uganda to revisit this village. It had been built to house people who had to make way for the rising waters of the new dam, people whose lives and communities were turned upside down so that the city could get more electricity. I was here to listen and to take the photographs that I hoped would speak louder and more clearly than my words ever could – about life as it should not be.

My colleagues from the African Rivers Network and I had arrived to a day filled with so much ceremony. The beautiful children in their shiny dresses and not so shiny shorts sang, 'This land is my land, this land is your land, from the Ruwenzories to the Eastern Highlands, this land belongs to you and me.'

And I wished it did. This land they just lost. This land that was taken away from them – close to the river, close to the road, close to the fishing grounds and markets and relatives and graves and shrines and clinics and history and schools and all the things that make everyday life worth getting out of bed for to say 'I will live another day'.

The World Bank, who financed the dam, said that the people would be better off than they were before the dam was built, and that adequate compensation would be given – land for land. But the people say a structure for a structure. A school for a school. A clinic for a clinic. A fruit tree for a fruit tree. It's so obvious. You don't need degrees or pieces of paper to understand this, to put yourself in their shoes. You just need common sense, wisdom, compassion.

'Can you imagine what it's like living with two wives under one roof?' The man showed me the tiny bedroom where one wife sleeps and the open-plan living room where the other wife sleeps. He talked about his former spacious homestead where each wife had her own hut, now drowned by the dam waters.

I asked the two women under the tree: 'What is it like?'

'Difficult,' they said, not looking at each other.

'Very, very difficult,' the older wife said when the younger wife had walked away. 'Very difficult.'

By Liane Greeff

The writing process

One of the things that discourages new writers is the high standard of writing they see around them in books, in journals, in pieces *other* people have written. What they often don't consider, is that they are seeing the *finished product* and have not been party to the endless drafts, the frustrations, the pages tossed in the bin – sometimes even tears! If you don't expect to write your final product the first time you sit down to write, you will be a much happier writer.

Writing is a process. Of course the process takes different routes for different writers. After a while you may begin to recognise your own preferences, patterns and approach to writing. Some people have a favourite time of day to write, some a favourite place or a favourite pen. Some like quiet. Some like to write in a busy restaurant. Some write a piece in one go then leave it lying for weeks before going back to it. Some people work steadily on a writing project. Some people feel compelled to write about something – as if it were inside them banging to get out. Others may have a strong urge to write, but have no idea what about. Some people are reluctant writers, obliged to write for work purposes, looking for any and every possible distraction to postpone it until tomorrow.

When writing something for others, you may find it helpful to think of the writing process as a journey with a beginning, middle and end. In the *beginning* the writer's emphasis is on exploring her topic by writing about it, reading about it, speaking to others about it. It includes all the research she needs to do – but most importantly it's about actually beginning to write (not just thinking about writing or planning to write, or tidying her desk, but actually writing). In the *middle* of the writing process the writer reworks his draft having read it with both an appreciative and a critical eye. It may be necessary to rework it a number of times. Feedback from trusted others helps the writer see his writing with an outside eye. Perhaps his main points are not clear. Perhaps they are lost in too many words. Perhaps he is writing in beige and needs to let his own voice and personality into his writing. At the *end*, the writer's focus is on polishing her text. She pays attention to small, but important details and gets it ready to be printed, published or distributed.

Novelist and non-fiction writer Anne Lamott refers to these three main phases as the down draft, the up draft and the dental draft.

The down draft

When writing something for others to read, I begin with exploratory writing. For example I might free-write for six minutes about my feelings on the topic (feelings, not thoughts), beginning with the prompt 'I feel…'. Or I might begin by free-writing a story, taking a specific example as my starting point.

Other prompts I find really useful at the beginning of writing a paper, article, or report for others are:

- I really want to write this story because …

- The real issue I want to capture or explore is in this article is …

- The questions my report answers are …

- The purpose of this paper is to …

You can also begin by brainstorming a list of words or phrases associated with your topic. Choose three or four of the most important or significant words and/or phrases and free-write for six to ten minutes on each of the words or phrases you have chosen. After each piece of writing, stop and read over your work, underline what you like, what surprises or bothers you. Then write a twenty to fifty word summary of all your free writing, beginning with the prompt: 'My topic (or story) is about …'. Writing a title for your article, report or story will further help to identify the crux or heart of what you want to say.

I sometime use a timed mind-mapping exercise at the beginning of a writing assignment. It's timed so that I am under pressure and have to work with first thoughts and random associations. To create a mind map, draw a circle in the centre of your page and write your (topic) key word or phrase in the middle. Then radiating out from the centre circle write words or short phrases you associate with your key word, drawing linkage lines where appropriate. A mind map doesn't generate the depth or quality of writing that free writing does, but it is a great technique for creating an overview, and for

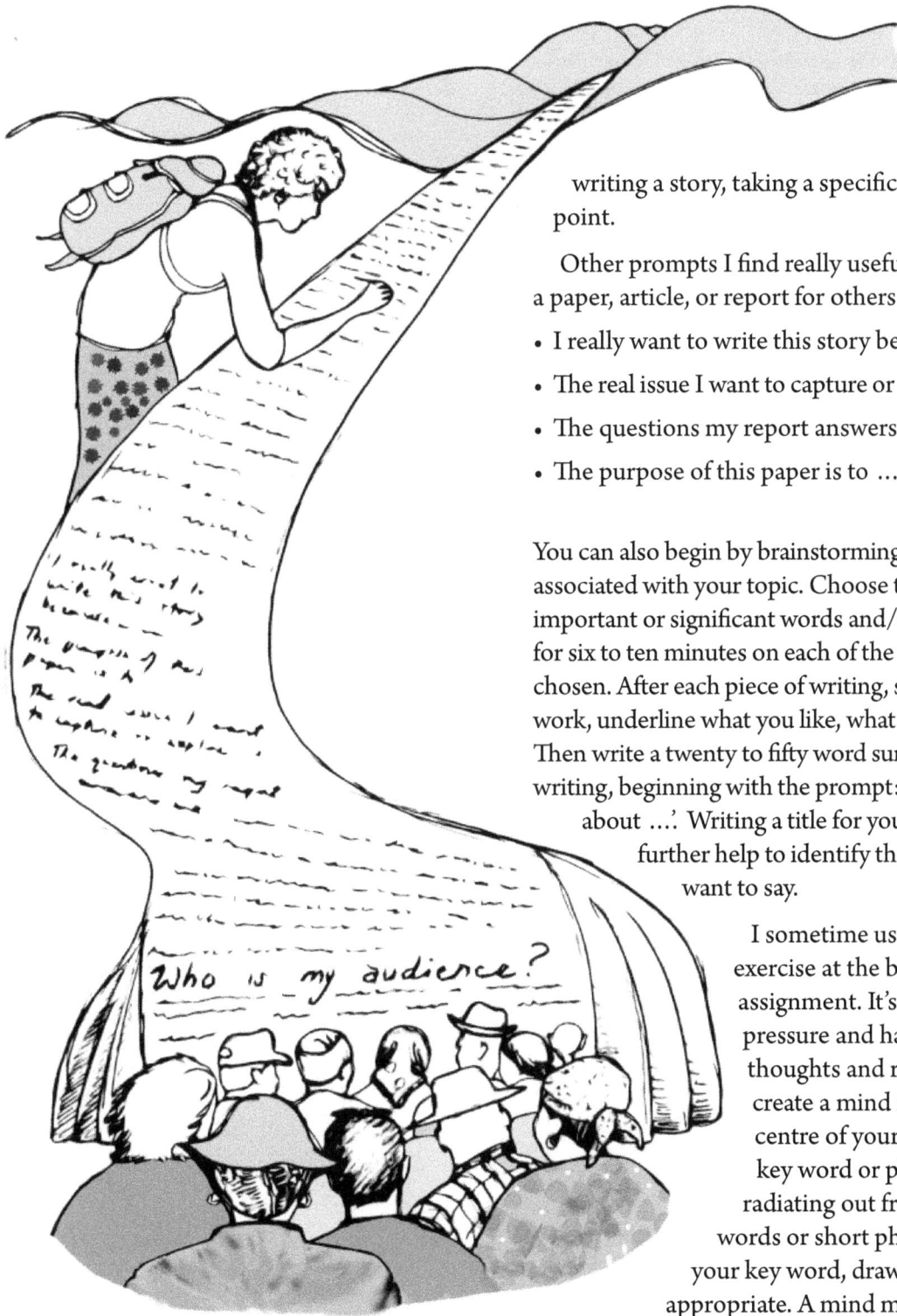

Who is my audience?

visualising all the interconnecting parts of your topic. It may even help you see connections you never thought of before.

It is important to now stop and think about who you are writing for. Ask yourself: 'Who is my *audience*?' Free-write a brief description of the people you are writing for. Be specific. Or free-write from the prompt 'My reader is …'.

Finally I begin writing the actual down draft (first draft or rough copy). I try to write it fast without too much agonising about whether it's coming out right or not. The down draft is about getting everything you want to say down. If you remember information you want to include, but can't remember all the details, make a note to yourself in the margin or on a separate piece of paper. For example, you may quickly jot down 'Look up Margaret Wheatley's stuff on communities of practice' or 'Ask Nathi about her workshop on gender'. Then just keep going. Although you may be writing a lot of stuff you won't use in your final paper, think of what you are generating as raw data, or *source material*. It is better to write too much and then cut down your writing rather than trying to stretch it out later.

Working on your down draft is a very creative stage in the process. Keep the critic out of it. Don't worry about spelling and grammar either. Don't worry about form, logic or sequence (order). Concentrate on content and meaning – what is it you want to convey? What's in your heart?

Once you have a couple of pages, it's a good idea to leave your writing for a while and take a break.

Then go back to your paper – as its first, friendly reader. Read your draft looking for and underlining what you like in colour. Then read it again, noticing where it is strong, where it captures your attention, and where your interest begins to droop. Use a different colour pencil to underline things that disturb you, gaps, and areas that need further attention. See if you can identify the key messages in your draft. Ask yourself, 'Is this what I want to say? Is it serving the purpose I intended?'

Go back to your notes and, if necessary, do some more 'homework' – read, look up references, or speak to colleagues.

It is a good idea to keep a list of anything you read on your topic, detailing the author, title, date of publication, publisher and page number of quotations. You will need this information if you want to reference your paper properly.

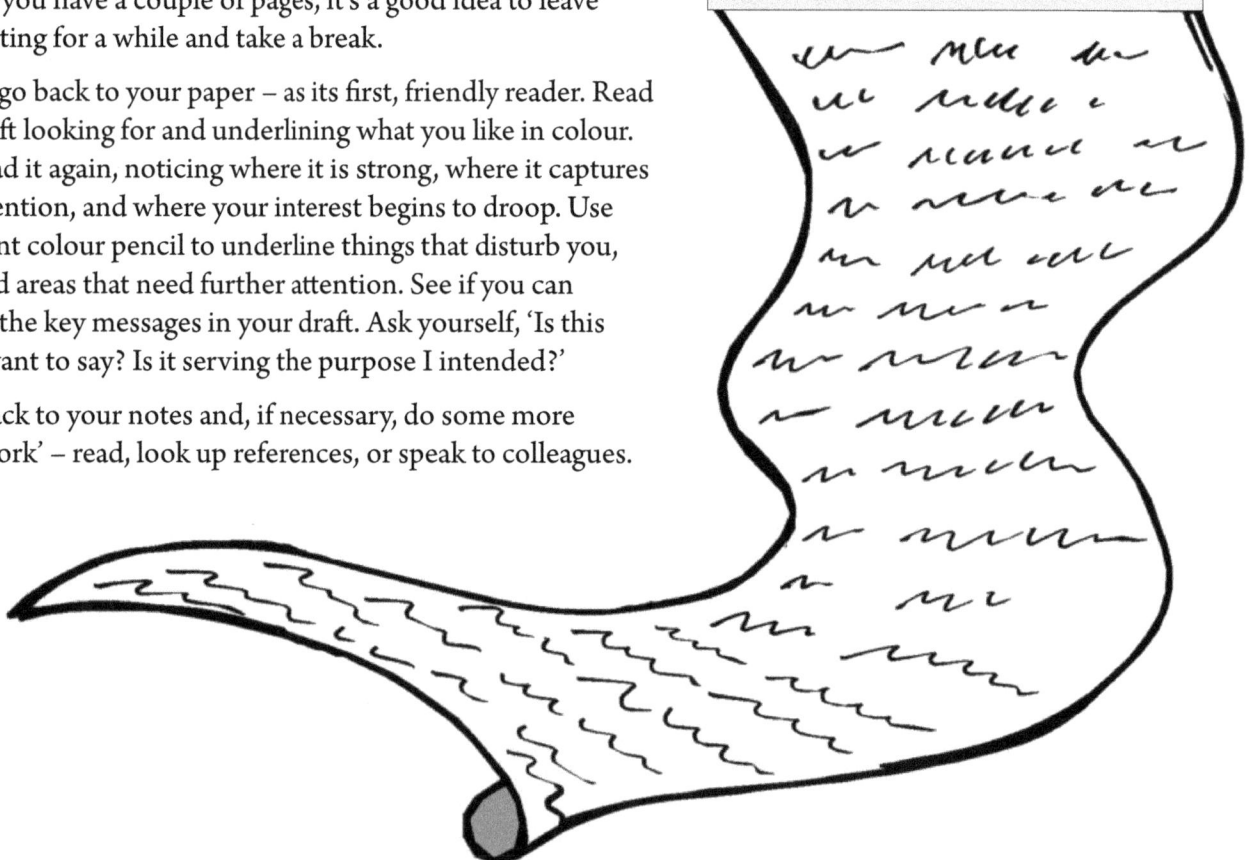

The up draft

Rework your paper, based on your own critique of it. Write and rewrite until you are reasonably happy with what you have.

Focus on content but now also on how you present your content. The shift from exploration to presentation becomes more of a priority in this phase of the process. Peter Turchi, in his 2004 book, *Maps of the Imagination: The Writer as Cartographer*, put it like this: 'That is to say, at some point we turn from taking the role of Explorer to take on that of Guide.' The information you have written may be important, but is it inviting to read? Will it touch your reader's heart, intellect and will? What's the *pace* like? Do you cover too many points too quickly or is it very wordy and long-winded? How have you *hooked* your reader's attention? Are you spoon-feeding her? Is there enough 'space' for her to draw her own conclusions?

Check if the way you have ordered the information needs changing. Do paragraphs or sentences need moving around? Check if you are repeating yourself and whether some sentences could be deleted altogether. What kind of language are you using? Is it appropriate for your audience? Is it full of jargon or shorthand names of organisations? Is there too much detail? Or too little? Can you hear your own voice or is it too impersonal?

Share your up draft with two or three others you trust. 'Oh, how lovely' or 'This is the worst thing I've read in years,' is not helpful feedback. You want them to be *critical friends*, people who will make the time to engage with your writing thoughtfully and honestly. It's pretty scary handing over a paper you've been labouring over for days, weeks or months. I always feel vulnerable. I am learning to ask for the kind of feedback I find useful, and the more specific I can be about what I want or need, the more useful the feedback I get.

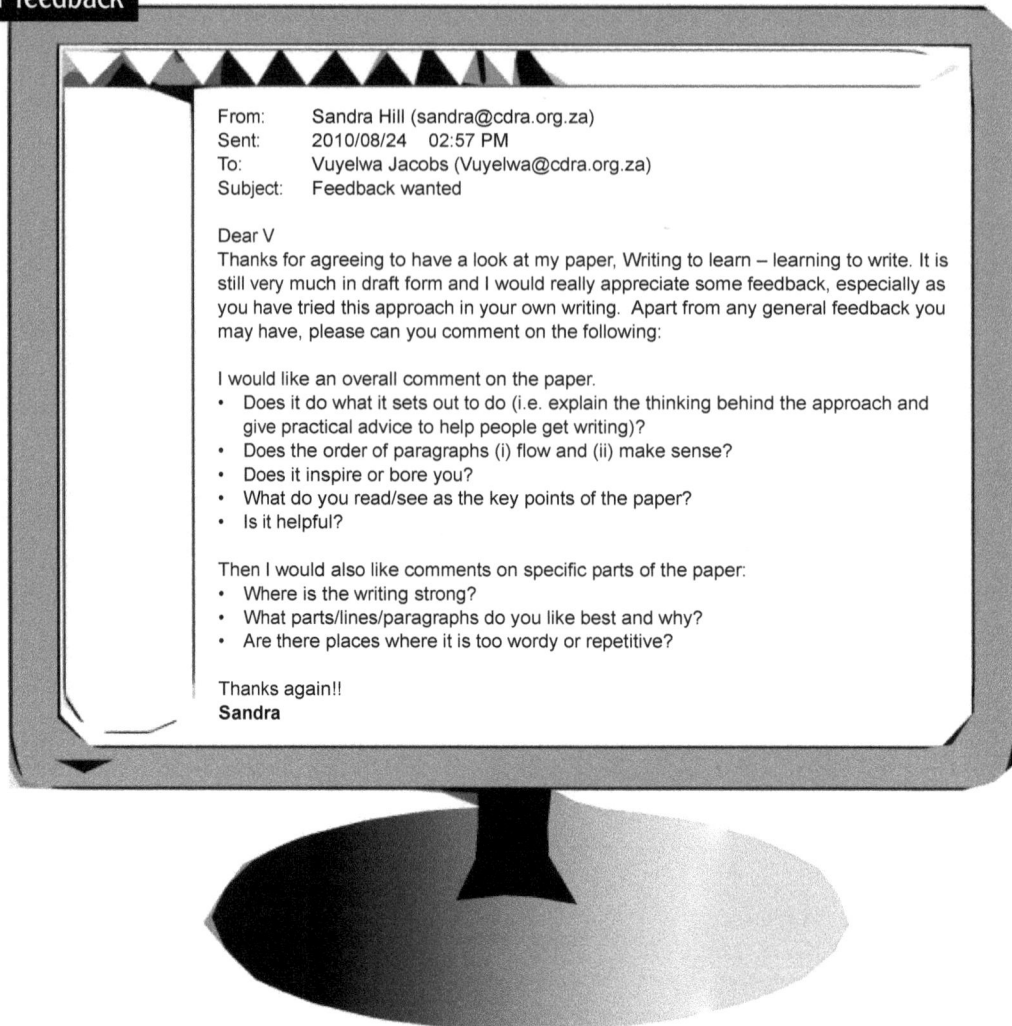

From: Sandra Hill (sandra@cdra.org.za)
Sent: 2010/08/24   02:57 PM
To: Vuyelwa Jacobs (Vuyelwa@cdra.org.za)
Subject: Feedback wanted

Dear V
Thanks for agreeing to have a look at my paper, Writing to learn – learning to write. It is
still very much in draft form and I would really appreciate some feedback, especially as
you have tried this approach in your own writing. Apart from any general feedback you
may have, please can you comment on the following:

I would like an overall comment on the paper.
•   Does it do what it sets out to do (i.e. explain the thinking behind the approach and
    give practical advice to help people get writing)?
•   Does the order of paragraphs (i) flow and (ii) make sense?
•   Does it inspire or bore you?
•   What do you read/see as the key points of the paper?
•   Is it helpful?

Then I would also like comments on specific parts of the paper:
•   Where is the writing strong?
•   What parts/lines/paragraphs do you like best and why?
•   Are there places where it is too wordy or repetitive?

Thanks again!!
Sandra

Remember you are not obliged to follow other people's feedback. The final decision as to what to cut out, what to change and what to keep the way it is, is yours.

If you get stuck: a word on writer's block

Some days the words just pour out of me and writing is a pleasure. Other days it is a complete struggle.

If I get stuck on a particular section, I go back to free-writing about it; if I hit writer's block, I free-write about it. If I hate writing the paper, hate the paper, hate the computer … I free-write about that too. It releases the stress and emotion, and hopefully gets the creative juices flowing again … or at the very least it fills up the time until I feel justified to take another break! Then I get on with the job. Or I give up; sometimes it is better not to fight it, but to go for a walk, a coffee, a sleep. Take a break.

Sometimes I feel inspired. Sometimes not. But I have been told that as a writer, your job is to show up at your desk, to show up at the blank page or computer screen, and write – never mind how you feel. The artist Picasso said, 'Inspiration exists, but it has to find you working.'

When feeling stuck, all you do is write one paragraph. Not the whole paper, just that one paragraph, that one idea. And then the next one.

by Anne Lamott

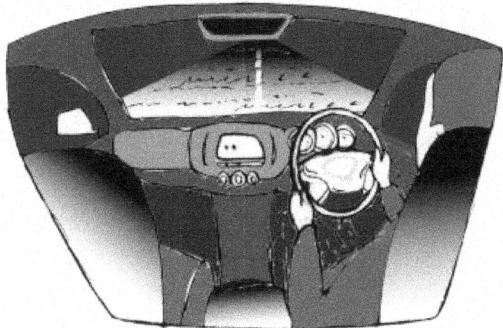

'Writing is like driving a car at night. You can only see as far as your headlights, but you can make the whole trip that way.'

EL Doctorow

Dental draft

It's time to polish and print. Enough is enough! At some point you have to stop writing and hand over your paper. It is always a good idea to have a third party read it carefully, looking not at content, but at grammar, spelling, layout, numbering, consistency, and so on. This is often called proof-reading or copy-editing. It is a particularly good idea if you are writing in a language other than your mother tongue. Make the corrections indicated and avoid the temptation to fiddle with your paper. Print it, and hand it over to the person you wrote it for or to whoever is publishing it.

In conclusion

On our way to a 2010 Soccer World Cup match at the Cape Town Stadium, my eight- year-old son casually announced that he was going to play for Brazil when he grew up. I agreed it was a fantastic idea, but pointed out that he would need to begin practising now. He was astounded by the very idea! I have met many people who want to be writers, grown-up people, who are similarly astonished by the idea of having to practise writing. Sure, talent helps, but even the most talented of writers, like musicians, dancers, even soccer players, have to practise. So, if you want to write – whether it is for yourself or for others – make time to write. If not every day, then every week.

CHAPTER 15

Creative Space:
designing and facilitating learning activities

This chapter goes with the *Designing and Facilitating Creative Learning Activities - The Barefoot Guide 2 Companion Booklet,* which you can also download from the Barefoot Guide website. Together they cover principles of designing and running organisational learning activities, but this chapter is aimed at dealing with the deeper challenges – like working with diversity or including the right people. These are the issues that you need to revisit again and again to make sure that your learning foundations are strong.

The *Learning Companion Booklet* looks in more detail at typical elements of many learning processes, such as 'how to begin a process' or 'how to ask good questions'. It also presents ideas about different kinds of learning processes and events, for example case studies or strategic planning.

Now however, let's go through seven important principles for creating strong learning foundations.

Principle 1: Include the right people

Back to square one

It was a great workshop. We came up with a new way of working. We were all excited. But the next day when we went to tell our manager he said we couldn't afford the changes. So now we are back to square one.'

They rejected our suggestion

After a long workshop it became obvious to us, as programme managers, that the monitoring and evaluation team would be more effective if they were split up and based in country offices. Their relationships with the field staff would be stronger and the information richer. After the workshop, when we informed the M&E team what we had realised, they totally rejected our suggestion and are now complaining to the union.

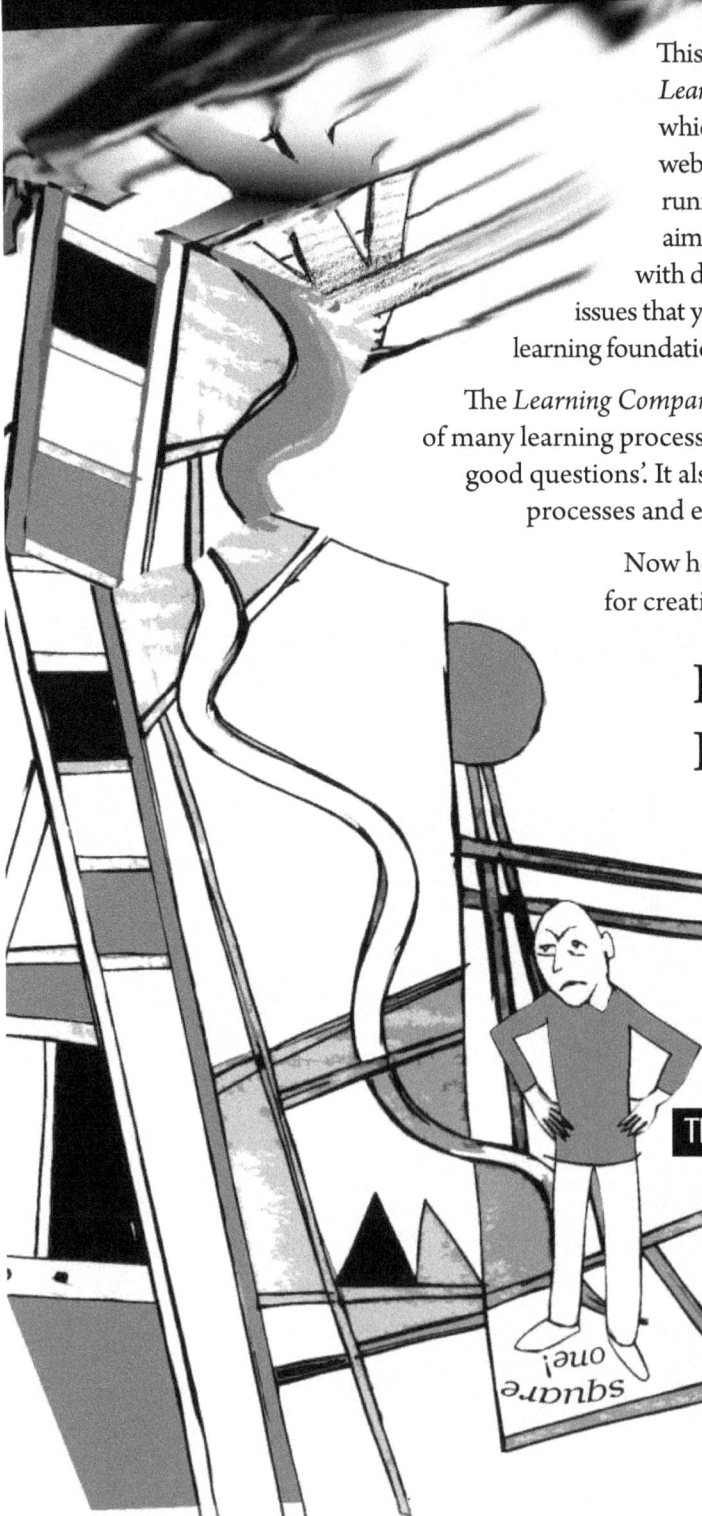

It is crucial to involve the right people in a learning event or process…

Whether you like it or not, whether you have the time or not, it is crucial to involve the right people in a learning event or process, or you too could 'end up back at square one'. But how do you know who should or should not be there?

The *purpose* of the activity should be your main guide. What do your values and principles say about participation and involvement? Who has important information and who will be affected by the issues? What will happen if you do not invite certain people? Who can offer useful or different ideas?

Nothing about us without us!

This heading is a slogan and a principle from disability movements that are tired of other people coming up with solutions to their problems, without fully involving them. Those affected by any changes need to be involved in the process – both because it is morally right and also because it makes common sense to seek guidance, ideas and leadership from those most affected.

Those who come are the right people

This principle from Open Space Technology is put into practice through an open brainstorm. It aims to enable groups to freely discuss questions and ideas that really matter to them, and from which they may kick-start new projects. Often, the aim is to find people who will champion an idea and bring their enthusiasm and commitment. You don't want to force people to come who are not interested, who would rather be somewhere else. They may drag the energy down and pour cold water on the idea.

Get the whole system in the room

This is a principle we hear more and more these days. If we want holistic, integrated and sustainable change we need to get everyone in the room, everyone who is involved or affected in any important way. This builds on 'nothing about us without us' to include a wider range of contributors.

Build confidence before engagement

Sometimes people who are not confident of their own power need some space to meet together to prepare before they meet with confident people or groups, so that they can engage on a more equal footing.

Participation doesn't necessarily mean having everyone in the same room together at the same time. In hierarchical organisations, it may be better initially to speak to people individually or in peer groups. Then you can design the next stage of the process so big issues can be raised without causing resentment. Learning processes can help to break down hierarchies but this takes time and careful thought.

Principle 2: Explore 'the whole elephant'

Three blind men touched an elephant, one touching at the front, one at the side and one at the back. The first told his friends: 'An elephant is long and about as thick as a man's arm.' The second one said, 'No, it isn't. It's flat and feels like paper. It is very thin.' The third one said, 'You're both wrong. It's large and hard and hot, smelly stuff comes out of it.'

What's a client?

We were neatly divided into three different programme groups, each with our own funding sources and reporting requirements and our own team dynamics. So we focused on our own programmes, ignoring each other's work. But we often had the same clients. Sometimes we would meet our colleagues at the client organisations, not really knowing what each other was doing there.

One day, our manager announced that we would have meetings based on client organisations, instead of programme meetings. You could almost hear the collective groan.

At the first meeting, focused on one shared client, each person had to explain the work they had been carrying out with that client. The first person shared their programme objectives and main activities. But when they began explaining the difficulties they were experiencing, a hush came over the room.

As person after person spoke, a much richer picture of the client organisation started to emerge. The stories built on each other and fresh insights began to bounce around the room. It was marvellous to see everyone doing their best to deepen their understanding of this client organisation – and also to hear laughter and notice knowing smiles.

These meetings became regular, always resulting in new insights only made possible by the different inputs. Indeed, it also enabled new kinds of learning conversations throughout the office.

When working with systems and complex situations, if we only deal with problems or specific parts, we may miss the root causes of the problem or we may fix one part, only to find this has a negative effect on the other part. We may spend time trying to address issues that could more easily be addressed elsewhere.

Mapping systems and people and exploring relationships between them can be very helpful in making sure you are not missing information and input. Often it is the relationships that need work, rather than the separate parts of the system.

> *Often it is the relationships that need work rather than the separate parts of the system.*

Principle 3:
Work with the whole person – head, heart and feet

We can't work with half a person! If we want to work holistically, if we want to engage with the whole person, the whole team or the whole organisation then we have to think about what we are neglecting, where we need to pay more attention.

So often learning is taken to be only about facts and figures, thinking, ideas and theories, opinions and thoughts – you know, *head level* stuff. These things *are* critical to being clear, scientific, intelligent and strategic.

But what we think is not the only thing that makes us human. Imagine if we had no emotions? In a way we would be little more than walking computers. Our emotional life, our *heart level*, is a key part of who we are – we experience and respond to the world through our emotions, as much as our thoughts. If you want to really discover what is important to someone, whether experiences or thoughts, one way to do this is to find out what they feel, to follow their emotions.

But at times you need to dig even deeper than emotions to a hidden level where our true motivation, will, or energy lies. This is the *feet level*. (Have you heard the expression, 'They voted with their feet'? It means: they walked out, they left because they wanted to!) Sometimes when we are trying to understand why something happened, in order to learn from it, we may be puzzled because things just don't make sense at a head or a heart level. For example, the community leader said that she and the others supported the project, for all the reasons you had discussed with them, and expressed happiness and appreciation for your interest. But when the time came to do the work, no-one arrived; no-one really had the energy or will. It had made logical sense to them to be involved (your plan was good) and everyone was friendly, but actually it was not that important to them; there were other priorities. So what was their motivation? Perhaps it was to be agreeable, not to offend you, so they happily went along (their heart level, emotional response), maybe not consciously realising themselves that they were not so interested. This disinterest was at their feet level, their 'will' response.

So, when we design learning activities it is important to pay attention to all three levels: head, heart and feet.

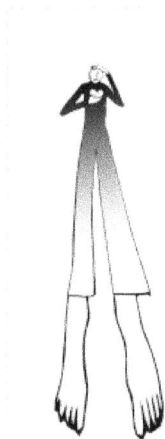

Head-level learning

This involves collecting good information and thinking logically about what happened to develop knowledge, theories and ideas.

Heart-level learning

When learning from an experience, we pay attention to the emotions or feelings that were part of the story, looking for how these guided thinking and doing. This also applies to the feelings of the person listening and learning. Do both people feel safe to speak honestly, to share what really happened, without fear of being punished?

Feet-level learning

Often we cannot really understand and learn from an experience until we uncover the will, the different motivations and energies that drove the situation. What did people really want? This also applies to the learner – do they really want to learn?

Principle 4: Appreciate and encourage diversity

In the context of a learning process, 'diversity' means the varied types of cultural experience, acquired skills, natural talents and physical and mental ability that people bring to the learning event. If we do not consider this diversity and unconsciously prevent people from participating fully, then we are limiting how much learning can take place.

For example, a programme manager attends a meeting where his colleagues are discussing what kind of database should be used to monitor government spending to address poverty. Because a PowerPoint presentation is used and he is blind, he is unable to fully share his experience of designing databases. Nor is he able to learn about the particular data that is needed to carry out this kind of monitoring.

You can find out as much as possible about the people who will come to your learning event. And you can create the conditions that will enable them to participate. Here are a few simple suggestions.

Before the event:

- Ask if people need anything in order for them to fully participate or if they have any particular requirements for food or amenities.

- Ask what experience and skills they can bring.

- Check there is no religious or cultural festival that might prevent some people from attending.

- Choose a venue that is as accessible as possible.

During the event:

- Don't assume what people can or can't do – ask them.

- Have alternatives for people who might find some activities difficult or inappropriate – for example modelling clay instead of drawing materials for someone who is visually impaired.

- Ask quiet people individually if they have anything to contribute.

- Listen to and try to understand all opinions respectfully.

- Create an atmosphere where everyone is listened to and acknowledged, to enable people to overcome any barriers.

After the event:

- Get feedback afterwards so you can learn from the experience; you may inadvertently have excluded people.

> *... looking again at the purpose ... may help them to see that their differences are not worth getting so heated about!*

Principle 5: Help people to find common ground

There is huge *diversity* in the world and we must appreciate and work with it. But there is also huge *commonality*. We may be different and want different things but we are human, we all need to feed our children, to live in peace, to be free of oppression, to work in solidarity. There is so much to disagree about, and it is important to disagree, but it is just as important to find agreement, to look for common ground. If we do not have agreement we often cannot move ahead together.

When we are facilitating a discussion it can easily become an argument. Our diversity becomes a source of conflict, which can be healthy, but it can also become stuck, with people trying to win the debate. One way to open things up is to ask people to pause and ask themselves where they *do* agree, and to share this. They may not easily see it, so you may have to suggest where there is common ground.

Sometimes people love to disagree – they like the energy of arguing – but often their differences don't matter that much. Your task might be to bring them back to the purpose of the discussion, to ask them how important their disagreements are for the actual work that needs to be done. Sometimes looking again at the purpose of the work or the bigger vision of the organisation may help them to see that their differences are not worth getting so heated about!

It could be that their disagreement lies somewhere else. Perhaps they are having a personal conflict and bringing this to the discussion. Maybe they are working from a different set of values or theories and so they will never agree unless they explore and acknowledge these.

You may also see that they are both right, that it is not an either/or situation, but that – depending on the situation – both of them have a point. Help them find a win-win solution.

Principle 6: Work with the left and right brain

Our brains are divided into two halves or hemispheres. The left half deals mostly with logical thinking processes while the right half deals more with imaginative and emotional processes. Using both sides of the brain well enables us to think and act creatively.

QUESTION TO THINK ABOUT

- Think of a meeting or workshop you have recently been to in your organisation, and look at the table. What percentage of what you did is left brain- and what percentage right brain-oriented?

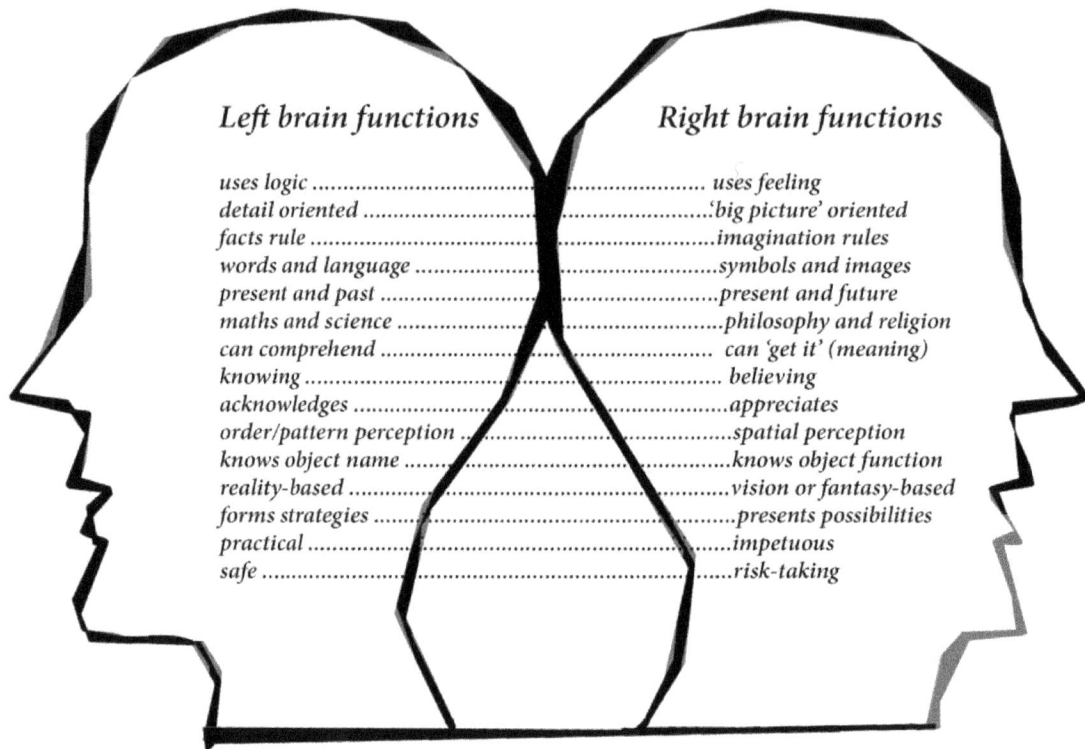

Left brain functions	*Right brain functions*
uses logic	*uses feeling*
detail oriented	*'big picture' oriented*
facts rule	*imagination rules*
words and language	*symbols and images*
present and past	*present and future*
maths and science	*philosophy and religion*
can comprehend	*can 'get it' (meaning)*
knowing	*believing*
acknowledges	*appreciates*
order/pattern perception	*spatial perception*
knows object name	*knows object function*
reality-based	*vision or fantasy-based*
forms strategies	*presents possibilities*
practical	*impetuous*
safe	*risk-taking*

Most organisations encourage their people to be left-brained, ignoring their right-brain capacities and thinking in their processes and activities. Many of their learning processes follow the same pattern.

The way you organise your learning activities will influence how people address an issue or learn from their experiences. If the activities are too left- or too right-brained, important insights and learnings may be missed. You wouldn't use half your body to play football, although one leg may be stronger than the other. The two parts of the brain support each other and focusing exclusively on one is like playing football with one leg. (For more on this see 'The Master and his Emissary': a think piece on the *Barefoot Guide* website.)

If you include creative activities in your workshop or learning process this can bring new ideas and dimensions to the learning. For example, asking people to see a situation as a picture can produce an 'Aha!' moment that enables people to move forward from being stuck after hours of discussion.

> *If the activities are too left- or too right-brained, important insights and learnings may be missed.*

We are often resistant to thinking in different ways and automatically think with our left brain. As the facilitator we will need to nudge people out of their comfort zone by introducing unfamiliar activities. Don't be put off if everyone groans when you suggest something new. Once they are fully involved, they may find – to their surprise – that they are enjoying it and learning in new ways as well!

Principle 7: Keep an eye on the 'real work'

Sometimes we can get so involved in the details of the activities that we forget about some of the deeper work that we are responsible for in facilitating learning. Consider the following key roles:

Inspiring people to learn

Are people inspired to be learning? Do they believe that it is worth investing time and energy in this activity? Is it meaningful for them?

Energising people to learn

It might be that people are inspired to learn but they don't show the will. Perhaps the space is not safe. It might be that they are afraid to be honest. Or they feel stupid and don't want to expose themselves. They might be exhausted. What is de-energising them from fully and willingly participating in the learning activity?

Focusing the learning on what matters

Are the learning questions clear? Are the activities focusing on the things that matter to the people trying to learn?

Grounding the learning in experience

Do the learning activities really draw on people's experience, valuing and using it? Are 'mistakes' seen as an opportunity to learn? Are people forgiven for these mistakes?

Challenging learning

Is the activity challenging enough to help people to break out of their comfort zones, to think out of the box? Are the difficult questions being asked or avoided? Are they being asked in a positive or a negative way?

Supporting learning

Is there good human warmth? Are people feeling supported enough that they are open to being challenged?

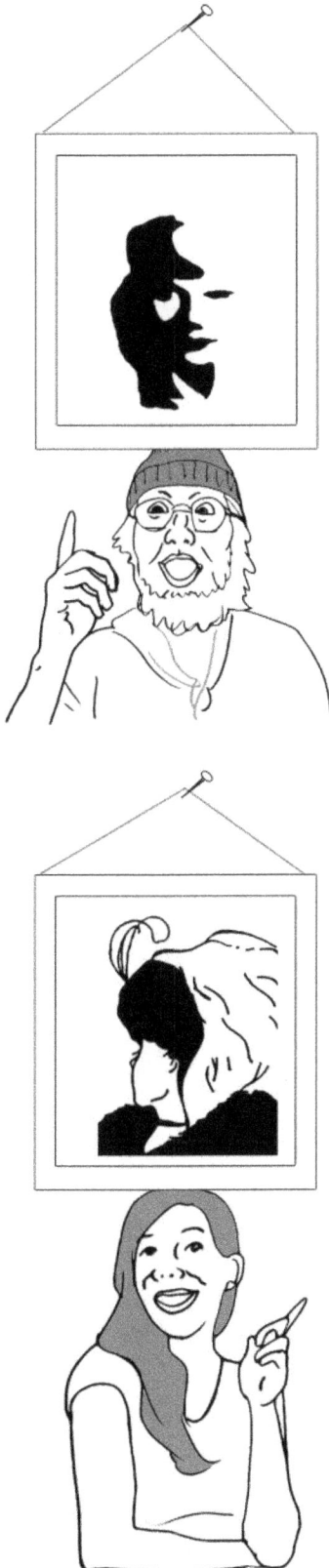

Don't forget to download the...

**Designing and Facilitating Creative Learning Activities
The Barefoot Guide 2 Companion Booklet**

www.barefootguide.org

Containing thoughts and suggestions on:

A. Principles of Design and Facilitation (as in this book)

Include the right people
Explore 'the whole elephant'
Work with the whole person - head, heart and feet
Appreciate and encourage diversity
Help people to find common ground
Work with left and right brains
Keep an eye on the "real work"

B. Key elements of learning processes

Beginning a process
Future Springboard... how to end a process well
What's the point of Powerpoint?
Creating a learning space
Seating and tables
Helping people tell their stories well
Collecting better information from a story
Tips on asking good questions
Better reflections, deeper learnings and more effective action
Guiding questions for the Action Learning Cycle
How to use creative and artistic activities in learning processes
How to work with resistance and "difficult" people
Interpersonal conflict – some basics tips

C. Tips for different learning processes

Action Learning Sets
Study circles
World Café
Team building
Learning from Case Studies
Supervision, Mentoring and Coaching
Skills development
Strategic thinking, strategic conversations
Management meetings

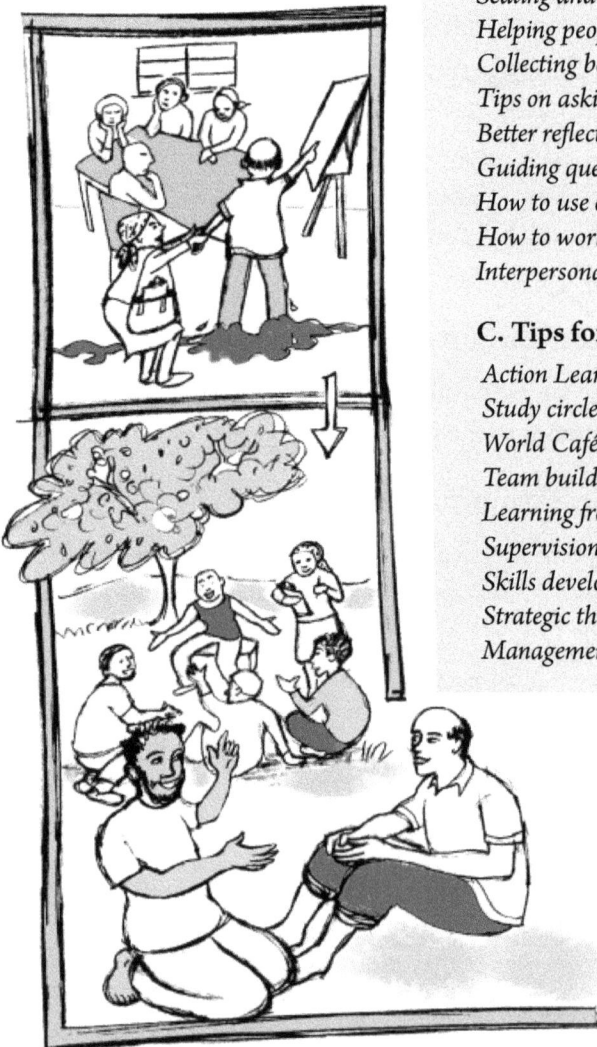

Acknowledgements

Chapter 1: First Steps: Preparing for our learning journey

Page 16, under Enabling Change to Happen, is inspired by the concept of "Nudge" as put forward and practised by James Wilk What is particularly appealing is his interest in minimalist change interventions and the idea of *flux and constraint* in the place of the kind of the kind of cause and effect thinking that many development practitioners struggle with.
See http://www.interchangeassociates.com/wp-content/uploads/2010/09/Wilk-on-the-Nudge.pdf

Chapter 2: I am, we are: Linking individual and organisational learning

Schön, Donald A 1987:3 *Educating the Reflective Practitioner* San Francisco: Jossey-Bass

McGilchrist, Iain 2009 *The Master and His Emissary* Yale University Press Publication

Chapter 3: Lively Spaces: Creating a learning culture

Farago, J and Skyrme DJ 1995 *The Learning Organization* http://www.skyrme.com/insights/3lrnorg.htm

Hofstede, G, Hofstede, GJ and Minkov, M 2010 *Cultures and Organizations: Software of the Mind* New York: McGraw-Hill USA

Chapter 4: Moving tapestries: Learning in organisational systems

Kellner-Rogers, M & Wheatley, MJ 1998 *Bringing Life to Organizational Change* Journal for Strategic Performance & Measurement

Pearson, J 2010 *Seeking Better Practices for Capacity Development: Training & Beyond* at www.oecd.org/dataoecd/35/53/44696077.pdf

Semler, R 1994 *Maverick* London: Random House

Chapter 5: Weaving learning into change: Planning, monitoring and evaluation alternatives

Davies, R and J Dart (2005) *The Most Significant Change* (MSC) *Technique; A Guide to Its Use*, see: www.mande.co.uk/docs/MSCGuide.pdf

Earl, S, Carden, F, and Smutylo, T (2001) *Outcome Mapping: Building learning and reflection into development programs* Ottawa: International Development Research Centre (IDRC)

Westley, F, Zimmerman, B, & Patton, M (2006) *Getting to maybe: How the world is changed* Toronto: Random House

Wendy Quarry & Ricardo Ramirez (2009) *Communication for another Development: Listening before Telling*, Zedbooks, New York

Chapter 6: Humble Offerings: Donors' practice and learning

Cambridge Advanced Learners' Dictionary http://www.dictionary.cambridge.org/dictionary/british/donor

The Free Dictionary http://www.thefreedictionary.com/donor

Ken Schofield, head of the Philippines USAID mission, 4 March 2010 (ref in Natsios, A (2010) *The Clash of the Counter-bureaucracy and Development* Washington, DC: Centre for Global Development

ActionAid (undated) *Grounded Advocacy: Donor-funded projects & advocacy: a resource book for staff*

The Big Push Forward Initiative http://www.bigpushforward.net/

Chapter 7: Our feet on the ground: Learning with communities

Several sections of this chapter are based on the work of Reflect, a global collective of practitioners developing and working with the Reflect approach:

> "*Reflect, or Reflect-Action* as it is also known, is an innovative approach to adult learning and social change, which fuses the theories of Brazilian educator Paulo Freire with participatory methodologies It was developed in the 1990s through pilot projects in Bangladesh, Uganda and El Salvador and is now used by over 500 organisations in over 70 countries worldwide Organisations working with *Reflect* won UNESCO literacy prizes in 2003, 2005, 2007, 2008 and 2010" From the website: http://www.reflect-action.org/

Chapter 8: Horizontal Learning: A sideways approach to change

Reeler, D 2005 *Horizontal Learning – Engaging freedom's possibilities* Community Development Resource Association from the 2004/2005 CDRA Annual Report www.cdra.org.za

Chapter 9: The Heart of Change: Stories of learning

Marilyn Ferguson - http://www.worldtrans.org/whole/wsquoteshtml

Chapter 10: Unlearning: Letting go for a change

Reeler, D (2001) *Unlearning - Facing up to the real challenge of learning* Community Development Resource Association www.cdra.org.za

Chapter 11: In the sea of change: Understanding your context

Batliwala, *Srilatha From Evaluation to Learning in Social Change* – the challenges of "Measuring Development, Holding Infinity" accessed from www.jassassociates.org/associates/sri_from_evaluation_to_learning.pdf in July 2010

Dey, AK and Abowd, GD 2000 *Towards a better understanding of context and Context Awareness* Accessed in July 2010 from www.cc.gatech.edu

Clarke, P and Oswald, K (researchers) as part of Participation, Power and Social Change team Facilitating Learning and Action for Social Change – June 2006 to March 2009 Accessed in May 2010 from www.ids.uk

Chapter 12: Harvesting experience: Learning how people learn

Peter Honey and Alan Mumford – variation on Kolb's learning styles

Honey, P and Mumford, 1986 *A Manual of learning styles* 2nd ed Honey (this is the original place of publication but difficult to access – the book below is easier to access and does have the learning style very nicely defined)

Mumford, A 1989 *Management Development: Strategies for action* London: Institute of Personnel Management

Kolb's Learning Styles/cycle:

Kolb, D 1983 *Experiential Learning* Harlow: Prentice-Hall

Chapter 13: Mirror Mirror: Knowing and changing yourself

van Houten, C 1999 *Awakening the Will: Principles and Processes* in Adult Learning Temple Lodge: London

Chapter 14: Writing to learn – Learning to write

Goldberg, N 1986 *Writing Down the Bones* Boston: Shambala Press

Bolton, G 2001 *Reflective Practice: Writing & Professional Development* London: Paul Chapman Publishing

Hill, S 2006 *Networking People and Nature in the City* Cape Town: Cape Flats Nature

Environmental Monitoring Group 2007 EMG *Organisational Report* Cape Town: EMG

Lamott, A 1994 *Bird by Bird* New York: Anchor Books

Turchi, P 2004 *Maps of the Imagination: The Writer as Cartographer* Texas: Trinity University Press

Doctrow, E source www.goodreads.com

See Reeves, J 1999 *A Writer's Book of Days* California: New World Library for more on free writing

See Rico, G 2002 *Writing the Natural Way* New York: Tarcher/Putnam for a more detailed explanation of and guide to the kinds of mind maps referred to on page 12.